The Pre-Biblical Narrative Tradition

SOCIETY OF BIBLICAL LITERATURE
Resources for Biblical Study

Edited by
W. Lee Humphreys

Number 24
The Pre-Biblical Narrative Tradition

by
SIMON B. PARKER

THE PRE-BIBLICAL NARRATIVE TRADITION

Essays on the Ugaritic Poems *Keret* and *Aqhat*

By
Simon B. Parker

Scholars Press
Atlanta, Georgia

The Pre-Biblical Narrative Tradition

LIBRARY OF CONGRESS
Library of Congress Cataloging-in-Publication Data

Parker, Simon B.
The pre-biblical narrative tradition : essays on the Ugaritic poems Keret and Aqhat / by Simon B. Parker.
p. cm. -- (Resources for biblical studies ; no. 24)
Bibliography: p.
ISBN 1-55540-300-X (alk. paper). ISBN 1-55540-301-8 (pbk. : alk. paper)
1. Keret epic. 2. Aqhat epic. 3. Narrative poetry, Ugaritic--History and criticism. I. Title. II. Series.
PJ4150.Z77K4737 1989
892'.6--dc19 88-31148
CIP

**Printed in the United States of America
on acid-free paper**

To
Sonia
Jonathan and Jeremy

ltbrkn alk brk
tmrn alk nmr

ACKNOWLEDGMENTS

Besides the patience of my family, to whom I dedicate this book, I should like to acknowledge the support of a Graves Award, which enabled me a number of years ago to do some basic work on these two poems and on studies of oral tradition in general; and of Boston University and (then) Dean Nesmith of its School of Theology, who more recently granted me a two-month leave in which to begin the writing of the present work. On both occasions I benefitted especially from the use of the Griffith Library of the Ashmolean Museum in Oxford.

CONTENTS

INTRODUCTION

The following essays are primarily descriptions and interpretations of features of the Ugaritic poems *Krt* and *Aqht*. Since their discovery in the early thirties and publication in the thirties and early forties, there have been scores of studies of these two poems and hundreds of studies of various parts of them. Philological investigations in the narrow sense—that is, investigations of lexical and grammatical matters—have, appropriately, predominated; but there have also been numerous discussions of the larger significance of the poems, especially in terms of the history of religions.

The angle of vision in the following essays is literary. The adjective is not defined narrowly. I take it as a given that the poems as we have them are the products not only of some copying of earlier written version(s) but also of a period of oral transmission; and that as oral poems they used traditional sources. None of the evidence at our disposal suggests that they were transmitted in a fixed form. Rather, as the following studies suggest, the traditional material was handled rather freely in the developing of new narratives and in the extending and transforming of old ones. Transmission and composition went hand in hand. Once we recognize that the composition of *Krt* and *Aqht* has a history and that we have but a snapshot of a long process of transformation, it follows that a proper appreciation must be sensitive to the diachronic movements that have produced the present static objects, and must see the poems in the context of the larger narrative tradition out of which they have grown and been formed. The paucity of material for the study of the tradition in Ugarit requires (unless one simply fills in the gaps on the basis of one's own prejudices) that one turn to comparative evidence in the larger narrative tradition beyond that preserved at Ras Shamra for support for or correction of any analysis of the poems.

Further, I take it for granted that literature always implies a linguistic medium and a social context. Therefore, though we have only limited knowledge of the language and society of Ugarit, I attempt to remain alert to both. Obviously, some understanding of the language of the poems is a prerequisite for the study of them as literature. But it is not necessary that literary study await complete understanding of the language. If it is true that literary analysis depends on linguistic understanding, it is equally true that the understanding of obscure words and constructions presupposes literary understanding—that is, knowing what literary form is the context of the obscurity, knowing what is going on at the level of plot. While such literary knowledge will not provide the means for linguistic analysis, it will suggest possibilities and limits for hypotheses about the meaning or function of a word or phrase, and eliminate total ignorance or wild guesses. Thus if these studies can advance our knowledge of the literary structure and movement of the poems, they may in a small way also assist further philological study.

The poems are here viewed as *poems* and as *narratives*. The book progresses from the smallest scale to the largest scale features of the works. Their smallest and most pervasive poetic and literary forms are explored in chapter one. The object of interest here is those conventional features of the Ugaritic narrative poems that may be designated their essential characteristics. Excluded are occasional stylistic features and rhetorical devices, such as chiasmus and alliteration. The second chapter investigates some unique non-narrative forms (speeches) in the poems and pursues similar forms in other literatures in order to discover their usual *social* form and setting, which in turn permits a more just appreciation of the artistry of those who adapted such typical social expressions to their present narrative, poetic context. The last two chapters, after proceeding through each poem, identifying its major narrative structures, comparing these with similar narrative structures in the broader Near Eastern literary tradition, and then noting the particular treatment of the common structures in their present Ugaritic contexts, attempts to define the particular theme, purpose and setting of each poem.

The treatment of *Krt* and *Aqht* together and apart from other narrative poems requires some justification. First, neither *Krt* nor *Aqht*, has been the subject of a major study in recent years. (Their treatment in Del Olmo Lete 1981 comes closest to such.) Second, as the basis for ongoing investigation of narrative in other Ugaritic literature and for comparative narrative study, it appears best to concentrate on those texts which use narrative most extensively and consistently, and in which narrative seems to be of central interest and significance. I take narrative to be essentially an account of human acts and experiences, only by extension applied to gods (myths) or animals (fables; on fables in the Bible see Daube 1973; Solomon 1985). (Clearly, however, both gods and animals may be portrayed in essentially human terms, so that the extension may be immediate and the difference trivial. On the other hand, myth may take the form of narrative about humans; but then it betrays its non-narrative interests in its use of fantastic, oneiric elements, in its fracturing of normal human experience—cf. Kirk 1970.) Narrative is essentially a structuring of human experience—and thus serves aesthetic and social ends. It is not essentially a means of achieving some loftier programmatic or more immediate practical end, such as an exposition of (or effective renewal of) the order of the universe, or the curing of a disease.

While narrative is to be found in several other Ugaritic poems, especially in the first twenty-four texts of *CTA* and *KTU*, it is nowhere else at once so extensively developed and so directly devoted to human experience as in *Krt* and *Aqht*. I should like to claim that a detailed description of the features of these two narratives will contribute to our appreciation of the use of narrative in other Ugaritic texts in which other interests may be paramount, as well as to ongoing comparative study of ancient Near Eastern narratives. Among the latter, it is perhaps Hebrew narrative—practically devoid of myth and fable—that will most benefit from such comparison.

The title of the book also requires justification. What was the character of the narrative tradition to which the writers of the biblical narratives were heirs? Rough answers to this question have long been attempted by internal analysis of biblical narrative literature and some general comparisons with more or less remote homologues. The hypothetical character of these reconstructions has always been clear. But since 1931 we have had in these Ugaritic poems representatives of late bronze age narrative in a northwest Semitic language from the East Mediterranean littoral. The exploitation of these as the ancestors of Israelite narrative has been strangely neglected. Admittedly, a striking general difference between the Ugaritic literature that we have recovered and that of Israel is that in the former narrative takes the form of poetry, while in the latter narrative is prose and poetry is non-narrative (apart from a few approaches to narrative in cultic or spiritual poetry). I recognize that the definition and identification of "prose" and "poetry" is not always as simple and straightforward as is often assumed. Nevertheless, the general contrast seems to hold. As poetry, the Ugaritic poems have much in common with Israelite poetry, and these connections have been intensively studied for decades. But as narrative they have more in common with Israelite narrative, and these connections have received very little attention at any time (with the exception, in recent years, of the work of Del Olmo Lete). It is the investigation of these narrative connections that the present volume wishes particularly to encourage.

It should be clear, however, that I do not wish to claim any direct connection between *Krt* and *Aqht* on the one hand, and Hebrew narrative on the other, nor to imply anything about the date or origins of the latter. *Krt* and *Aqht* simply happen to be the only two representatives we have of what was doubtless a rich narrative tradition spread throughout the Northwest Semitic-speaking settlements of the Eastern Mediterranean countries; and that tradition would have continued in such communities long after the collapse of the late bronze age communities of northern Syria.

A continuing need in Ugaritic studies is for an authoritative text. In the case of damaged letters the various editions based on the actual tablets—the *editiones principes* of Virolleaud and subsequent collations—often do not agree on what is there and read the remains quite differently. Those who are able travel to where the tablets are presently housed and collate to their own satisfaction. (To such we owe some checking and evaluation of the major recent editions. "None of them is absolutely reliable," according to Dressler 1983. On Herdner 1963 in particular, see Horwitz 1972; on Dietrich, Loretz and Sanmartin 1976, see Dressler 1983.) An adequate publicly available edition based on the best current photographic technology (i.e. high resolution macro-photography using various light-sources and angles) remains the great desideratum of Ugaritic studies (see provisionally Friedman 1980, Pls. 1-12; Pitard and Zuckerman 1987). It is to be hoped that the Northwest-Semitic Photographic Project that Bruce Zuckerman has undertaken at the University of Southern California will at least begin to remedy this situation.

Under present circumstances, it seems to me that it is precisely the investigation of conventional and typical features of the texts, and of their larger-scale components, that is least affected by uncertainty about the readings of odd letters or words in badly damaged parts. I have adopted a skeptical, agnostic position towards such doubtful readings. What follows is based in general on that great part of the text the reading of which is universally agreed upon. On the basis of the structure of well-preserved parts of the text and comparable structures in other works I have formed broad hypotheses about the general outlines of large missing portions. The reasonableness of such hypotheses must be judged by the requirements and possibilities given by the context, and by the validity of the comparisons. I have taken isolated words or fragments of words into account, not as a basis for the construction of hypotheses—the identity of the words, the grammar and the versification are often ambiguous in such cases—but rather as checks on such larger surmises, asking the question: do these remains disallow this view of the general course of the narrative?

Some recent writers have reacted differently to the situation, supplying letter by letter restorations in incomplete lines, making decisions about doubtful readings on the basis of these hypothetical restorations, and even passing judgement on the literary quality of the resultant constructed text ("the literary result of the restoration and reconstruction proposed in this study represents one of the finest pieces of narrative description to be found anywhere in Ugaritic literature, it recalls and rivals the level of achievement in the Homeric classics"—Margalit 1983b, 106). But who is to say this is not self-congratulation? *Pace* Margalit (later on the same page), literary quality is not a criterion for judging the correctness of a reading or restoration. The only criteria—apart from the obvious ones of consistency with the discernible remains on the tablets and fit with the present context—are the evidence of similar expressions and collocations elsewhere, whether beautiful or ugly from a literary point of view.

The focus on the literary character of the poems is reflected in the bibliographical references. By and large these are limited to studies that are directly related to the literary interests of this book. I have not attempted to list the more narrowly philological treatments of each verse or passage. Ugaritic scholars are now well served by the bibliographies of the *Newsletter for Ugaritic Studies* and its indexes. The annual *Ugaritforschungen* has for nearly twenty years served as the main forum for Ugaritic scholarship. Finally, Del Olmo Lete 1981, now an indispensable handbook for any study of the Ugaritic poems and narratives, is equipped with generous bibliographical references.

It is obvious to anyone working in the field that we all reap what others have planted and watered. We are, however, dependent on our own best judgment for distinguishing the good plants from the weeds. Doubtless many will think that, in sometimes disregarding or dismissing the suggestions of others, whether for the construction of meaning in difficult parts of the text or for the reconstruction of text in missing parts of the tablets, I have been too conservative. On the other hand, some will find my own analyses and comparisons too bold. No work on these incomplete, damaged, partially understood texts can be regarded as authoritative or final. What I hope to do with these essays is to focus attention on a level of analysis and comparison that I consider neglected and yet fruitful for the understanding and appreciation of the Ugaritic narratives; and at the same time to suggest the value of this kind of study of the Ugaritic narratives for the nicer appreciation of the tradition and artistry of biblical narratives. If others are stimulated to make better or more careful comparisons, they may discover new clues to the composition and purpose of these two Ugaritic poems, and may enhance our appreciation of the peculiar transformation in the rendering of narrative that we find in ancient Israel.

Ugaritic texts are cited according to their numbering in Dietrich, Loretz and Sanmartin 1976 (*KTU*). Texts in syllabic cuneiform, except where particular editions are cited by author, are designated according to the conventions of the Chicago Assyrian Dictionary (*CAD*).

Chapter 1

SOME CONVENTIONS OF UGARITIC NARRATIVE POETRY

It quickly becomes clear to anyone reading the major Ugaritic poems that the poets who composed them were working with some well-established conventions. While these conventions are clearly related to those of other poetic and narrative literatures in the Ancient Near East, and a comprehensive study of such conventions in all the literatures would lead to a clearer view of the kind and degree of relationships among those literatures, a thorough exposition of the particular forms and uses of the conventions that appear in the Ugaritic narratives will both lay the foundations for the broader comparative study and help us to determine the tradition, techniques and purposes of the composers and the sensibilities and interests of the audiences of the two poems.

The following review of the formal conventions of the Ugaritic narrative poems proceeds from smaller-scale, more pervasive features to those on a larger scale that are used more freely. It attempts to identify and describe the general character of the conventions and particular cases of variations from them. It also seeks to avoid a purely formal presentation, by interpreting them wherever possible in terms of the sensitivities and purposes of the poets who used them and in terms of their impact on the audiences who heard them.

A. Parallelism and Versification

There is little disagreement that the most obvious and pervasive convention of the Ugaritic poems is parallelism. We shall return to this shortly. What is vigorously disputed is whether or not Ugaritic poetry also exhibits a metre of some kind (see recently Wansbrough 1983). Various metrical systems have been proposed—of quantity or stress, of syllables or words or other specially defined components of the verse—but none has been shown to the general satisfaction of students of the texts to be as regular and predictable as would be necessary for them to be described as metrical.

In 1950 G. D. Young put to the test a metrical system favored by many scholars at that time, demonstrating its inadequacy and further claiming that metre was "beyond [the] aims and experience" of the Ugaritic poets (Young 1950). The model which Young disposed of was one in which one stress was assigned to each word. His attempt to dispose of metre altogether as a category appropriate to Ugaritic verse was evidently unsuccessful, since new theories or variations of old theories continued to be published.

Recently Pardee has undertaken a review of the question, and a critical appraisal of two currently promoted metrical systems (Pardee 1981). He begins with a useful clarification of what is meant in standard parlance by terms such as metre. While the term may be used variously to refer to systems based on the alternation of short and long syllables, the number of syllables per verse or the number of stressed syllables per verse, it *always* implies the regularity of the pattern and hence its predictability. None of the metrical systems proposed for Ugaritic poetry has in fact exhibited these last two features. Pardee turns his attention to a relatively widely accepted system based on the number of syllables per verse. He takes Stuart (1976) as representative of this system. The other system—much more complicated—appraised by Pardee is widely and vigorously exhibited by its proponent, B. Margalit, but does not appear to have been wholeheartedly embraced by anyone else. (For Margalit's initial exposition of his various theories of Ugaritic poetry see Margalit 1975.) Pardee shows that neither system, on the terms of its prononent, is in fact either regular or predictable. (The fact that the metrical analysts of Ugaritic poetry sometimes handle the text rather freely and inconsistently, even to achieve the irregular patterns they do present, is of secondary importance, though it surely confirms the inadequacy of the system.)

An attempt to redeem Margalit's description of Ugaritic metre was published in Zevit 1983. Zevit simplifies and modifies Margalit's system, and finds that it is then supported by syllabification and non-distinctive stress in Proto-Northwest Semitic. On this linguistic basis Zevit would favor a system of word-meter, in which "word" is understood to include semantic-syntactic units such as construct chains. This brings us back to theories that are at once earlier, simpler and less apparently arbitrary than Margalit's. While Zevit's proposal is plausible, the construction of a hypothetical metrical system on a hypothetical system of stress in a hypothetical form of Northwest Semitic is not likely to prove convincing. (A fuller, judicious criticism of Margalit's several theories concerning various aspects of Ugaritic poetry, including prosody, strophic structure and alliteration, appeared in Pardee 1981/82, 267-70.)

As Pardee notes, a metrical system based on stress remains a possibility, but is scarcely discoverable or demonstrable, given the nature of the evidence. If the poems were sung or chanted, as they may well have been, metre is also a possibility, but a possibility of a different kind. For there need be no correspondence between the rhythm of the music and the linguistic form of the text. One has only to think of Anglican chant, in which a varying number of words and syllables may be sung to a single note and a single syllable may be extended over several notes (cf. de Moor 1978, 129-31; O'Connor, 1980, 40-41; Pardee 1981, 125-6).

Two phenomena in the poetry may be adduced to confirm that the presence of metre in Ugaritic narrative poetry is highly unlikely (see further de Moor 1978, 123-28). First, lines which are realizations of a formula such as *w* √ *ʿny* PN "then up spoke PN" may use relatively short or long personal names and epithets, e.g. *wyʿn krt ṯʿ* "then up spoke Keret the Noble" or *wtʿn pǵt ṯkmt mym* "then up spoke Pughat, the bearer of water," lines of seven and thirteen syllables respectively. Here one line is virtually twice as long as the other, as measured by syllables. Such formulaic lines normally stand alone between immediately preceding and succeeding parallel bicola, so that there is no question of the lines being divided at different points in different contexts.

A second phenomenon arguing against the existence of metre in Ugaritic poetry is the parallelism of a verse such as:

tgly ḏd il — she journeyed to the *ḏd* of El
wtbu qrš mlk ab šnm — and entered the *qrš* of the King, Father of Years

1.17.6.48-49 and six times in 1.1-6

Again, the difference measured in syllables is seven to thirteen. In this case, one could divide the line differently, say *tgly ḏd il wtbu//qrš mlk ab šnm* (as many have done), but then one has contravened the parallelism. The question then is: which is the more firmly established criterion for the division of the verse into cola: parallelism or metre? I have no hesitation in acknowledging the claims of parallelism, with its describable syntactic and semantic features, over any alleged metrical constraints.

Admittedly, if construct chains could be treated as having

optionally one *or* two stresses, it would be possible to achieve a balanced line of three stresses in both the above cases. Thus the construct chain *ḏd il* could be counted as two stresses and the construct chains *qrš mlk* and *ab šnm* could each be counted as one. I note this simply to concede that stress remains a possible basis for a metrical system in Ugaritic poetry. But to demonstrate this would require not only a knowledge of stress that is not accessible to us, but also an uncomfortable degree of flexibility in the handling of identical grammatical constructions with words of identical length. Such a division into stress units would achieve an equal number of three stresses in each line; but it would also militate against the syntactic and semantic parallelism: *ḏd//qrš*, each in the construct state; *il//mlk* (*ab-šnm*), each in the genitive case, dependent on the preceding noun (with *ab-šnm* in apposition to *mlk*).

While it cannot be demonstrated or recognized that metre is an essential feature of Ugaritic poetry, it must be granted that the length and rhythm of cola may be occasionally significant. For example in the thrice-repeated account of Danel's examination of the eagles' viscera there appears the expression *in šmt//in ʿẓm* "(there was) no fat//no bone" (and finally *iṯ šmt//iṯ ʿẓm* "(there was) some fat//some bone"). Whether this expression is considered one colon with internal parallelism, or a bicolon, it nevertheless appears to exhibit a striking change of rhythm and phrasing in comparison with the surrounding cola. The particular conjunction of form and content suggest that a speaker would pronounce these words after a moment's pause and with some deliberation, and that an audience would listen with corresponding intensity, as the result of Danel's examination is announced in each case.

That parallelism is in fact the primary observable structural principle of Ugaritic narrative verse is, I think, universally admitted, and has certainly been forcefully stated in a series of studies (Young 1950; Parker 1974; Pardee 1981; Segert 1979; 1983). Recently both Pardee and Segert have expressed themselves in almost identical terms: parallelism is the primary structural principle of Ugaritic poetry. What distinguishes it from prose, which may also use parallelism, is its pervasiveness. It also appears to be more pervasive in Ugaritic poetry than in any other Ancient Near Eastern poetry. Further, the parallel clauses are, *in general*—though not regularly enough to warrant the conclusion that metre is involved—of approximately equal length (Gordon 1965, 138-44; Parker 1974, 287; Pardee 1981, 126; Segert 1979, 730). It is of course this latter feature which leads many to the hypothesis that some kind of metre must inhere in the poetry. Normally the cola of comparable length are composed of two, three or four words of varying length. But, as we have seen, there are some verses in which the parallel structure creates great inequality in the length of the two parts of a bicolon. In other rare cases unusually short or unusually long parallel clauses appear. But here the sense of "approximately equal length" may permit a restructuring of the verses that does not do violence to the parallelism. Thus instead of being regarded as two parallel cola *in/iṯ šmt//in/iṯ ʿẓm* may be treated as a single verse with internal parallelism, and *[lm] ṣbi nrt ilm špš [ʿ]r[bt] pǵt minš šdm//lm ʿrb nrt ilm špš mǵyt pǵt lahlm* (1.19.4.46-50) as a verse of four cola of which the first and third and the second and fourth are parallel. But variations of these kinds—whether of length between the two cola of a bicolon, or of length of both parallel units as compared with length of surrounding cola—suggest that strict consistency of length of parallel units may have been experienced as monotonous in the long term, and that deliberate variation may have been cultivated to stimulate interest and enjoyment. Hence the poets worked with a flexible, approximate consistency of length of cola, which allowed for occasional extension beyond the normal boundaries.

But what is parallelism? It would seem to be a relatively simple phenomenon that has been defined and analysed in rather different ways. To my mind the most satisfactory account of Ugaritic parallelism to date is that of Segert (briefly and generally, 1979; with more detail and examples, 1983), and I shall follow him in the next few paragraphs.

Parallelism refers to common semantic and/or especially syntactic features shared by (usually) two or three cola. The discernment of this structure accordingly requires both semantic and syntactic analysis. (A proposal for a more sophisticated analysis of Ugaritic poetry, based on O'Connor's system of analysis of biblical poetry, has been proposed in Wansbrough 1983.) But further definitions are in order before we can proceed—and here I follow Segert completely, reserving "line" for a numbered line of the text on the tablet; calling the poetic units of approximately equal length "cola"; and recognizing that such cola usually occur in pairs ("bicola") but also in threes ("tricola") and in isolation (without parallelism—"monocola"). Cola paired or grouped by parallelism form a "verse." The definition of the first and last terms—line and verse—contrasts appropriately with their definition in descriptions of biblical poetry, for there "verse" refers to the numbered subdivisions of "chapters" (dating from medieval times), so that "line" is the suitable term for a poetic unit. I would defer to Pardee in avoiding the term "prosody" because of its metrical implications, and in substituting terms such as "poetic structure" for the formal features that establish the verses.

The relationship between cola is closest when the words in the cola correspond in meaning, syntactic function and order. But this is not common, and may have been avoided as monotonous. The establishment of a degree of parallelism, but also of a constantly changing variety in semantic or syntactic relations between parallel cola, in the number of words paralleled or in word order would demand the constant attention and energy of the audience. The listeners would need constantly to discern correspondences and differences in order to recognize the composition and boundaries of each verse—monocolon (without parallelism), bicolon or tricolon.

The semantic relations among parallel cola are most frequently synonymous, but also complementary. Segert terms the two "thetic." This recognizes that "synonymous" is not a sufficiently broad term to subsume such pairs of expression as silver//gold, heaven//earth, which nevertheless belong together and bind cola together in the same way as house//palace, brothers//peers. The alternative to thetic parallelism in Segert's terminology is "contrastive," which is rare. Repetition or identity of words in parallel cola is also rare, except in tricola, where it is both the means to construct the tricolon and a force giving coherence to the tricolon. (For a more penetrating discussion of the semantic relations in [biblical Hebrew] parallelism see Kaddari 1973.)

Syntactic structures, while normally coinciding with semantic relations, are more fundamental to the poetic structure, and the best basis for identifying semantic relationships. (Greenstein sees syntactic structures—at the level of deep structure—as the essential ingredient in parallelism: Greenstein 1983, 43-46.) The first colon in a bicolon is usually a self-contained clause. The second colon then supplies additional information of lower syntactic rank. Occasionally a sentence will transcend an individual verse, but then the different clauses within the sentence will be distributed among different verses. Consider:

hm ḥry bty iqḥ	If I take Hurraya into my house
aš'rb ǵlmt ḥẓry	bring the girl into my court
ṯnh k!spm atn	I will give her double in silver
wṯlṯh ḫrṣm	her triple in gold

1.14.4.38-43

The first bicolon forms a dependent (conditional) clause, the second the main (independent) clause. Within each bicolon the first colon gives the complete syntactic information for identifying the clause, and thus for establishing the relationship between the two bicola. Also within each the second colon omits a significant element of the clause—the conditional particle in the first bicolon, the verb in the second. It is thus dependent on the first colon. In other words, it is only as the constituents of the second colon are related to their parallel constituents in the more complete context of the first that they can be satisfactorily construed. Parallelism binds together the component cola of a verse, marking it off from neighboring cola by the internal correlation of syntactic and/or semantic elements. Recognition of the parallelism is therefore a crucial step in understanding the poetry.

Bicola are the most common manifestation of parallelism. There are various ways of describing the forms it takes. Segert uses several categories based on the semantic relations between cola—synonymous and complementary (thetic); disjunctive and antithetic (contrastive). He also introduces a category of "relaxed" parallelism to describe cola with strong semantic parallelism but largely different syntactic structures, and cola with complete syntactic parallelism, but little common semantic ground. The establishment of a pattern of short clauses, each paired with a complete or partial clause with which it shares some semantic and/or syntactic features produces the bicola of approximately comparable length with which we began. Once that pattern is established, some variety in the semantic and syntactic relations between the cola was possible and—evidently—desirable. The establishment of the pattern means that we can recognize and enjoy such occasional features as internal parallelism—the repetition of semantic or syntactic features *within* a colon, e.g. *ištmʿ wtqǵ udn* "attend and let your ear be alert" 1.16.6.29-30—or the divergence in the number of words in parallel cola, e.g.:

abk!y waqbrnh	I will weep and bury him
ašt bḫrt ilm arṣ!	will place him in a pit of the Earth-gods
	1.19.3.5-6 (and repetitions)

or:

lqḥ imr dbḥ bydh	He took a sacrificial lamb in his hands
lla klatnm	a kid in both
	1.14.3.159-61

It is also observable and understandable that the poets would at times extend the parallelism beyond the individual bicolon, so that sometimes two bicola sustain similar semantic and/or syntactic relations (Segert 1983, 302):

sʿt bšdm ḥṭbt!	those gathering firewood rush from the countryside
(w)bgrnt ḥpšt	those collecting (chaff) from the threshing floors
sʿt bnpk šibt	those drawing water rush from the spring
(*w*)*bmqr mmlat*	those filling (their vessels) from the well

1.14.3.7-10=4.51-5.2

(Cf. 1.14.2.43-7=4.21-25; for justification of this translation see Clines 1976.) The two bicola of 1.14.1.31-35 exhibit only a partial semantic connection, while the five cola of 1.19.3.44-47 are bound together by their syntactic consistency, greater in the case of the first three—which thus may be classed as a tricolon—and the last two—which form a bicolon. The four cola of 1.14.3.16-19 form two bicola, each firmly established by several common semantic and syntactic features, some of which persist through all four cola. But they are incomplete clauses, all syntactically dependent on 1.14.3.15-16: *wl yšn pbl mlk* "and Pbl the king could not sleep." Thus not only do the two bicola by their common parallelism form a unit, but by their common dependence on the preceding colon they form part of a still larger unit. The bicolon comprising Danel's name and epithets is always dependent on a following bicolon for completion of a clause. Larger groups of bicola sustaining common parallel features appear in the refrain listing the duties of the pious son in the first two columns of *Aqht*. The cola listing the daughters that El promises to Keret in 1.15.3.7-12 are best described as just that: a list of cola of identical structure.

As already noted, a common alternative to the bicolon as the most common parallelistic structure is the tricolon. By my rough count of the adequately understood complete verses in the two poems the ratio of tricola to bicola is approximately 1:4 in *Aqht*, 1:6 in *Krt*. Segert claims that tricola are usually created by the addition of a third line related to the second (Segert 1983, 302). I find that not be be so (cf. already Loewenstamm 1969). Of Segert's example:

tqḥ yṭpn mhr št	She took Yutpan the *št* marksman
tštn knšr bḥbšh	she placed him like a bird of prey in her girdle

km diy bt'rth	like a bird in her sheath
	1.18.4.27-29

the last two cola are attested as a bicolon in the corresponding passage 1.18.4.17-18:

aštk km nšr bḥbšy	I will place you like a bird of prey in my girdle
km diy bt'rty	like a bird in my sheath

From this bicolon a tricolon has been constructed by the *prefixing* of a third colon, composed out of a verb parallel to *tšt* and a nominal object (name and epithets). In 1.17.6.26-28 (cf. 17-18) an additional colon, here created solely out of a (vocative) personal name and epithet, is again prefixed to a bicolon in order to produce a tricolon. Frequently the new line is created by repeating (rather than paralleling) some words from the following line, and supplementing these with a subject or vocative: 1.15.2.21-23 (cf. 14.4.40-42); 16.6.27-29; 54-57; 14.1.21-23 (cf. 10-11); 17.1.6-8 (and repetitions) (cf. 2-3; 21-22); 13-15 (cf. 3-5). Where both tricolon and corresponding bicolon are attested, the tricolon is used when the preceding context has not mentioned the subject or vocative; the bicolon when the subject or vocative has just been expressed.

In other cases we are faced quite simply with what may equally well be described as the expansion of the first line of a bicolon into two cola or the compression of the first two lines of a tricolon into a single colon. Thus, of the bicolon 1.14.3.55-56, the first colon *lqḥ imr dbḥ bydh* "he took a sacrificial lamb in his hand(s)" corresponds to the first two cola *qḥ imr bydk//imr dbḥ bm ymn* "take a lamb in your hand(s)//a sacrificial lamb in your right hand" of the tricolon 1.14.2.13-15. There is nothing in the context (identical in both cases) to explain why one form should have been preferred to the other. They appear to be free variants. The variation between the bicolon of 1.16.4.3-4 and the tricolon of the following 1.16.4.7-9 (and 10-12) appears to be equally arbitrary.

However, when a common, formulaic bicolon such as:

verb+*(l)ksi mlk(h)*	*verb*+(on) (his) royal throne
(l)nḫt (l) kḥṯ drkt(h)	(on) the seat, (on) the/his ruler's chair

—attested four times in the Baal and Rephaim texts—is extended in 1.16.6.22-24 by prefixing to the first colon a parallel colon: *yṯb krt l'dh* "Keret sits on his dais," it seems clear that the poet is creating a tricolon out of a standard bicolon. A similar case of the extension of a common bicolon may be found in 1.16.6.45-48 (cf. 33-34; 17.5.7-8; 19.1.23-25).

On the other hand,

tntkn udmʿth	his tears spilled
km ṯqlm arṣh	to the ground like quarters
k mḫmšt mṭth	to the couch like nickels
	1.14.1.28-30

looks like an original tricolon. The closely parallel second and third cola are both phrases syntactically dependent on the first colon, which is not in any respect parallel to them. However, had the subject been understood, the remaining words could have formed a bicolon, beginning with the verb *tntkn*. 1.17.5.16-19, transposed in 22-25, is not susceptible of such adaptation:

ʿdb imr bpḫd	prepare a lamb in flour
lnpš kṯr wḫss	for the appetite of Kothar-and-Khasis
lbrlt hyn dḥrš yd	for the palate of Hayin, skilled of hand

In this tricolon, as also in 1.15.3.2-4 = 13-15, the parallel prepositional phrases and the preceding clause on which they depend each contain an amount of discrete information that it is difficult to imagine being compressed without loss into a bicolon. In other words it is arguable that not all tricola were created out of existent or potential bicola. The tricolon was a sufficiently established convention for the poets that they might compose sentences in that form without building on a bicolon in the back of their minds or on the surface of the tradition.

If tricola may be seen as slowing down the pace of the narrative and demanding a little more attention from the listeners, compelling them to construe and relate a larger body of material over a longer period, we might expect the poets to use this form of verse when they particularly wished to claim such heightened attention and involvement. In fact tricola seem to cluster in more formal contexts: descriptions of rituals and ritualistic utterances, as in 1.17.1.1-16 (an account of an incubation—four tricola in sixteen lines); accounts of divine visits and pronouncements, as in 1.17.5.13-31 (a mortal couple's hosting of a visiting deity—four tricola in eighteen lines), and 1.15.2.12-3.19 (the gods' visit to a wedding and pronouncement of a marriage blessing—five tricola in thirty-six preserved lines); other formal and momentous speeches, e.g. 1.16.6.41-54 (a prince's indictment of a king—two tricola in thirteen lines); 1.16.6.54-8 (the king's responding curse—one tricolon in four lines). However, the name and titles of Pughat form a tricolon (used both as subject and vocative in different locations), appearing in as wide a range of contexts as the bicolon composed of the name and titles of Danel.

Another feature of the occurrence of tricola is their use in conjunction with monocola. Each tricolon in 1.17.1.1-5 is preceded by a monocolon (which numbers the days of the duration of the action described in the tricolon). Three of the four tricola in 1.17.5.13-31 are preceded by a monocolon. Many other tricola are juxtaposed to a monocolon. Perhaps the composers tended to conform these less frequent verse types to the prevailing rhythm of pairs of cola by creating a larger unit comparable to two pairs (1+3=2+2).

B. Poetic Formulae

Monocola, being by definition outside the predominant pattern of parallel cola (bicola and tricola), may be supposed to be in some sense non-poetic, *extra metri*, or prose interludes, symptomatic of some slippage in poetic creativity or tension. But before jumping to such a conclusion, we must determine whether their distribution in relation to bicola and tricola discloses any pattern or purpose, or whether, regardless of distribution, their formal or functional characteristics are in any way consistent with or complementary to parallelistic verses.

As mentioned at the end of the previous section, monocola often occur alongside tricola, for example: 1.15.3.5-6, 16; 1.18.4.26-27 (following a tricolon) and 1.14.1.20-21; 1.15.2.25 (preceding a tricolon). This might suggest that poets and audiences had a feel for a dominant rhythm based on multiples of two cola. However, monocola also fall between bicola: 1.16.1.38-39; 1.14.2.26-27=4.8-9; 1.14.1.37-38; 1.19.3.47, 4.5; 1.19.4.50. Moreover, 1.14.3.55 occurs between two tricola, and *ištmʿ wtqǵ udn* "listen and let your ear be alert," found between tricola in 1.16.6.29-30, is combined in 1.16.6.41-42 with the formulaic monocolon *šmʿm ʿlkrt ṯʿ* "here, now, Keret the Noble" to form a bicolon. Thus there is probably as much variety in the position of monocola in relation to bicola and tricola as one might expect if they were used randomly.

There are three features of monocola that argue for their deliberate, consistently poetic use. First, they conform to the "approximately consistent" length of cola identified above as an aspect of parallelistic versification (as distinct from parallelistic prose). In other words they consistently fall within the same spectrum of lengths as that of bi- and tricola.

Moreover, monocola seem to fall into two distinguishable classes, each of which has a characteristic function in the poetry, and each of which forms another argument for the purposeful, poetic use of monocola.

The first class is formulaic, consisting of stereotyped expressions which occur several times in different poems, but in particular predictable contexts, e.g. at the departure or arrival of a character, or to introduce direct speech. These formulaic monocola are readily available to the poets to assist them quickly and easily to move through standard, transitional situations in the narrative, while concentrating on the outcome of a visit or the content of a speech.

The second class of monocola consists of unique cola which stand out against both parallelistic cola and formulaic cola as stating something only once and stating it in a completely novel way. Corresponding to their character is their use: they appear most frequently at strategic points in the progress of the narrative—as the significant last verse of a speech (e.g. 1.15.3.16; 1.17.6.32-33; 1.18.4.26-27), to introduce a particularly significant speech (e.g. 1.14.4.36-38) or to emphasize the central element within a speech (e.g. 1.19.3.47; 4.5: the individual curse in two of Danel's three, otherwise repetitious speeches against places near the site of Aqhat's murder—the curse in the third speech is a bicolon).

All three observations together tend to confirm that monocola belong to the same poetic system as bicola and tricola; that, depending on their character, they take one of two contrasting forms and serve one of two contrasting purposes. Those of the first class are designed to facilitate the poets' progress by providing them with formulaic, easily adaptable phrases and clauses that they can use in standard narrative situations. Those of the second class arrest the attention of poets and audiences by their novel form and content. While the former may be used freely in the innumerable recurrences of the standard narrative situation which they describe, the latter are unique to the one context in the one poem for which they were composed.

By formulae are meant stereotyped expressions used recurrently in different narratives and poems (on Ugaritic formulae cf. Whitaker 1981; Segert 1983, 297-8). There are two types of formulae. Repetitive formulae are identical in every occurrence (e.g. personal and divine epithets). In transposable formulae some of the syntax and some of the words used are constant, but the form of some classes of individual words varies with context: different proper names and epithets may be used, pronouns may vary in person, number or gender and verbs may vary in person, number, gender, mood or aspect. (Cf. the "formulaic systems" of Parry and Lord—Parry 1928; Lord 1960, 30-67. However, it is debatable whether it is helpful to apply to non-metrical poetry terms that were coined to describe formulae functional in a metrical system.) The two types of formulae correspond to the two types of epic repetition discussed below (sections C and D).

The formulae of Ugaritic narrative poetry are found not only as monocola, but also as phrases within cola and as bicola or in larger groupings of cola. They may thus range in length from two words to several cola, the latter corresponding to Parry and Lord's "clusters." (As long as clusters are defined in terms of formulae, the term may apply as well to non-metrical as to metrical formulae.) Excluded from the category of formulae are the so-called "parallel pairs," which do not have the fixity, either of words or of word order, that is characteristic of formulae. Parallel pairs should be regarded as the products of normal linguistic association and of the demands of parallelism (Berlin 1983b).

The shortest formulae are those phrases which are associated with particular proper names—personal, divine or geographical epithets. References to characters and places in the narratives are in fact usually formulaic; reference by name alone is rare. Such formulae are invariable. Most frequently the formula consists of the name and a single epithet: *mṯt dnty, mṯt ḥry, aqht ǵzr, ǵzr ilḥu, yṣb ǵlm, krt ṯʿ, btlt ʿnt, aliyn bʿl*. Sometimes the epithets consist of two words: *yṭpn mhr št, dnil mt rpi, lṭpn il dpid, ṯr abh il, ngr il ilš, pǵt ṯkmt mym*. Such formulae are frequently used in transposable formulae consisting of one colon: √ *ʿny* PN, √ *šmʿ* PN, *apnk* PN, etc., where PN includes name and epithet(s).

But the epithets may be extended by parallelism beyond one colon. Danel appears as *dnil mt rpi//ǵzr mt hrnmy* (bicolon); his daughter as *pǵt ṯkmt my//ḥspt lšʿr ṭl//ydʿt hlk kbkbm* (tricolon). *Ilš* appears as *ngr il ilš//ilš ngr bt bʿl*, which is further extended into a tricolon by the additional formulaic reference to his wife/wives: *waṯth ngrt ilht*. In such cases the first epithet may be used within a colon consisting of a transposable formula, such as √ *šmʿ* PN. The parallel epithets of Danel appear in the formulaic bicolon: *apnk* PN//*aphn* PN_1.

The same phenomenon appears in the case of place-names. *Udm* may stand alone in a regular bicolon (*udm ytnt il//ušn ab adm* "*Udm* is a gift of God//a donation of the Father of Humankind"), but is repeated and expanded into formulaic epithets to produce a bicolon out of the transposable formula √ *mǵy l*GN:

ymǵy ludm rbt — He came to Great *Udm*,
wudm ṯrrt — *to Little Udm*

(Keret's city is likewise *ḫbr rbt//ḫbr ṯrrt.*) The name of the town near which Aqhat is murdered is extended by repetition and an additional (formulaic) epithet to fit the same transposable formula:

ymǵ lqrt ablm — He came to the town of *Ablm*
ablm qrt zbl yrḫ — to *Ablm*, the town of Prince Yarikh

It is clear from such examples that formulaic epithets are not haphazardly or arbitrarily imposed on the poetry. They are adapted both to the transposable formulae and to the predominantly parallelistic structure of the poetry. One obvious, yet often ignored corollary of this for the interpretation of the narratives is that the substantive relevance of any such epithet for a particular narrative context may be nil. While the poets may have coined or adopted an epithet with a particular narrative context in mind, there is no reason to think that we now have that context. Thus there is nothing in the epithets of Pughat that bears on her role in the preserved part of *Aqht*; Danel's epithet is "man of Rapi'u," but Rapi'u makes no appearance on his own account in our material.

The most common formulae consisting of one colon—the monocola already mentioned—are transposable, many of them used with the personal or divine formulaic epithet. The following are the chief transposable formulae used in *Krt* and *Aqht*, arranged according to situation described. I cite only such as are attested in more than one poem. The number of attestations in each of the three major poems is given for each formula.

	Krt	*Aqht*	*Bʿl*
Introduction of character			
apnk + subj.	3	8	2
Arrival			
bnši ʿn + pron.sfx. *w √ ph*		7	1
√ mǵy l + GN	3	2	(6)

—In *Bʿl* the formula does not use geographical names but refers to reaching the place where Baal fell, the fallen Baal himself, or another deity.

	Krt	*Aqht*	*Bʿl*
aḫr √ mǵy + subj.	1	1	3
Departure			
√ tbʿ + subj./*l* + voc.	3	2	2

—When the subject/vocative is not a proper name, the formula appears with the additional phrase *(w)l/al √ ṯb*, found twice in *Krt* (with *mlakm*), four times in *Bʿl* (twice with *ǵlmm*, twice with *ilm*). The additional phrase is placed at the end of the colon except in *Bʿl*, where it follows the verb.

tdʿṣ pʿn(m) wtr arṣ		1	2

—All three occurrences are followed by the next formula:

idk l √ *ytn pnm*		3	13

—*Bʿl* has four further cases with *al* in place of *l*.

idk pnm l/al √ *ytn*	3		3

—This is clearly a variant of the preceding. One of the occurrences in *Bʿl* has a personal suffix on *pnm*. The same formula also appears in 1.100.63. The line following both variants begins with *ʿm* or, sometimes in *Bʿl*, *tk*.

<u>Introduction of speech</u> (cf. Watson 1983)

gm l + object (subj.) *k* √ *ṣyh*	3	2	3

—Cf. *gm* √ *ṣyh* (subj.) *l* + object, found three times in the *B'l* texts.

√ *nšʾ g* + pron.sfx. *w* √ *ṣyh*	5	16	18
w √ *ʿny* + subj.	14	12	36
wrgm l + object	3		8
√ *šmʿ* PN	2	2	4

—Cf. below.

<u>Opening of speech</u>

tḥm + genitive	4		13
√ *šmʿ (mʿ) l*PN	4	6	6
ap mṯn rgmm argm(k/n)		1	2

—this has been compared with the Homeric *allo de toi ereō*: Gordon 1953, 93; Ullendorff 1977, 149.

Like formulaic epithets, transposable formulae may extend across parallel cola. In this case, since each transposable formula occupies an entire colon, their pairing produces a complete formulaic bicolon. It is no longer possible to say whether a formulaic monocolon acquired a parallel colon, or whether certain useful bicola became formulaic. Examples of formulaic bicola are:

(l) √ *dn dn almnt//(l)* √ *ṯpṭ ṯpṭ qṣr-npš/ytm*	2	2	

—Three things suggest caution in claiming this as a poetic formula: the discrepancy between *Aqht*'s *ytm* and *Krt*'s *qṣr npš*, the fact that the two occurrences in each poem are found in a repeated passage, and the fact that the general idea of the bicolon—with some similarity in wording—is found in a wide variety of contexts in Ancient Near Eastern poetry and prose. Perhaps we should think rather of two realizations of a common topos.

lpʿn DN √*hbr w* √*qīl* // √*štḥwy* (*w*) √*kbd* +pron.sfx./indep. pron.	1	8
subj. + *(l)bt* + pron.sfx. √*mǵy* // √*štql* + same subj. *lhkl* + pron.sfx.	2	1

Loewenstamm (1980) has shown how the formulaic *šmʿ (mʿl)* + voc. appears as a monocolon thirteen times, but is extended into a tricolon through the amplification of the vocative *pǵt ṯkmt my* (see above on formulaic epithets), and into a bicolon by the use of a parallel imperative and further synonymous expression in 1.16.6.41-42 (to cite only the examples from *Krt* and *Aqht*).

The bicolon *bph rgm lyṣa//bšpth hwth* occurs four times, but always in the same context in *Aqht* (Danel's search for Aqhat's remains in the eagles' viscera). However the first colon is very similar to the Homeric *ou pō pan eireto epos*, as pointed out by Gordon 1953, 92-93 (see also Ullendorff 1977, 149), and even closer to the Akkadian *amātam ina pīšu ul uṣa* (and its Sumerian counterpart) in "Enlil and Ninlil: The Marriage of Sud" line 26 (for which see Civil 1983, 51). It means essentially the same as the Aramaic *ʿwd mlt' bpm (mlk')* (Dan 4:28), or, though formally more removed, even the Hebrew *ṭrm klh ldbr* (Gen 24:15, 45) or *ʿwd zh mdbr* (Job 1:16, 17, 18; cf. 1 Kgs 1:22, 42). It thus looks like the Ugaritic version of a common Eastern Mediterranean narrative formula, which in *Aqht* has been extended by parallelism into a bicolon.

The tendency toward parallelism is well illustrated in the tricolon:

wyʿn [dnil m]t rpi	Then up spoke Danel, Man of Rapi'u,
yṯb ǵzr m[t hrnmy	Came back the hero, Man of the Harnamite
y]šu gh wyṣḥ	Raised his voice and cried:

There is clear parallelism, semantic and syntactic, running through all three cola, yet the first and third are well-attested transposable monocola, normally occurring independently. The middle colon appears to have been created as a close parallel to the first in order to produce a clear tricolon.

The formulaic monocolon *tḥm* PN "message of so-and-so" (1.14.3.21; 5.33; 6.3) is built into a bicolon by the creation of a second colon composed of a parallel to PN (twice in *B 1*) or a parallel to the whole formula: *hwt* PN_2 (in 1.14.6.40-41 and ten times in *B 1*). But we know from correspondence in the various archives that *tḥm* PN is also the opening announcement of the source of a message. This epistolary usage confirms that not only is the formulaic bicolon a poetic extension of a formulaic monocolon, but that the latter was adopted directly from the standard language of messengers (cf. chapter 3 below).

The poets also have a tendency to pair formulaic monocola, even when they have no common parallel structures. The formulaic monocolon *w* √ *ʿny* PN appears between tricola, and between two speeches in 1.14.6.16, but is followed by the formulaic monocolon √ *šmʿ(mʿ) l* PN, with which it is in effect paired, in 1.18.4.11-12. In 1.17.6.32-3 a monocolon ends a speech and an immediately following one introduces a speech. Was there a significant break between speech and narrative introduction of speech, or would the two monocola tend to fall together, maintaining the dominant rhythm of pairs of cola, and hastening the reader on? *apnk* PN is a monocolon in 1.17.5.28 (preceding a tricolon), as is *gm l* + obj. + subj. + *k* √ *ṣyḥ* in 1.19.1.49 (also preceding a tricolon), but the two appear in sequence in 1.14.5.12-14 between the end of one speech and the beginning of another. (The are followed by another formulaic monocolon, √ *šmʿ(mʿ) l* + voc. as the first colon of the following speech.) A similar pairing is effected in 1.16.5, where the repetitive structure of the passage puts between a repeated bicolon the two monocola: *in bilm ʿnyh//yṯny yṯlṯ rgm* (with numerically ascending verbs at each repetition of the second colon, until it is finally replaced by *wyʿn* + subj). *aḫr* √ *mgy* + subj., as a subordinate clause, is necessarily syntactically dependent on a following colon. In 1.15.2.10-11 this is another formulaic colon: *wyʿn* + subj. However in 1.17.5.25-28 the main clause consists of a unique bicolon.

Sometimes the association of two or more formulaic monocola is probably to be interpreted in the same way as "clusters." The occurrence in the poems of stock situations, actions and reactions produces clusters of formulaic cola, which may exhibit parallelism, or may be devoid of any traces of parallelism. Frequently such clusters will consist of transposable formulaic monocola, but they will also include fixed formulae, invariable phrases dependent on contiguous cola for completion of a clause, e.g. *balp šd rbt kmn, ʿm* + nominal phrase. The poets draw rather freely on the stock of formulae pertaining to a given situation—that is, they may use fewer or more of the monocola in the traditional stock for that situation, and they may vary the order in which these appear from passage to passage.

One example of such a cluster is the reaction to good news (cf. Del Olmo Lete 1984, 93-104):

bdnil pnm tšmḫ *šmḫ lṭpn il dpid*

w l yṣhl pit
yprq lṣb wyṣḥq
pʿn lhdm yṯpd
yšu gh wyṣḥ . . .
aṯbn ank wanḫn
wtnḫ birty npš
1.17.2.8-14

pʿn lhdm yṯpd
wprq lṣb wyṣḥq
yšu gh wyṣḥ
aṯbn ank wanḫn
wtnḫ birty npš
1.6.3.14-19

As compared with the *Aqht* passage the *Bʿl* passage omits one colon and inverts two others. In both the cluster extends over the narrative description of the reaction and its expression in speech. A shorter version of the same cluster in 1.4.4.28-30 begins with the second pair of cola in the *Aqht* passage and inserts a new colon before *yšu gh wyṣḥ*. The use of several of the cola belonging to the pool associated with a particular situation is sufficient to give the general idea, and that, rather than an account of a precise sequence of actions, appears to be the purpose of the cluster.

A second example portrays a journey (cf. Del Olmo Lete 1981, 39-40):

idk lttn pnm
ʿm aqht ġzr
balp šd rbt kmn
wṣḥq btlt ʿnt
tšu gh wtṣḥ
1.18.1.20-24

With appropriate transpositions the same passage appears in 1.4.5.22-26, and the first three cola in 1.3.4.37-38. To the third colon of the latter are added three other cola (39-40), describing the traveler's approach from the point of view of the one at the destination. The third colon of the original cluster cited above introduces the first two of these other three in 1.17.5.9-11, and all are set in the perspective of the person at the destination by the preceding transposable formula:

bnši ʿnh wyphn
balp šd rbt kmn
hlk kṯr kyʿn
wyʿn tdrq ḫss

Another selection of cola from the same pool and serving the same purpose occurs later in 1.18.4.5-7:

ttbʿ btlt ʿnt
idk lttn pnm
ʿm yṭpn mhr št
tšu gh wtṣḥ

The journey of messengers between the sender and the recipient of a message is conveyed through a version of the same cluster:

ttbʿ mlakm lyṯb
idk pnm lytn
ʿm krt mswnh/ʿm pbl mlk
tšan ghm wtṣḥn
tḥm pbl mlk/tḥm krt ṯʿ
1.14.6. -3 and 35-40

A transposition of this is used in the king's instructions to his messengers (1.14.5.29-33), which lacks the first colon and substitutes for the fourth the instruction attested elsewhere in copies of letters (*rgm l* + obj.).

A cluster of four cola found six times in the mythological Baal texts describes the journey of various gods to the residence of El. Four of those times the cluster is extended by a bicolon describing the obeisance of the god(s) on arrival before El (also used elsewhere twice on arrival before Anat, twice on arrival before Kothar, once on arrival before Mot). Once the same four-colon cluster is preceded by a colon describing Anat's departure on a journey (and used once elsewhere in connection with a journey to Baal's residence). In 1.17.6.46-51 *Aqht* boasts the longest cluster composed of all three elements—Anat's departure, the journey to El's residence, obeisance before El:

[tdʿṣ pʿ]nm wtr arṣ
idk [lttn p]nm
ʿm il mbk! nhrm
[qrb ap]q thmtm
tgly ḏd il
[wtbu q]rš mlk ab šnm
[lpʿn il t]hbr wtql
tštḥ[wy wtkbd]nh

A third cluster treats of the reaction to bad news (see Hillers 1965; Del Olmo Lete 1984, 93-104). In 1.19.2.44-47 Danel's reaction to the news of Aqhat's murder is depicted in the following formulaic cola:

[bh pʿnm] tṭṭ
ʿl[n pnh tdʿ
bʿdn] ksl yṯ[br
tǵṣ pnt kslh]
anš d[t ẓrh

The same cluster (transposed for a female subject) reappears in 1.4.2.16-20 and 1.3.3.32-35 with reversal of the second and third cola. The first of these is preceded by a version of the cluster referring to the sighting of the approaching visitor, the second by a monocolon on the same subject. This larger cluster is reduced to three cola in 1.16.1.53-55:

hlm aḫh tph
[ksl]h larṣ ṯtbr
[ ]a*ḫh tbky*

The passage cited from *Aqht* thus appears to break with convention in describing Danel's reaction not at the sight of the bearers of the bad news, but after their delivery of it.

The poets thus had at their disposal a repertoire of cola relating to each of several stock situations, such as the reaction to good news, a journey, the reaction to bad news. They drew on these without great respect for the production of bicola or tricola, giving the impression rather of an ad-lib accumulation of monocola. They may compress these clusters to a few representative cola, or extend them by adding additional cola associated with the same situation or with another stock situation in narrative proximity to the first one. The shorter versions—generally preferred by the composers of *Krt*—would hasten the narrative on, merely alluding to the fuller image of the conventional transition. The longer versions—favored by the composers of *Aqht*—would slow down the pace of the narrative and present common narrative developments in rich, familiar detail. In both poems the clusters seem to have served, not restricted the composers. The latter, far from being bound by the clusters, were free to handle them as they wished.

C. Epic Repetition I: Transposition

What is generally known as epic repetition is familiar to all who have read Genesis, the Iliad, Gilgamesh or Beowulf. Within Ugaritic poetic narrative it may be considered in relation to other forms of repetition of different dimensions, such as parallelism, as proposed by Segert. Yet it is also significantly different from other forms of repetition. In epic repetition the precise form of the repeated passage is generally predictable, as the second (or third) colon of a verse is generally not. Unlike clusters of formulae that may be identical in different narrative poems, each instance of epic repetition is unique in its wording, which is determined by the particular narrative context. Finally, epic repetition is, unlike parallelism, peculiar to narrative, and equally at home in non-parallelistic poetry (e.g. Homer) and non-poetic (prose) narrative (e.g. Genesis).

Epic repetition was recognized early in Ugaritic narrative literature (e.g., Montgomery and Harris 1935, 29-30), and has proved invaluable not only for the restoration of damaged or lost lines of text, but also for grammatical and lexical studies. Though it has been well exploited for such purposes, it does not seem to have been closely examined in its own right. The fullest analysis for many years was that of Aistleitner (1964, 9-10), who listed four types: command and execution, advice and action (only in 1.16.6.26-38 and 41-53; which is a special case of the first category), plan and promise and recognition (1.17.1-2); failure and success. More recently Del Olmo Lete has laid out a fuller description of the forms of repetition in his "morfologia literaria" (Del Olmo Lete 1981, 31-62, esp. 58-60). The following is an attempt to provide a complete typology of epic repetition in *Krt* and *Aqht*, with a view to discovering those types that are standard, conventional, commonplace but also those that are rare, novel, idiosyncratic; and in both cases to note deviations from the strict observance of the phenomenon and to interpret these. I distinguish two gross categories: transpositions and repetitions.

Transpositions involve repetition with consistent, systematic alterations, as in the transposition of a musical subject from one key to another. In this context transposition connotes the repetition of a passage with predictable grammatical adjustments to a different literary and grammatical situation (cf. the presentation of transposable formulae above). Thus the imperatives or second person jussives of a set of instructions are transposed into the third person in the subsequent narrative account of their execution by the addressee(s).

Repetitions, on the other hand, are either identical, as in the case of a message first entrusted to a messenger then delivered by that messenger, or largely identical. In the second case, unpredictable, arbitrary, significant alterations are introduced into the second (or subsequent) version. The effect of these depends on the recognition of the initial identity of the versions. Most commonly, repeated passages occur in twos or threes. Larger numbers of repetitions usually involve very short passages, and are set within the framework of a sequence of numbers.

The further classification of the occurrences of epic repetition in the poems requires the separate treatment of transposition and repetition. Following a summary presentation of the classification in each case is a complete listing of the examples according to the same scheme. While it seems unnecessary to cite each example in full, a brief description of the content of the passage and, where necessary, the narrative context accompanies each reference. Particular attention is paid to variations from the expected pattern.

TRANSPOSITION

1. Of Speech into Narrative
   a. Instructions and execution
   b. Prediction and fulfillment
   c. Conjuration and (divine) response
   d. Announcement and fulfillment of intention
2. From One Speech into Another
   a. Question and answer
   b. Request and response
   c. Announcement and acknowledgment
   d. Offer and rejection
3. Of Narrative into Speech (?)
   Activity and response (?)

1. Transposition of Speech into Narrative

a. Instructions and execution

1.17.5.16-21 and 21-25; 28-31. On seeing the approach of Kothar, Danel instructs his wife (1) to prepare for Kothar's visit and (2) to minister to him. He does not refer explicitly to Kothar's arrival. His wife's execution of the two sets of instructions is appropriately interrupted by a report of the arrival of Kothar.

1.19.2.1-5 and 5-11. Danel instructs his daughter to get his ass ready for him. *mdl ʿr//ṣmd pḥl* "equip the ass//harness the donkey" (a monocolon with internal parallelism) in Danel's instructions is expanded—by prefixing *bkm* to each clause—into a full bicolon in the account of Pughat's execution of them. The final bicolon of Danel's instructions—concerning the fastening of the silver//gold trappings onto the beast—is replaced in the account of their execution by a tricolon describing Pughat's assisting her father to mount the animal. (Cf. 1.4.4.2-7 and 8-15 which is a slightly different version of the same passage, in which the deviations of the execution from the instructions are also different.)

1.19.4.53-54 and 54-56. *Yṭpn* bids Pughat drink with him. While the basic form here is undisputed, several different constructions of the grammar are reflected in the translations. Assuming that the first colon of the execution is to be understood as: "Pughat took and drank it," the first line of the instructions must read: "Take, and drink wine," with the verbs interpreted as fem. sg. imperative and 2 fem. sg. jussive, both with the energic ending (so Jirku 1962, 46). *Yṭpn* is here understood, not to be replying to the servants who have just informed him of

Pughat's arrival, but to be abruptly addressing Pughat herself. This abruptly implied presence of Pughat before *Yṭpn*, when only "word" (*rgm*) of her arrival has been brought to him, and we might imagine her to be still on the outskirts of the camp, is an awkward moment in the usually smoothly flowing narrative. Familiarity with the hazards of copying successive pieces of similar text suggests a possible solution to the problem. Perhaps there was a brief passage intervening between the announcement of Pughat's arrival and *Yṭpn*'s invitation to drink. Such a passage would have begun *qḥn* "Take her," in which the person announcing her was told to bring Pughat to Yutpan; and then did so. This passage would have been omitted by homoioarkton.

Alternatively, one might follow Ginsberg in translating the first line of the instructions: "Take her and let her give me wine to drink," and the first line of the execution: "Pughat takes and gives . . ." (Pritchard 1969a, 155). This makes a smoother transition—from an announcement by the messengers to a response to the messengers—but it also posits a striking divergence between instruction and execution in the interpretation of the first verb (one person is instructed and another executes), and also envisages an anomalous situation: the guest gives wine to the host rather than the reverse.

On balance I think the construction implied by Gibson (1977, 121) has most to commend it. According to this *Yṭpn* responds to his servants' announcement of Pughat's arrival by addressing them: "Take her and give her wine to drink." The verbs are construed as masculine plural imperative and jussive (second person) with the third person feminine singular "energic" suffix. Correspondingly: "They take Pughat and give her to drink," with the first verb in the short form and the second in the imperfect with the simple feminine suffix. Jer. 25:15 and 17, though recounted in the first person, are comparable in subject and vocabulary and in the instruction-execution sequence: *qḥ . . . 't-kws . . . hz't mydy whšqyth 't . . . w'qh 't-hkws myd yhwh w'šqh 't . . .* " 'Take this cup . . . from me and give it to . . . to drink' . . . And I took the cup from Yahweh and gave it to . . . to drink." This interpretation of the ugaritic passage provides for continuity both within each tricolon, and between the two tricola: the servants are the addressees of all three verbs in the first and the subject of all three in the second. The address to and action by the servants follows on nicely from the servants' preceding announcement, and the giving of wine to Pughat leads her into the role of audience of *Yṭpn*'s next speech (lines 57ff.).

1.15.4.3-9 and 14-20. This is another case of a husband—this time Keret—giving instructions to his wife. There is a minor deviation in the wording of one bicolon. Keret says: "Summon my seventy bulls//my eighty gazelles (i.e. nobles, lords)." Hurraya then "brought into his presence his bulls//brought into his presence his gazelles." There is also a question as to the content and function of the intervening lines 10-13. These do not correspond to the lines following 14-20. It is an open question whether these were further instructions whose execution was for some reason postponed (cf. above on 1.17.5.16-21 and 21-25, 28-31) or whether they are a passage of some other nature intervening between instruction and execution.

(?) 1.16.1.43 and 2.53. The former line occurs in instructions Keret tells *Ilḥu* to convey to Thitmanit. The sequel contains some gaps. *Ilḥu* conveys at least part of Keret's message to Thitmanit at 1.16.1.61-62. If the text according to Virolleaud and Herdner is correct in 1.16.1.43, the *škn* of Keret's instructions, presumably delivered to Thitmanit by *Ilḥu* in the damaged passage following, could be fulfilled by her in the *šknt* of 1.16.2.53. However, for the *škn* of 1.16.1.43, read as certain by Virolleaud and Herdner, *KTU* reads *šr* (registering both signs as damaged).

(?) 1.16.2.26 and 34. See Chapter 4.

1.16.4.3-4 and 6-8. Following a command to summon *Ilš*, the summons is delivered, and El addresses *Ilš*. *ṣḥ* is the verb used in the instruction, as it was in 1.15.4.6-7. But whereas 1.15.4.17-18 has Hurraya fulfill Keret's instruction by a periphrastic expression (see above), here the expected transposition *yṣḥ* appears. The rest of both passages consists of epithets of *Ilš* and his wife/wives. The bicolon of the instruction is expanded into a tricolon by extension of the epithets of *Ilš*.

1.16.4.10-? and ?-?. El's instructions to *Ilš* begin with the formulaic *šmʿ PN* (PN here representing divine name and epithet). The sequel is lost, but we may suppose that it included an account of *Ilš'* and his wife's/wives' execution of El's instructions.

1.16.5.?-6.2 and 6.2-14. Column 6 begins with the last two cola of a speech beginning *at š[ʿtqt*] (1.16.5.4)—i.e. addressed to El's created agent of healing, Shaʿtiqat—and concluding with the feminine imperative *li* "prevail." The following account of Shaʿtiqat's activities ends with a transposed version of the same bicolon (lines 13-14)—assuming that the text's *lan* is an error for the 3 fem. perf. *lat* "she prevailed" (cf. *dt* for *dm* in line 1). It is likely then that the last ten lines of column 5 contained El's instructions to Shaʿtiqat corresponding to her actions in 1.16.6.2-

12. (Cf. Kothar's instructions to his created agents of destruction, beginning *šmk at ygrš/aymr* [1.2.4.11-12/19] and concluding with second person jussives/imperatives [1.2.4.13-15/20-22], and the transposition in the subsequent account of their performance in the hands of Baal [1.2.4.15-17/23-25].) But this leaves some eight lines of instruction in excess of the number occupied by the execution. For further discussion see chap. 4 B.

1.16.6.16-18 and 19-21. Keret instructs his daughter—beginning with the formulaic *šm*ʿ*(m*ʿ*) (l)*PN—to prepare food for him, and she exactly executes his instructions.

1.16.6.27-29 and 39-41. This is a special case of the pattern, in which a character instructs *himself* in a plan of action which he then executes. In this case the character is Yassub, and he is proposing to challenge his father's capacity to govern. There is a lack of precise verbal correspondence in the two passages: the tricolon of the instructions is replaced by three formulaic monocola in the execution. The readily available cluster prevails over the specific local language of epic repetition.

1.15.6.?-? and 16.1.11-14. In 1.16.1.11-14 Keret's son goes weeping to his father. His following speech is virtually identical with that with which the column begins, the latter lacking only the first two lines, which, it is reasonable to assume, formed the concluding two lines of tablet 15. As in the preceding case, here too we appear to have a person conceiving of a plan of action in the form of instructions to himself. The lines preceding the beginning of the proposed speech to his father would have corresponded at last in general import with those reporting his subsequent action in 1.16.1.11-14, transposed into the imperative mood—something to this effect: "Go weeping to your father and say."

There remains one doubtful case that should be mentioned briefly: 1.14.5.14-?(?). *Pbl* begins an address to his wife using the same formula that Danel used in instructions to his wife (1.17.5) and daughter (1.19.2)—see above. The sequel is entirely lost, but the convention would suggest that *Pbl* directed his wife to do something, and that there followed a corresponding account of her execution of his instructions. But this is problematic. Speech continues through line 21 (*išlḥ*-first person singular verb), and then another speech is introduced in lines 22-23 (*gm*[ ]*yṣḥ* "he cried"). There appears to be no space for a third person narrative account of any action by *Pbl*'s wife. See further chap. 4 A.

b. Prediction and fulfillment

1.17.5.2-3 and 12-13. 1.17.5.2-3 concludes a speech in which (evidently) Kothar announces that he will deliver the bow. Such first person predictions might be termed announcements of intention, but in the mouths of deities first, second and third person predictions are probably best treated as a single category (see the next two examples, and below on "announcement and fulfillment of intention"). The account of the fulfillment transposes the verbs into the third person, as expected, but also inverts the order of verb and object. The correspondence of the two bicola within the general pattern of prediction-fulfillment constrains the interpretation of the initial word of each colon as an adverb of place: *ṯmn* "there" in line 2 and *hlk*//*hl* "here" in lines 12-13 (rather than "eight," "behold," etc.).

1.18.4.17-27 and 27-37 . . . Anat announces her plan for killing Aqhat and the narrative then reports its fulfillment. Here again first person verb forms appear, as several of the actions are performed by Anat, but so do second and third person forms. The prediction is preceded by an address to Yutpan in the opening colon of Anat's speech, so that, as the object of the first verb of the prediction, he can be referred to by the second person suffix. The account of the fulfillment is not preceded by any recent reference to Yutpan, so the first bicolon of the prediction is here expanded into a tricolon in order to introduce him. The first colon of the fulfillment then balances the first colon of Anat's speech (addressing Yutpan). Lines 37ff. (at the end of the account of the fulfillment) are both sufficiently well preserved to reveal that that account did not have a colon corresponding to the last colon of the prediction, and sufficiently damaged to prevent certain reconstruction of what they did have.

1.14.2.9-3.49 and 3.52-15.1.?. El's long, complex speech to Keret consists of both instructions and predictions. A categorized list of the differences between the speech and the following narrative of actions is presented in Lichtenstein 1969-70. The major variations are:

1.14.2.12-14, El's prohibition against Keret's use of missiles against *Udm*, is omitted at the corresponding place in 1.14.5.5-6.

1.14.3.59-60, the first colon of a bicolon, corresponds to the first two cola of a tricolon in 1.14.2.13-14.

The bicolon 1.14.2.37-38 is lacking between 1.14.4.16 and 17.

The episode in which Keret makes a vow to Asherah—lacking in El's predictions—has been interpolated into the account of their fulfillment by splitting the skeletal seven-day sequence of 1.14.3.2-4 (see below) into a three-day sequence (introducing Keret's arrival at the shrine of Asherah) and a four-day sequence (bringing his journey to its final destination) in 4.31-46. For the significance of this for the larger composition of *Krt* see Chapter 4.

1.14.5.8-? is interpolated between 3.18-19 and 19-20 in the account of the fulfillment, and includes an address by *Pbl* to his wife, and whatever devolves from that. El's prediction moves directly from the noises that kept *Pbl* from sleeping to *Pbl*'s commissioning of an embassy to Keret.

In 1.14.3.19-32 El describes *Pbl*'s sending of messengers to Keret with a message, while 1.14.5.29-6.15 includes *Pbl*'s instructions to his messengers to convey the message to Keret, a reference to their journey to Keret, and then their delivery of the message to him (see below on repetitions).

The bicolon 1.14.3.27-29, in the middle of *Pbl*'s speech, appears instead at its end in 1.14.5.44-45 and 6.14-15.

In 1.14.3.32-49 El directs Keret to send a message back to *Pbl*. The account of the fulfillment again treats this more fully, recounting first the delivery of the message to the messengers, then their return to *Pbl*, then their repetition of the message to him (1.14.6.16-15.1.?).

Finally 1.14.3.44-45, an elaboration of Hurraya's beauty in El's predictions, is omitted between 1.14.6.30 and 31 in the account of their fulfillment.

c. Conjuration and (divine) response

In this category the third person jussive form is used to conjure a deity to do something, and the narrative mood to describe the deity's responsive action.

1.19.3.1-3 and 8-10; 16-18 and 22-24; 30-32 and 36-38. Danel effectively conjures Baal to break the wings of the birds of prey so that they fall at his feet. His similar conjuration of Baal to mend the birds' wings so that they fly away lacks a corresponding transposition narrating Baal's active response. But the narrative does not depend on the mending of the wings as it does on their breaking.

d. Announcement and fulfillment of intention

This consists of a first person form (used in the same speech as the conjuration) expressing a person's intentions and a third person narrative describing the fulfillment of those intentions. While only one passage is cited here, it is appropriate to recall the first person-third person sequence in the first two examples of "prediction and fulfillment," which might also be subsumed under the present category. In the second of those cases, first, second and third person verbs allow for different classifications. However, in both cases the fact that the speech is put in the mouth of a deity perhaps lends to statements using all three forms a degree of authority and certainty that justifies the distinction between "prediction" there and "announcement of intention" here.

1.19.3.3-6 and 10-11; 18-21 and 24-25; 32-25 and 38-41. These passages concern Danel's intentions following Baal's felling of the birds of prey. The last of them in each case is contingent upon his finding Aqhat's remains. The contingency, expressed by *hm iṯ* "whether there is" in the announcement of intention, is transposed into the simple *in* "there is not" or *iṯ* "there is" in the subsequent narrative account. Since the contingency is not met in the first two cases the account of the fulfillment of Danel's intentions is cut short at that point. In the third case the contingency is met, but the fulfillment of his remaining intentions is only in part a transposition of his announcement. In part it is an expansion of the announcement, and in part a substitution of material of greater concreteness, describing his removal of the remains and burial of them in a specific location. (On this whole passage see below on repetitions.)

2. Transposition from one speech into another

a. Question and answer

1.16.1.56-57 and 59-60. Thitmanit says to *Ilḥu*: [ ]*mrṣ mlk*//[ ]*krt adnk* (*CTA* restores the first *m* and *KTU* reports traces of ʿ or *š* after *mlk*). To this *Ilḥu* replies: [ ]*mrṣ mlk*//[*k*]*rt adnkm* (*CTA* does not report a final *m*). *Ilḥu* has been told of Keret's sickness and Thitmanit has not. She anticipates bad news when she sees *Ilḥu* coming (lines 53-55). Her speech is accordingly best interpreted as an enquiry whether Keret is sick, and *Ilḥu*'s as an affirmative reply to her enquiry (though most commentators assume that his reply is negative). We do not know what interrogative/affirmative particles may have introduced the two bicola. However, it is probably appropriate to restore, on the basis of the following example, *dw* in the second colon of each speech.

1.16.2-19-20 and 22-23. Someone (Thitmanit again?) enquires: *mn yrḫ kmr*[*ṣ*]//*mn kdw kr*[*t*] "How many months has he been ill//how many has Keret been sick?" to which *Ilḥu* replies: *ṯlṯ yrḫm km*[*rṣ*]//*arbʿ kdw k*[*rt*] "Three months he has been ill//four Keret has been sick." The numerals in the second bicolon are the appropriate "transposition" of the interrogative *mn* in the first.

1.16.5.10-12 etc. and 25-28. El asks the assembled gods seven times who among them will drive out Keret's sickness (*my bilm ydy mrṣ//grš̌m zbln*). Finally, failing the expected conventional response (**ank ady mrṣ//gršm zbln* "I will drive out the illness//dispel the sickness"), El answers his question himself, by proposing to make a creature who will do the job: *aškn ydt [m]rṣ//gršt zbln* "I will make one who will drive out the illness//dispel the sickness" (expanded into a tricolon by the prefixing of an additional line: *ank iḥtrš waškn*).

b. Request and response

Both examples are requests for a blessing. In the first case the speaker requests a blessing for herself, in the second the (divine) speaker requests a blessing for a third party.

1.19.4.34-35 and 39-40. The first bicolon occurs in the speech in which Pughat asks Danel for his blessing, and specifies in the first person (short form of the verb) what she hopes to accomplish with his blessing, namely to dispose of the one who disposed of her brother. Danel's blessing then includes the same bicolon transposed into the second person (also short form).

1.17.1.25-26 and 42-43. Baal here intercedes for Danel, requesting El to bless him. The verbs are in the third person, to be read as a short form (jussive) in the first bicolon, and as a long form (narrative) in the second. (The blessing of the deity is a simple prediction, where that of the father in the preceding example is a wish: "May you . . .")

There is no common material shared by Anat's requests of Aqhat and his (negative) responses in 1.17.6.16-41.

c. Announcement and acknowledgment

1.17.2.?-8 and 14-23. Someone announces and Danel acknowledges El's promise of a child. The second person references of the announcement are transposed into the first person pronouns of the response. All except the first bicolon of the announcement can be restored with certainty (since this a version of the four times recurring list of characteristics of the dutiful son). The case for restoring the first bicolon on the basis of lines 14-15 is made below in the discussion of the birth announcement (Chap. 2).

d. Offer and rejection

qḥ . . . and *lm ank* . . . is a consistent transposition in pairings of the frequently repeated refrain listing royal wealth in text 1.14. For the whole passage and the larger structure of relations in which it is involved see below on repetitions.

3. Transposition from narrative into speech(?)

Activity and response(?)

1.19.4.22-25 nd 29-31. Danel performs a sacrifice to which Pughat's speech is a response. Although the latter part of her speech is addressed to Danel in the second person, this tricolon refers to his action in the third person. In certain other respects the grammar of the transposed response is uncertain, and since the published editions of the text disagree on their reading of the tablet here, a firm foundation for a decision on the matter is lacking. If this is simply a repetition in Pughat's speech of the activity described in the previous narrative, it should presumably be classified with the repetitions that follow. On the other hand, there are several differences between the two passages, including especially imperfect verb-forms in the first passage and infinitives or perfect verb-forms in the second. Interpretation is rendered more difficult by the presence of almost three damaged lines between the two passages. It is contested whether the sacrifice which is the subject of both passages is the conclusion of the period of mourning treated in the preceding lines 9-22, or the initiation of the mission of vengeance which Pughat is prompted to undertake in her speech beginning with the reference to Danel's sacrifice. For further discussion see chap. 3 D and E.

1.19.1.36-37 and 46-48. The rending of Danel's garment is mentioned immediately preceding and immediately following his announcement concerning the clouds. The two occurrences are identical except for the addition of a *k* at the beginning of the second. For this reason I am inclined to see this as the final bicolon of Danel's speech, referring to his preceding activity as grounds for the effectiveness of his speech. But the interpretation of this section of text is very difficult and disputed.

It is clear from the preceding list that certain types of transposition—especially the first two—are common. These two are in fact among the best known types of "epic repetition" from other literatures. The next most common is the "question and answer" type which is found three times, but only in text 1.16. The remaining "types" occur rarely or only once. A thorough comparative study would give grounds for discriminating between those which are well known from epic repetition elsewhere, and those which are not. A provisional conclusion from the contrast between those types which occur several times within these two poems and are well-known elsewhere, and those types which occur only once or in one context within the poems, is that the composers of these poems exploited what I have called transposition in a variety of situations that were amenable to that treatment. In other words, we can probably credit the poets with seeing in the different relationships between speeches or between speeches and narrative new opportunities for introducing the technique of transposition, and so producing patterns and relationships within sequences of text by ad hoc creation of new types of transposition.

It is also clear that the poets were not bound to a rigid observation of the convention. They felt free to introduce diverse additional variations into the transposed passages, expanding bicola into tricola or reducing tricola to bicola, omitting cola or bicola, adding additional material, rearranging cola, etc. The esthetic virtue of the phenomenon strictly observed would be its effective binding together of related passages and its recognizable recapitulation of familiar material with predictable variations. The slightly freer handling especially of the longer transpositions suggests a clear sense that repetition and predictability could be overdone. The use of transposition in passages related in other ways than the familiar instruction-execution or prediction-fulfillment, and the introduction of minor—and sometimes very significant—unpredictable variations exhibit the poetic inventiveness of the composers and maintain the attention and stimulate the appreciation of the audience.

D. Epic Repetition II: Repetition

The various cases of simple repetition may be classified as follows:

1. Multiple repetition
2. Threefold repetition of narrative with deliberate variation
3. Twofold repetition in different speeches without variation
4. Miscellaneous twofold repetition
5. Repetition with a numerical framework

Unlike transposition, as defined above, repetition resists a rigorous typology. Admittedly there are two or three recognizable and definable types, but beyond these repetition is an open-ended category. The poets were apparently quite free to repeat a passage when and wherever they deemed appropriate.

1. Multiple repetition

Occasionally passages recurring in standard forms of repetition or transposition are by combinations of such forms effectively repeated several times, thus forming a refrain or motto theme in a section of text.

Thus in 1.17.1-2 the list of filial duries is repeated four times, as part of an appeal for blessing and the response (the actual blessing) and as part of an announcement and the response (for both pairs see above under "transpositions"). It thus dominates the narrative leading up to the birth of Danel's son and raises expectations which are the more grievously frustrated when Aqhat is killed.

In 1.14.3-15.1 the messages of Keret and Pbl to each other, entrusted to and delivered by their messengers, are the second and third occurrences of the speeches in question, the first of each having been already given in El's predictions and instructions to Keret. Further, two bicola in each set of three speeches are identical except for the first words:

lm ank/qḥ ksp wyrq
    ḫrṣ yd mqmh
w ʿbd ʿlm ṯlṯ sswm
    mrkbt btrbṣ bn amt

Beyond these six occurrences there is a seventh in a rather different context—Keret's response to El's opening question (1.14.1.51-2.3 partially restored). This refrain thus extends from almost the beginning to almost the end of the narrative concerning Keret's acquisition of a family, binding that extended and repetitive narrative together. It perhaps also emphasizes the rejection of wealth, a traditionally desirable benefit of monarchy, in favor of a family.

As noted above in the preceding section, 1.15.6.?-1.16.1.11 appears in a speech to be understood as *Ilḥu*'s "instructions" to himself. They recur in *Ilḥu*'s execution of his instructions in which he addresses these words to Keret. But beyond this they recur in a speech Thitmanit addresses to her father. Apart from some minor variations there are some substantial differences among the three versions. All three are virtually identical through the seventh colon (*bd aṯt ab ṣrry*). From there on, the first and second versions diverge, the third partially combining them:

A(1.6-11)	B(1.20-23)	C(2.43-49)
	ikm yrgm bn il krt	
	špḥ lṭpn wqdš	
	uilm tmtn	*uilm tmtn*
	špḥ lṭpn lyḥ	*špḥ lṭpn lyḥ*
tbkyk ab ǵr bʿl		*tbkyk ab ǵr bʿl*
ṣpn ḥlm qdš		*ṣpn ḥlm qdš*
any ḥlm adr		*any ḥlm adr*
ḥl rḥb mknpt		*ḥl rḥb mknpt*
ap krt bnm il		*ap krt bnm il*
špḥ lṭpn wqdš		*špḥ lṭpn wqdš*

It is noteworthy that the last bicolon of A and C is adopted for the first bicolon of B, where it is made an explicit question: "How has it been said . . .?" Version A, after raising the problem posed by Keret's death (*ik mtm tmtn* 1.3-4), continues with the mythological reference to the weeping for Keret by the Mountain of Baal, and concludes by restating the conventional piety in the final bicolon—Keret is indeed the son of El. But in version B, *Ilḥu*'s delivery of this proposed speech, the possibility of Keret's death leads immediately to a questioning of conventional piety. How could it have been said that Keret is the offspring of El? Or alternatively, and more radically, do gods die? This speech concludes with this catastrophic thought. The third version in the mouth of Thitmanit seems to presuppose both the earlier versions. It acknowledges the radical question about divine immortality (1.16.2.43-44), but then immediately quashes it by turning to the first version's mythological language, and concluding with its final assertion that Keret is indeed the son of El (having ignored B's earlier transformation of this into a question). Nothing in the context of the three passages, so far as it is preserved, appears to explain these divergences. There is certainly nothing in Keret's reaction to the second that reflects its more radical character. Perhaps it is most judicious to interpret them as hesitant and inconsistent explorations of a rather sensitive religious topic—particularly in the world of temple and priesthood in which the tablets were found. Their possible function in this section of *Krt* will be explored in chapter four.

All the repetitions in this category appear to be the poets' deliberate *extension* of conventional pairs of repetition or transposition for the purposes of the particular narrative in question.

2. Threefold repetition of narrative with deliberate variation

1.19.2.56-3.14 and 3.14-28 and 3.28-45. Danel sees the birds of prey in the sky and, invoking Baal's aid, inspects their viscera to determine whether Aqhat's remains are there. Finding they are not he invokes Baal to restore the birds' wings, broken for the purpose of his inspection. In the first repetition the poet isolates *hrgb ab nšrm* "*Hrgb*, father of the birds of prey" as the object on which Danel's eyes alight. All references to the birds in the first version are adjusted accordingly (to m.sg.). Otherwise the two passages are identical. In the third version Danel see *ṣml um nšrm* "*Ṣml*, mother of the birds of prey." This again effects a change in the form of the references to the birds (now f.sg.). But this time, when he inspects the viscera, the previous *in šmt in ʿẓm* "there was no fat, no bone" is replaced by *iṯ šmt iṯ ʿẓm* "there was fat, there was bone." The search is now ended. This affects the remainder of the third version. Instead of the immediate introduction of direct speech and the tricolon:

knp nšrm bʿl ybn	May Baal restore the birds' wings
bʿl ybn diyhmt	may Baal restore their pinions
nšrm tpr wdu	birds, take wing and fly!

the poet describes Danel's removal and burial of Aqhat's remains (1.19.3.39-41). The whole episode is then concluded, after the introduction of direct speech, with

knp nšrm bʿl yṯbr	may Baal break the birds' wings
bʿl yṯbr diyhmt	may Baal break their pinions
hm tʿpn ʿl qbr bny	if they fly over my son's grave
tsḫ!ṭann bšnth	disturb him in his sleep

(1.19.3.42-45)

The first two cola here are the reverse of the two that have concluded each of the previous versions (calling for the restoration of the birds' wings). They are also identical with the first two uttered by Danel at the beginning of each episode (with *nšrm* replaced by *hrgb* in the second version and *ṣml* in the third), so that the audience might be led to wonder, as they hear them coming round again, how much longer this episode will last. But with the last two cola it becomes apparent that this time the invocation of Baal to break the birds' wings is a curse, conditional upon the birds' disturbance of Aqhat's rest. In effect then, these cola, by their reiteration of the opening cola of all three versions (calling for breakage), and by their reversal of the concluding cola of the first two versions (calling for restoration) recall the preceding pattern even as it has been broken and convert the motif into a closure. This appears to be a case in which, through the recognition of the way repetitive devices are used, we have some relatively firm ground for appreciating the aesthetics of the tradition other than through our personal or modern taste.

But beyond that, the content of the passage makes clear that the purpose of the repetition is to express the main character's repeated efforts to accomplish something—repeated because previous attempts have ended in failure, and concluded because the third attempt ends in success. The same narrative structure—two activities ending in failure and a third ending in success—seems to inform the next example.

1.19.3.45-49; 3.50-56; 4.1-7. Following his recovery and burial of Aqhat's remains, Danel curses three places. In the first colon of the second and third versions he comes to a named site to which he addresses a curse. (The first colon of the first version remains a conundrum—the cursed site is mentioned at the beginning of the colon, followed apparently by the words *mlk yṣm*— or *lk yṣm* according to Dressler 1984a.) The poets introduce a different curse for each site: a single colon for sites one and three, a bicolon for site two. Otherwise the passages are identical (except for a minor variation of the wording of the last bicolon in the third version). Only the larger narrative context tells us that, as in the preceding example, so here Danel is twice unsuccessful in finding the right target for his curses, but the third time hits the mark. It is in fact the third site, *qrt ablm*, that is the place where Anat and *Yṭpn* accomplished the murder of Aqhat.

There is a measure of repetition in 1.15.4, 5 and 6, though all three columns are too badly damaged to permit a sure correlation. In what survives of them there is sufficient common material to encourage us to think that here again certain narrative actions and speeches were repeated three times. However, the state of the text does make clear that there was considerable variation among the three versions, and so discourages attempts at restoration. The following repetitions can be extricated from the remains: 1.15.4.15-16 and 5.1-2; 15.4.24-5 and 5.7-8; 15.4.26-27 and 5.9-10 and 6.3-4; 15.4.21 (cf. 17-18) and 5.12-13 and 6.6-7(?). However, the function of these repetitions could not, as in the previous examples, be to present two failures followed by one success, since we know that Keret's sickness was not cured until 1.16.6 (always assuming that his sickness was the occasion for the sacrificial meal that is the subject of these columns) .

3. Twofold repetition in different speeches without variation

Perhaps the most common form of repetition in epic literature generally is that of the message first entrusted to a messenger and then delivered by the messenger to the destinee. This form is so well known, and *Krt* and *Aqht* use it in such a standard, conventional way that it will suffice simply to list its occurrences.

1.14.5.33-45 and 6.3-15.

1.14.6.17-35 and 1.15.?-? (safely restorable following 1.14.6.35-41—note that 40-41 is an addition).

1.16.1.39-41 and 61-62 (the remains of the succeeding lines in 1.16.2.1ff. suggest that these did not repeat 1.16.1.41ff.).

The following two cases constitute a special use of this formal pattern: the message is entrusted by a person to himself. This adaptation of the relationship is the poets' means of penetrating terrain that is otherwise obscure—the thoughts and intentions of the actors.

1.16.6.29-38 and 42-54 (Yassub's "message" entrusted to and then delivered by himself; cf. his "instructions" to himself above under "Transpositions").

1.15.6.?-16.1.11 and 16.1.14-23 (*Ilḥu*'s "message" entrusted to and delivered by himself—this interpretation is based on Yassub's proposal to address his father in 1.16.6).

Two other passages deserve comment in this context: 1.17.1.37-? is El's blessing of Danel in response to Baal's request. 1.17.2.?-8 is an announcement of this to Danel. The two speeches share the list of filial duties, but we do not know how much more. The pronominal suffixes change with the different addressee. Formally there is nothing in the surviving text that stamps the relationship between these two speeches as that of message entrusted and message delivered. However, the context implies that the relationship between the two is very similar. Baal, or whoever conveys El's blessing to Danel, perhaps takes it upon himself to bear the message without being formally commissioned. Since the message is a response to Baal's request, based in turn on Danel's appeal, Baal would not need to be directed to report the response back to Danel.

1.15.1.1-7 is also a candidate for classification as a message delivered. It is the next preserved piece of text following the messages exchanged between Keret and *Pbl* at the end of 1.14.6. Each of those messages is first entrusted to messengers and then delivered by them. Since, when 1.14. ends, Keret is sending a message to *Pbl*, we would expect his reply to follow; and since there is room for *Pbl*'s reply to be first imparted to his messengers, and its delivery then introduced prior to 1.15.1.1-7; and since after 1.15.1.1-7 Keret again initiates a speech; it is reasonable to conclude that these seven lines constitute the last part of *Pbl*'s reply, here delivered by his messengers to Keret (see further chap. 4A).

4. Miscellaneous twofold repetition

The following repetitions appear to be not fixed, conventional types, but individual cases of poetic use of repetition.

1.19.2.12-18 and 19-25. Danel's tour of the cultivated land occurs twice, with a change in three words, those referring to cultivated land (*palt* and *aklt*), to desirable vegetation (*bṣql* and *šblt*), and to the poor condition or environment in which the vegetation now is (*yǵlm* and *ḥmdrt*). There are several uncertainties in the interpretation of this passage. We do not know, for example, whether the two versions (the three pairs of words) are synonymous or complementary in the same way as parallel cola, so that no significant difference in meaning or referent is intended (cf. Jirku 1960, who sees them as dialectal variations), or whether in fact the two versions refer to two different agricultural situations. In any case, the outcome is the same, so the purpose of the full repetition is likely to be aesthetic—to elicit appreciation of the repetition and its variation, and to slow down the action and heighten the suspense: when is Danel going to learn the real cause of the conditions he deplores? (Contrast Gray 1965, 301: "to indicate persistence in ritual.") The reference to Aqhat as the harvester in the repeated wish that there may be a harvest conduces to this effect by its dramatic irony.

1.17.6.17-18 and 26-28. These may be formulaic, but since they are not attested elsewhere, they should be mentioned here. The repetition is strictly *irš* X *watnk*//Y *wašlḥk*. In the first version X//Y = *ksp//ḫrṣ*, in the second *ḥym//blmt*. The second version expands the bicolon into a tricolon in order to introduce the vocative. This repetition is one device in the portrayal of the development of the conflict between Anat and Aqhat.

1.14.10-11 and 21-23. The first passage is a simple statement of the collapse of Keret's household; the second, following notice of the various forms of death suffered by Keret's family, is cast as the object of what Keret sees, and is expanded for that purpose into a tricolon:

10-11	21-23
	yʿn ḥtkh krt
krt ḥtkn! rš	*yʿn ḥtkh rš*
krt grdš mknt	*mid grdš ṯbth*

Since lines 1-25 seem to be a prologue—current action begins with line 26—the repetition serves to bind this section together. The first statement may be a summary statement of Keret's condition described in lines 6-11; and the second, succeeding the list of specific developments recording how that condition came about, and putting the situation as the object of Keret's view, may be designed to lead us more directly into his reaction, which is the focus of the following lines. In any case the repetition is rather loose. (Even looser, perhaps better noted as a faint echo, is the connection between lines 1.14.1.7-8 and 24.)

1.15.2.2-4 and 13-15. El's pronouncement of a marriage blessing on Keret promises him greatness among his ancestors. This promise is found after his enumeration of Keret's sons (though the text is lacking after his characterization of the first son) and again after his enumeration of Keret's daughters. Its reiteration emphasizes Keret's comparative status as the ultimate purpose of the blessing (cf. chap. 2 C).

(1.19.4.46-50 and 51-2. This narrative report of an action subsequently reported in a speech might have been an appropriate occasion for simple repetition. In fact, despite a large commonality in general substance, only one or two words are identical. Since journeys are only transitional between scenes, it is inappropriate to dwell on them; hence the report to *Yṭpn* of Pughat's arrival here is brief and summary, moving the audience rapidly on to the encounter between *Yṭpn* and Pughat.)

Before a review of repetitions within a numerical framework, some general conclusions on the previous uses of repetition may be appropriate. Even more than transpositions, repetitions may be handled quite freely by the composers. Admittedly some types, such as the message (entrusted and delivered), are treated rather rigidly. Another example of a more rigidly observed form of repetition is the refrain—defined here as a passage which may be repeated twice as a message or as a standard type of transposition, but which is then deliberately used much more extensively through a particular narrative unit. In repetitions with significant variations, such as an action repeated twice without, and a third time with success, the variations are neither arbitrary nor specifically predictable by the audience, but form a rational, purposeful pattern, which becomes recognizable as the repetitions succeed one another and can be appreciated in full at the end of the sequence.

The recognition of these conventional types of epic repetition, as well as of those cases of repetition which do not appear to fall into any general type, has long been seen to be invaluable for the approximate restoration of damaged or lost passages.

Variations from type or from strict repetition expose the creative freedom—or sometimes laxity—of the poets in relation to their conventions. Such variations occasionally give grounds for hazarding judgments about the aesthetic effects sought, an enterprise always freighted with the risk of imposing on the poems personal or modern tastes quite alien to this archaic literature.

Given the ubiquity of transposition and other forms of repetition in the poems, and the widespread use of the same devices in other ancient narrative poetry (e.g. Akkadian, Hittite, Homeric), the literary character of these devices must be regarded as well established. The burden of proof lies on any who would claim that sometimes the repetition of a passage is evidence of its roots in ritual, expressive of the repetitiveness of a ritual or the solemnity of an imprecation, or reflective of the repetition of an incantation. Gray in particular has made such claims (e.g. Gray 1965, 298-301). While he recognizes that various kinds of repetition are literary conventions, and sees their literary character as arguing against their literal interpretation (Gray 1965, 302-3), he claims that they are significant for the specific social setting of the poems and connects them with ritual acts and pronouncements. Admittedly the ritual acts and pronouncements reported in 1.19 may reflect actual ritual acts and pronouncements as used in the society, but as they figure in this text they all have their place in the progress of the narrative, and their repetition (or transposition) has narrative functions. There are no grounds for supposing that their repetition is a reflection of their social use. As described, several of the actions are clearly not realistic, and in fact stand in contrast with the actions described in Ugaritic (and Hittite, Akkadian, etc.) ritual texts. Consequently an individual case of repetition cannot be taken to be descriptive of actual practice in social life, nor indicative of the use of the poem in actual social life.

While the preceding account of repetition in the narratives has been largely descriptive, the evidence for the poets' freedom and creativity in handling the standard types of repetition, and of using repetition other than where the conventional relationships between passages are found, has a historical corollary. Different successive performances—or copies—of a narrative might, while retaining the same overall structure, use variation within a standard pattern of repetition, add or remove multiple repetition, or repeat a particular passage in an unconventional way so as to produce different emphases, motifs or themes. These would in turn imply different purposes, audiences and settings. The poems as we have them are but one realization of the several that successive generations of poets would have produced.

5. Repetition with a numerical framework

Although the sequence of numerals has been regarded as a formula, it is perhaps more satisfactory to treat it as a framework for the repetition of a subject. A sequence of numerals is no more a formulaic peculiarity of narrative than conventional pairs of words are a formulaic peculiarity of parallelistic poetry.

The full repetition of a verse of text in conjunction with a sequence of numerals is well known in Mesopotamian narrative literature, being attested from Sumerian to Neo-Assyrian writings. (On this and on the relationship between the Mesopotamian and West Semitic, specifically Ugaritic, conventions see Freedman 1970-71.) This means of repetition is used in a wide variety of ways in Ugaritic: to construct a self-contained episode, to extend a transition and thus suspend entry into a new episode, and ultimately without repetition to hasten the plot along.

1.17.2.26-40. Following Danel's return home with the news that he has been granted a son, he is visited by the Kotharat:

26-27 The Kotharat arrive (*ʿrb*)
(27-29 Formulaic introduction of Danel as subject of the following verbs)
29-31 Danel gives food and drink to the Kotharat
31-34 "Now for one day and a second" he gives etc.
34-36 "A third, a fourth day" he give etc.
36-38 "A fifth, a sixth day" he gives etc.
39-40 Then, the seventh day the Kotharat depart (*tbʿ*)

The episode is enclosed by two bicola distinguished only by the verb (*ʿrb*/*tbʿ*). The activity is first spelled out in a tricolon, which is then repeated three times as a bicolon, each bicolon linked with a colon numbering off two days. The reference to the seventh day introduces the concluding counterpart to the first bicolon. Thus the sequence of days leads nowhere: the seventh day is not climactic. The numerical framework simply extends the basic activity into a length of text which conveys the repetitiveness of the activity. This thus becomes a distinct episode in the sequence of events leading up to the birth of Aqhat.

1.17.1.1-16. In the opening scene of *Aqht* Danel performs actions which are designed to bring to the attention of the gods his childless plight:

1-3 Formulaic introduction of Danel as subject

3-6 Danel gives some special food and drink to the gods (bicolon) and lies down for the night (bicolon)
6-9 "Now for one day and a second" he feeds the gods (tricolon)
9-12 "A third, a fourth day" he feeds the gods (tricolon)
12-16 "A fifth, a sixth day" he feeds the gods (tricolon) and lies down (tricolon)
16-17 "Then, the seventh day" Baal responds

The two different activities—feeding the gods and lying down for the night—constitute the largest block of repeated material in these numerical frameworks. In each of the repetitions the opening bicola are extended into tricola by the prefixing of Danel's name and the prolepsis of the first two words of the bicolon. But in the first two repetitions only the first action (bicolon) is resumed, the second being assumed. The use of two tricola in the last repetition have the effect of postponing the climax, which then follows quickly in a single colon leading directly into Baal's speech to El (which includes a quotation of the original bicolon referring to Danel's feeding of the gods: lines 21-22).

In none of the numerical frameworks is there a distinction between the initial statement of an action and its repetition, such as Caquot and Sznycer see here (Caquot and Sznycer 1974; Caquot 1979). They take the first two bicola to be the gods' order of the following action (jussive verb forms), which Danel then begins only in line 6. But as in 1.17.2 above and all the other cases to follow, the repeated action is itself always first stated before the numerical framework (so Loewenstamm 1980, 192-209). That this is no exception is confirmed by the traditional form of the narrative of which this is the opening (see chap. 3 A).

These are the only two full uses of the traditional framework in *Krt* and *Aqht*. Other examples appear in the Baal texts and in Akkadian narrative poems (Loewenstamm 1980, 192-209; Freedman 1970-71). A unique adaptation is found in 1.16.5.9-28. The formulaic *wyʿn* PN (DN) introduces a speech by El in which he enquires which of the gods will dispel Keret's sickness (bicolon). The following colon reports that none of the gods answered him. His speech and the gods' silence is then repeated three times, each introduced by a colon containing numerals. But there are two peculiarities of the numerals in this passage. First, the poet uses verbal forms of the numerals (*ytdṯ yšbʿ rgm* "he speaks a sixth, a seventh time")—presumably because the conventional days or years would be out of place here. Second, instead of starting with the first and second times, as is customary in the framework, the initial description of the action is taken as its first performance and the framework begins with the second and third times, presumably because the language did not provide a verb form meaning "to do once." But the consequence of this is that the final repetitions are the sixth and seventh times, so that there is nothing new in the usually climactic seventh unit. The climax—which follows in El's next speech—is postponed beyond the expected point, and the response to El's question is of a different order from that which the repetitions (and the underlying conventional scene) lead us to expect (see chap. 4 C). There is in fact no-one among the gods who will dispel Keret's sickness. Hence El bids them sit down (lines 24-25). El will create a being to do the job (25-28). The peculiarities of form and substance are thus perfectly matched.

Other versions of the numerical framework in *Krt* and *Aqht* are abbreviated in various ways. 1.14.3.2-4 has an opening verb followed by the bare numerals with the noun *ym*: *lk ym wṯn//ṯlṯ rbʿ ym/ḫmš ṯdṯ ym* "go a day and a second//a third, a fourth day//a fifth, a sixth day." The arrival at the end of the journey is introduced by *mk špš bšbʿ* "then at sunrise on the seventh." The measurement of time here is also a measurement of distance. The framework, without any undue delay, counts out how many days' journey is required to reach the destination. There is no interest in the journey itself, simply a superficial respect for tradition, with an eagerness to proceed with the plot.

The same is true of 1.14.3.10-16. Apart from the substitution of *dm* for *lk* the first three cola are identical with those just quoted. In this case, however, a bicolon is inserted prior to the seventh day, to give more substance to what is happening—or rather, not happening—during this passage of time: the besieging army is not to release its missiles against the town. In the later transposition of the passage (1.14.5.3-8) this bicolon is absent altogether. In neither context does the seventh day produce a climax, leading rather into the succeeding subject: *Pbl*'s inability to sleep because of the noise of the domestic animals enclosed within the town. The two passages are evidence of the decline of the traditional full-bodied version still found in *Aqht*. The repeated matter is gradually discarded, being retained immediately before the seventh day—perhaps to heighten the suspense—in some contexts, but finally jettisoned altogether as the poets' sense of the urgency of the narrative reduces the function of the framework to an indicator of the passage of time and a transition from one subject to another.

The transposition of 1.14.3.2-4 is a striking example of poetic creativity in the handling of convention. The poet wishes to introduce a new episode, and does so by making the third day of the seven-day framework a climactic one: *aḫr špšm bṯlṯ* "after sunrise on the third" (1.14.4.32-33; the three day sequence is also an established convention: 1.20.2.5; 1.22.2.24-25; cf. Bauer 1958). With the third day Keret and his troops arrive at the site at which the inserted scene is enacted. The numerical framework is then resumed, beginning with the first day again. This time it continues through "a third, a fourth day," at which point the fourth day is repeated in the climactic line: *aḫr špšm brbʿ* "at sunrise on the fourth." Both the repetition of the preceding number in the climactic line and the use of "four" as the climactic number are otherwise unattested. What has led the poet to these innovations and what he has accomplished by them is the introduction of the new episode and the maintenance of the total of seven days for the full journey from *Ḫbr* to *Udm* (cf. chap. 4 A).

Comparable to the visit of the Kotharat in the first tablet of *Aqht* is that of the mourners in the third tablet. This visit also occurs after Danel's return home, and is also framed by a verse (in this case a tricolon) reporting the arrival (*ʿrb*) and one concerning the departure (*tbʿ*) of the visitors—the latter in the form of a directive from Danel. The substance of the mourners' activity is given in a bicolon following the reference to their arrival. Following this the passage of time is conveyed by the expression *lymm lyrḫm//lyrḫm lšnt//ʿd šbʿ šnt* "from days to months//from months to years//until the seventh year," after which the bicolon describing their activity is repeated. The following climactic line *mk bšbʿ šnt* "then in the seventh year" leads into a tricolon introducing Danel's concluding, dismissive speech.

Here, while the climactic line of the traditional numerical framework is retained, the sequence of numbers is abandoned altogether in favor of a quite different sequence of prepositional phrases, that more directly describe the passage of time. This is used even more simply and realistically in 1.6.5.7-9, where there is no repetition, no reference to any activity, but the expression simply reports that seven years passed before the next development in the story.

In other contexts the remains of the numerical framework

are even more vestigial or apocopated. It is as though the poets vaguely recalled the convention and felt obliged to gesture toward it in passing, but were more interested in moving on with the substance of the narrative. In 1.17.5.3-4 the concluding line *whn šbʿ bymm* stands alone. It is preceded by a bicolon that is evidently a speech of Kothar, but the text is missing before that. Does the preserved text begin with the repetition of something Kothar had been saying for six days? That seems unlikely. It is preferable to take it as a minimal vestige of the old numerical framework, here simply alluding to the time that must have passed between Kothar's announcement that he would deliver the bow, and his actual appearance to Danel. (The displacement of the preposition *b* from the numeral *šb'* to *ymm* "days" remains a puzzle.)

The difficulties of 1.15.3.20-21 are probably also to be explained as the result of the compression and near elimination of a numerical framework:

wtqrb wld bn lh
wtqrb wld bnm lh
mk bšbʿ šnt
bn krt kmhm tdr
ap bnt ḥry kmhm

The last bicolon reports that the totality of the children born to the marriage by the seventh year (middle colon) were as many as promised (by El in the preceding marriage blessing). The first bicolon would be a gesture in the direction of the numerical framework—referring to one son (sg.), two sons (du.)—abandoned, except for the concluding formula, in order quickly to affirm the satisfactory conclusion to the whole affair. Any inclination to use a numerical framework here may have foundered on the difficulties of listing seven//eight sons (1.15.2.23-5) and six (1.15.3.7-12) daughters (or might the *ṣǵrthn* of the last line of the marriage blessing envisage a seventh?)! The whole passage is a good illustration of the irrelevance of the arithmetical value of numerals in poetic texts. What is important is their sequence and the symbolic value of certain individual numbers—three, but especially seven.

The numerical framework makes another vestigial appearance in 1.16.6.21-22. Thitmanit has just executed her father's instructions to prepare food for him (bicolon) following his healing by El. Keret then ascends his throne (tricolon). Between these two subjects the text has *hn ym wṯn* "then a day and a second"—and no more. One may speculate that Thitmanit prepared food for several days—scarcely that Keret kept on getting on his throne for several days! But the simplest explanation of the phrase is that it is used to allude to the passage of time between Thitmanit's preparation of food for Keret following his sickness and his resumption of his royal duties. Perhaps an earlier poet would have used the framework to describe Keret's eating of the food and growing stronger. But our poet/scribe wishes to hasten on to the next episode, Yassub's rebellion.

Two other passages deserve comment in this context. In 1.14.2.30-31 (corresponding to 1.14.4.11-12) Keret is told to bake grain "of the fifth//of the sixth months." As an isolated pair, five-six is unique. Further, its position in the structure of the verse does not accord with the situation of a pair of numbers in any other numerical framework; nor is there anything in the context to suggest that this is the third pair of months in a repetitive passage. We know from the sequel that the march to *Udm* and the siege of *Udm* lasted only six days each, so that the months in question can have had nothing to do with the length of the campaign. Presumably we have to do here with a realistic reference to the time when the grain became available, and hence to its ripeness and quality.

Finally in the prologue to *Krt* there is a sequence of numerals which has vexed interpreters throughout the history of Ugaritic scholarship. The range is unique: from three to seven; and the form is unique: each numeral has a prefixed *m* and a suffixed *t*. The numerals occur in successive cola with no repetition, and there is no discernible shift in direction or impact in the colon housing the number seven. Given these facts, the numerical framework appears to shed no light on this passage.

In sum, the use of the numerical framework with extensive repetition, well attested in both Akkadian and Ugaritic narrative poetry, is in Ugaritic often handled with considerable freedom. Frequently the repetitions are eliminated and only one statement of the repeated or persisting action is used. Sometimes that one statement is limited to one verb, or the framework is used without any action, simply to indicate the passage of time. Often only fragments of, or substitutes for the framework appear, suggesting either the rejection of fuller material formerly in the context or the deliberate use of allusion to suggest the passage of time between two episodes. The use of the numerical framework to build to a climax is clear and forceful only in 1.17.1 and 1.16.5, the latter being formally unique. The most creative, purposeful adaptation of the framework appears in Keret's execution of El's instructions (by contrast with the instructions themselves) in which the poet makes the third day of a seven-day sequence the point of entry into a new episode, introduced into the narrative although it was absent in the instructions, and then continues with an unprecedented four-day sequence in order to have Keret complete the predicted seven-day journey to *Udm*.

E. Larger Conventions and Conclusions: the World in the Poems and the Poems in the World

Formulae and epic repetition are both characterized by literal repetition. There are other, non-literal forms of repetition which are part of the stock-in-trade of the narrative poet. For example, the poets have at their disposal standard scenes or activities which they may use as they judge appropriate in different contexts. (I do not include here passages that recur in only one poem, on the assumption that such repetitions may be specific to the shape and theme of that poem, and therefore better considered within an analysis of its particular structure—see chaps. 3 and 4 below). The different instances of a given scene or activity may exhibit some verbal identity (and such common verbal elements are cited below), but this is not so striking as the subject and its location and use in the narrative. These narrative passages of conventional content—variously called themes, topoi, motifs, type-scenes, etc.—are not numerous.

1) The visit, including arrival and departure, of deities: *aḫr/mǵy* DN (so also 1.2.1.30; 1.4.3.23-24; 1.4.5.44) . . . verb + DN *lahl* + pron.sfx.//DN (verb) *lmšknt* + pron.sfx. (1.17.5.25-33; 1.15.2.11-3.19). In both cases the purpose of the divine visit is to confer something—a gift, a blessing—upon the hero. The visit of Kothar to Danel results in Aqhat's acquisition of the bow that will be the occasion of his downfall. The visit of the whole pantheon to Keret produces a divine blessing on his marriage, which in turn leads immediately into the superabundant fulfillment of his wish for progeny. But that too is a false security, since Keret immediately becomes ill, and one of his progeny later challenges him for the throne.

2) The approach (as distinct from the visit) of a deity in response to an expressed need: *wyqrb* (1.14.1.26-38; 1.17.1.1-16). In *Krt* the approach clearly takes place in Keret's dream. In *Aqht*, while the opening scene suggests an incubation, there is nothing in the surviving text to indicate that what follows occurs in a dream. In any case, in *Aqht* the verb is ambiguous: it may serve to describe Baal's response to Danel's appeal or Baal's approach to El in intercession for Danel—or both (see chap. 3A).

In both texts El ordains that the need will be met, and in the event it is met.

3) The appeal for a blessing: *ltbrk*//*(l)tmr* (1.17.1.23-24; 1.15.2.14-16—both cases an appeal by Baal to El for the blessing of a third party; 1.19.4.32-33—an appeal on her own behalf by a daughter to her father). In each case the act of blessing immediately follows the speech of the petitioner.

4) The act of blessing: *ks yiḫd il !b(y)d(h)* (. . .) *ybrk//ymr* (1.17.1.34-36; 1.15.2.16-20). In both passages the blessing leads directly into its fulfillment: the long-term fulfillment of Keret's blessing is reported immediately and briefly; the more immediate fulfillment of Danel's blessing is stretched out over a column or so. The act of blessing by Danel in 1.19.4 does not involve the cup nor a description of the act, but simply a speech which uses the language of El's blessing in 1.17.1. and of Pughat's request—which is presumably fulfilled in the following narrative of Pughat's expedition for revenge. The *ks*[ ]//*kr[pn]* of 1.16.5.39-40 may also be an act of blessing leading into the commissioning of El's new creature, Shaʿtiqat. The commissioning speech begins in the next line (41): *at š[ʿtqt]*, and apparently becomes the instructions that end with 1.16.6.1-2 and are executed in 1.16.6.2-14 (see chap. 4 B and the present chapter, C 1 a).

Other such standard scenes and activities, less fully or clearly attested in *Krt* and *Aqht*, but well known from other occurrences in Ugaritic literature, include the preparation of a banquet, invitation of guests and the actual feasting. Elements of this occur three times in the badly damaged last three columns of 1.15 (see above, D 2). For further examples see the presentation of ugaritic "morfologia literaria" in Del Olmo Lete 1981.

There are whole sections of narrative that may occur only once in the two poems, or indeed in all of the preserved Ugaritic literature, that nevertheless are comparable with narratives units elsewhere, thus revealing underlying stereotyped narrative structures. The traditional narrators might use one such structure to tell a single tale complete in itself; or they may, as here, compose or adapt tales based on several structures to form larger narratives. Obviously, the discernment of such structures or types will depend on the analysis of large-scale portions of the poems and comparative study of other narrative literature. As the analysis of the two poems in chapters four and five will focus on these larger entities, further elaboration of the conventions operating at this level will be postponed to those chapters.

To conclude: the Ugaritic narrative poets used a variety of

conventional forms ranging from formulaic epithets, phrases and cola to fixed tale types. The formulae were of two types: fixed and transposable, the two functioning efficiently in relation to one another. For example, formulaic epithets would fit neatly into the variable component of transposable formulaic monocola. Formulae were sometimes paired to meet the constraints of parallelism: the grouping of cola in parallel bi- or tricola. Parallelism allowed the relatively simple variation of a colon by any of a variety of semantic or syntactic analogues, also by abbreviation or extension, before the taking of the next step in the narrative. Beyond these verse by verse conventions, the poets would repeat verbally material that was repeated in the world created by the poet: messages were spelled out each time they were pronounced by the actors; a repeated action was not just referred to but described equally fully each time; as in the exercises in elementary language textbooks, a question was to be answered not with a single word but in a complete sentence that repeated or transposed the language of the original question. Beyond these verbal repetitions, the poets worked with a number of conventional situations and actions; journeys, visits, invitations, meals—material used commonly enough that here too some of the wording might become conventional, whether in the form of individual words or of whole clusters of formulaic monocola. The largest components of the narratives were fixed tale types—whole stories or episodes that may be attested elsewhere in simpler combinations of two or three, as in the Hittite *Illuyanka*, or built into more extended and complex narratives, such as *Gilgamesh* or Genesis.

All these conventional forms may be classified according to two broad types: specific formulaic phrases and cola, standard scenes and activities, and tale-types, that the poets might use in the development of any narrative; and general types of repetition that the poets might use in the development of a particular narrative to produce a variation on or repetition of unique cola or passages: parallelism and epic repetition.

In view of this pervasive use of repetition of one kind or another at one level or another, it is not surprising that the poems generally strike the modern western mind as repetitive, slow-moving and lacking in creativity. In fact, compared with most modern Western poetry (which we unconsciously tend to use as a basis of comparison) it may quite legitimately be so described. The narratives lack many of the features that we consider appealing and admirable in narrative and poetry.

There is, for example, no interest on the part of the Ugaritic

poets in the appearance of the physical world, whether of the physical appearance of their characters or of their characters' environment. The narrators do not depend on observation and description for their effects. They have no interest in the specific geography of the action. Only the most conventional and artificial reference is made to distance (e.g. in the seven days = four plus three days of Keret's journey to *Udm*), and orienting references to any of the major settlements of the known world—including the city in which the immediate transmitters and audiences lived—are totally lacking. (On the difficulties of identifying *ṣrm* and *ṣdynm* in 1.14.4.35-39 with Tyre and Sidon, see Astour 1973, 30-31.) Most of the place-names mentioned in the poems are either totally unknown elsewhere—as is the case with the artificial-looking *mrrt tǵll bnr* of 1.19.3.50-52—or they are so common, at least in the consonantal form of the Ugaritic script, that they could be equated with any of several sites attested elsewhere. Astour's equation of the place names in *Krt* with sites in the Khabur triangle known from other second millennium documents is as carefully done as any such study, yet finally he appropriately admits: "It is true that the existence of numerous toponymic parallels between that region and the contemporaneous Syria precludes a clear-cut solution [to the problem of identifying the locale of the action in *Krt*]" (Astour 1973, 38-39). *Ḫbr*, the seat of Keret's rule, is not mentioned in any Ugaritic texts outside *Krt*. *Udm*, the corresponding city of king *Pbl*, may be once referred to in the gentilic form, *udmym*, mentioned in the administrative record, 4.337.15 (but is not to be read in 4.693.7; see Ribichini 1982). *Ablm*, the only significant place-name in *Aqht*, appears in no Ugaritic text outside that poem (although the element *abl* is common in several Hebrew place-names). Significantly, then, the place-names that figure most prominently in the poems—those associated with the kings in *Krt* and the murder of the hero in *Aqht*—do not appear anywhere else as such in the Ugaritic texts. It is reasonable to conclude that, for the Ugaritic composers and audiences, the action of the poems takes place in an undefined zone, which, whether real or imaginary, derives its significance from the action of the poems, not from the audience's familiarity with their geographical setting (cf. Ribichini 1982; and contrast Margalit 1981).

Likewise the time and duration of the action are undefined in any real chronological sense. The preceding section laid out the conventional artifice and its variations by which the narrator indicted the passage of time. The action as a whole appears to take place in time as experienced by ordinary people (as distinct from some cyclical mythic time or magically suspendible or reversible time), but not at any defined point in the community's awareness of its past. Of course, we do not have the opening lines of either poem. Both may have opened with some temporal reference. However, comparative evidence would lead us to expect that, even if that were so, it would be the sort of reference that would tell us that the particular time of the action was irrelevant (on this see the quotations in Berlin 1983a, 23; and, contrasting the Sumerian and Akkadian conventions, Westenholz 1983, 336; on the whole subject of the internal setting of "epic" literature, Berlin 1983a, 20-24).

Recent attempts to specify the geographical or historical setting of the actions of the poems commit a major category mistake. They attribute to the poems a historical and geographical realism and precision that is totally irrelevant to these traditional compositions and to the interests of their composers, transmitters and audiences (similarly Del Olmo Lete 1981, 355-56). Thus to place the action of *Krt* in the Habur triangle in the Mari period (Astour 1973); or that of *Aqht* in the movement and settlement of the Amurru tribes in the Old Babylonian period (Dijkstra 1979, 206), around the south and east shores of the Sea of Galilee c. 1500 B.C. (Margalit 1981; but see now Dressler 1984b; also Sapin 1983, 172-73, n. 69), or in the Homs valley during the twentieth or sixteenth centuries (Sapin 1983) is equally valueless for the interpretation of the poems. For the latter, the only relevant settings are those created in the poems by the poets, and that in which we know the poems were transmitted, fourteenth century Ugarit.

Again the poets do not open up the mental or emotional lives of their characters, whose actions do not seem to devolve either from deliberate moral choices or from cosmic necessity. At least such choices or necessity are not explicit. Instead, where actions do not follow each other in conventional sequences, they strike us as arbitrary. However, it is the uniqueness or lack of context of the "arbitrary" actions or sequences of actions that leads us so to designate them. As soon as we can correlate the acts in question with a similar sequence of actions elsewhere, that is, as soon as we can place them in the narrative tradition, we can begin to discern the significance of the common or distinct features of the sequences. What cannot be compared cannot be understood.

In fact the characters of the poems move in a world already created by literary tradition, and only that tradition can provide the larger background and presuppositions of narrators and audiences that we—and the words of the poem itself—lack. It is to that tradition that we must turn again and again as we work our way through the poems. It is also vis-a-vis that tradition that we can define the modifications and variations in the tradition that are the peculiar work of our poets. These modifications and variations are our primary clues to the purposes of the poets and the expectations of their audiences, and it is our explanation of them as producing special effects or conveying significant messages that will permit us to approach an understanding of the poems as wholes.

To relate *Krt* and *Aqht* to the larger tradition requires some knowledge of the ways in which traditional narratives change, so that one can recognize related texts through the different dress in which they may appear. The study of such changes has been undertaken by anthropologists looking at the operation of live oral traditions (see especially Vansina, 1965) and by orientalists looking at the different versions of a narrative as they appear in writing centuries apart (see especially the study of the Gilgamesh tradition in Tigay 1982). From such investigations it is clear that the most unstable and variable elements in a narrative are the setting—the specific time, place and people referred to—and the theme. The most stable and durable features are the narrative structure, the plot, the sequence—though not necessarily the number—of episodes (Vansina 1965, 63-64 distinguishes these as the secondary and functional elements of a traditional tale). A nice illustration of this from the ancient Near East is the Sargon story, in which, at a time when Sargon himself was unknown to the oral transmitters of the tale, the more recent figure of Cyrus was substituted for the earlier hero (Drews 1974, esp. 391-93). Fontenrose has drawn a nice distinction between *variants*, in which the names of persons and places may be altered, but the basic structure remains stable—i.e. the same story with different settings; and *versions*, in which, though the setting remains the same, various mutations or displacements may take place; alterations of the status of the characters (their role, rank, relationship or class), of actions (e.g. of types of combat, deception, or punishment), of degree (emphasis or prominence, understatement or suppression of a feature), of connection between deed or trait and character, the fusion or combination of roles, or their expansion or duplication. Different variants or versions belong to the same tale type if the basic plot persists—the same series or constellation of episodes—a durable core, even though some episodes may be dropped or added or changed around (Fontenrose 1980, 5-9). Vansina has a more complex typology ranging from identity in all four categories of setting, theme, episodes and plot, to a total lack of commonality between texts (Vansina 1965, 126-28).

For our purposes, it will be sufficient to note the fact of change, the kinds of change, and the persistence of basic plot structures; and further to apprehend that the causes of the changes will include cultural presuppositions, the social use and function of the text, and the individual abilities and motives of the transmitters (cf. Vansina 1965, 76-113). Since we shall not be able to compare the narratives as wholes (which we do not have) with other whole narratives, much of our relation of *Krt* and *Aqht* to the narrative tradition will be through the simpler narratives or episodes of which they are composed. And since we have very little from Ugarit with which to compare these, we shall frequently have recourse to other versions found across social, cultural and even linguistic barriers. Narrative entities that move freely across such barriers are known as folk-tales or Wandersagen, precisely because of their wide and easy diffusion, their apparent rootedness in certain human experiences or interests that transcend the specific experience of individual societies and cultures.

Our knowledge of the transformations that ancient Near Eastern narratives undergo begins with the surviving, occasional, written versions, produced over centuries. But the transformations themselves begin with the individual poets and narrators who, in response to changing conditions, their own cultural or social situation, or their own unique vision or skill, modify what they have received or heard. We possess hard copy of the written versions, but know almost nothing of the generations who told and retold the stories. And yet, since it is they who have produced what we now have, we must almost remain aware of their presence and activity behind our texts.

One thin line leading us toward the activity of the poets, is the function and adaptation of the conventions discussed in this chapter. For those conventions as we have found them used were all functional for the oral poets who were undoubtedly the main tellers of these tales, even during the period of their written transmission. Such poets would depend on their mastery of a repertoire of formulae, on their skill in echoing cola with parallel cola, on their freedom to repeat with epic prolixity speeches or actions repeated in the plot, and on their knowledge of standard scenes and actions and tale-types—would depend on all these in order to perform a narrative. For these resources would enable them both to spin it out from memory and to vary it according to their own artistic sense, the demands of the situation and the reactions of the audience. Thus the traditional tale, in which various poets and audiences shared ownership, would be realized in fresh and vital ways from performance to performance. The small deviations from type, which we have noted again and again, may at times betray the poet's inattentiveness or resourcelessness—or that of the scribe, who may or may not have been a poet. But often such deviations play a clear aesthetic or rhetorical or narrative or thematic role, giving testimony to the poets' responsiveness, creativity or purposefulness even within the conventional culture of their art. Recognition of the limitations and possibilities of the poets may enable us to appreciate more fully even at our cultural distance the repetitiveness, slower pace, and conventionality of much of the poetry.

Chapter 2

SOME NON-NARRATIVE TYPES OF SPEECH IN THE NARRATIVE POEMS

A. Narrative Poetry and Social Speech

Large-scale narratives generally make use of a variety of other types of verbal expression, especially in the speeches of the characters in the narrative. The narratives of Genesis, for example, contain blessings and curses, promises and etiologies. The narratives of the books of Kings include prophetic oracles, prayers, and royal messages. These are all types of speech used in ordinary social life without any relationship to narrative. Within the poetic conventions and narrative movement of Ugaritic poetic narratives several such types of expression are discernible, though the linguistic difficulties of the texts as well as the demands and freedoms of poetic narrative style do not always allow easy recognition of their generic character. Further, the limited volume of the rediscovered Ugaritic literature does not usually provide multiple examples of such utterances. For congeners it is necessary to turn to other Ancient Near Eastern literatures. Two literatures are particularly valuable for this purpose: Israelite, since that is by far the most abundantly preserved northwest Semitic literature for more than a thousand years following the recording of the Ugaritic narratives; and Hittite, which, though using an unrelated language, was contemporary with Ugaritic literary activity, and a dominant political and cultural force for fourteenth century Ugarit.

A precise analysis of the internal structure of a Ugaritic passage, attention to the social setting implied by its narrative context and inferences about its purpose may be sufficient to formulate a hypothesis about its derivation from a type of speech used in ordinary social life. But the hypothesis will be greatly strengthened if other passages can be adduced which exhibit a similar fundamental structure, imply the same social context and serve a similar purpose, and if differences among the various passages can be explained by the demands of the particular context in which each is found. Such similarities among quite independent literary contexts are strong evidence either of a pervasive oral literary tradition or of highly conventional forms of speech in non-literary social settings. They may be rooted in fundamental institutional continuities, common cultural presuppositions or persistent poetic or narrative conventions. The differences, on the other hand, may be attributable to, and even predictable on the basis of the institutional or cultural or literary peculiarities of each text or its society. Such comparisons will sometimes confirm or elucidate our understanding of the less clear features of the Ugaritic text.

In each of the following sections of this chapter a passage in *Krt* or *Aqht* serves as the starting point for an exploration of several examples of the same type of speech. It is possible that the literary tradition had its own conventional form, setting, and use for a type of speech, but while that is more probable where the examples are limited to a particular literary tradition, such literary continuity is less likely where the examples come from different languages or societies and when they occur in quite different literary contexts. A stronger hypothesis in such circumstances is that institutions and situations common to the societies in question produced similar forms of expression for similar purposes, and that it is with those oral expressions that the various literary composers were directly familiar, rather than with literary adaptations of them in neighboring or antecedent literary traditions. This hypothesis better explains both the common elements of the genre that transcend the bounds of any individual culture, and the divergent elements that distinguish one literary example from another. In other words, the common material leads us to the primary social setting of the pronouncement; the divergent material leads us to the cultural presuppositions of the particular society and the literary, e.g. poetic or narrative purposes of the particular composer.

Of the three genres explored in the following three sections the first is a very brief saying that in Ugaritic literature is incorporated unchanged into an individual poetic colon; the second is a slightly longer and more complex utterance that is neatly adapted to the parallelistic structure of Ugaritic poetry, each of its three parts being cast in the form of a bicolon; the third is less fixed in its generic form (in part this perception may derive from the paucity of examples available for observation), but in one of the Ugaritic poems the discernible common features of the genre are developed into a speech considerably more lengthy and elaborate than anywhere else.

B. The Birth Announcement

At the beginning of the second column of 1.17 someone is announcing to Danel that El has granted him a son. The text then describes Danel's physical reaction to this news. Following this is his verbal reaction, in which the father-to-be expresses first his relief, and then the reason for it:

kyld bn ly km/aḫy for a son has been born to me as to my brothers
wšrš km aryy an offspring as to my peers
1.17.2.14-15

With the exception of the verb this bicolon is one of the refrains in columns 1-2, appearing twice in 1.17.1.18-21 (with the pronouns transposed to accommodate the different speaker). The repeated material may be represented as follows:

bn l + pron.sfx. *km aḫ* + pron.sfx. son to (pron.) as to (poss.adj.) brothers
wšrš km ary + pron.sfx. offspring as to (poss.adj.) peers

The basic structure of the bicolon is formulaic: other versions of it—with the nouns and pronouns replaced by different nominal elements—appear in the Baal poems (see below).

The nucleus of the bicolon as it appears in the mouth of Danel is the verbal sentence *yld bn ly* "a son has been born to me." The sentence consists of a third person passive form of the verb *yld* "to bear", the noun *bn* "son" as the subject of the verb, and the prepositional phrase *ly* "to me," referring to the father, in this case the speaker. The word order corresponds to that found by G. H. Wilson to be standard in *Keret* (Wilson 1982, 17-32). It also appears to be required by the structure of the bicolon. *km aḫy* now modifies the immediately preceding *ly*, thus comparing Danel with his brothers. Had *bn* followed *ly* and preceded *km aḫy*, the latter may have been misconstrued as modifying *bn*, and thus comparing Danel's son with his brothers. Apart from the word order, the form of this simple statement appears on the basis of comparative evidence in the Hebrew Bible to be neither necessary nor arbitrary. Rather it is possible to recognize in it the standard pronouncement of a father on hearing the news that his wife has given birth to a son.

The Hebrew evidence both confirms the basic form of the saying and fills out the succession of circumstances and corresponding transpositions in which it was used. In a personal lament in the book of Jeremiah the speaker curses the day he was born and the person who announced the birth to his father. The announcement is quoted, and reads in its entirety:

yld lk bn zkr A male son has been born to you

Jer 20:15

As in *Aqht*, so here the announcement consists of a passive form of the verb *yld*, the noun *bn* as subject, and the preposition *l* with a pronominal suffix referring to the father, in this case the addressee. The order of subject and indirect object is reversed—but the announcement in Jeremiah merely conforms to normal Hebrew word order. It also includes the supererogatory qualification of the son as "male," perhaps to emphasize the grounds for rejoicing (see below; ironic in this context), or for reasons of versification or rhythmic euphony. Allowing for the particular constraints of the two contexts, we may say that both use the same expression: *yld bn l* + pron. sfx. "a son has been born to (pronoun)." But the two also reflect in the pronominal element two different stages in the use of the saying: Jeremiah reports the immediate announcement to the father; *Aqht* records the father's response.

A third stage is represented in the announcement of the birth of a new ruler in Isa 9:5. Here Isaiah speaks for and claims the child for the larger community, by using first person plural pronouns:

ky yld yld-lnw for a boy has been born to us
bn ntn-lnw a son has been given to us

Here, as in the Ugaritic version, the poet has adapted the expression to poetic parallelism. In doing so he has used a different noun (*yeled*) in the first colon and a different verb (√*ntn*) in the second, thus creating the paronomasia of *yeled yullad* in the first and the assonance of *ben nittan* in the second. Behind the poetic bicolon the same simple statement can be discerned—in this case, *bn yld ln* "a son has been born to us." The word order is different again, but it conforms to one of the most common arrangements used in the prophets for bicola consisting of subject, verb and modifier (Collins 1978, 99-105)

Wildberger may well be right in claiming that this saying in Isaiah "reflects the message of the court to the general public" (Wildberger 1972, 379). But while the Isaiah example is clearly linked with a royal birth, the use of the announcement in the individual lament of Jer 20 removes any grounds for thinking that this might be a formula used only in court circles. The Jeremiah lament portrays the circumstances surrounding the birth of an ordinary member of the society. It is taken as a given that when a child is born, someone comes and makes the announcement to the father. It is the ordinariness of that task that makes the one who executes it a fitting object of a curse by the individual who wishes he had never been born. If behind Isa 9:5 we recognize not a specifically royal announcement, but a variant of the generic birth announcement, we may take a broader view of its use, namely as the announcement made by the members of any family to others who will share their celebration of the new birth.

The same expression appears a fourth time in Ruth 4:17, where Naomi's neighbors, following her adoption of Ruth's baby, proclaim the birth publicly:

yld bn ln'my a son has been born to Naomi

Here instead of a first or second person pronoun a personal name follows the preposition, as is demanded by the third person reference. The word order agrees with that of the text of *Aqht*, but here that is simply in accordance with the rules of Hebrew word order. Naomi takes the place of the father due to the special relationships involved in the plot of the book of Ruth—she, rather than the father, is the chief beneficiary of the birth (v. esp. 4:15a). Otherwise the pronouncement conforms to type.

In all four cases—from two different literatures; from poetry (narrative, personal lament and prophetic proclamation) and prose (narrative)—the essential elements of the saying are the same: a 3 m.sg. passive of the verb *yld*, the noun *bn* as subject, and the prepositional phrase *l* with a following suffixed pronoun or personal name referring to the chief beneficiary of the birth. Apart from the variation in the person of the prepositional phrase only the word order varies—apparently in accordance with the grammatical or literary demands and opportunities of each context.

One might suspect that such a simple, short statement could scarcely have been worded otherwise. But as the Isaiah passage shows, it would have been quite possible for people—and especially poets—to use another noun (e.g. *yeled*) or another verb (e.g. √*ntn*). It would also have been possible, at least in Hebrew, to use the *nip'al*, rather than the qal passive, form of √*yld*, the two being identical in meaning (Andersen 1971, 11); or indeed to use an active form of the verb with the mother as subject (as in 1.23.52-53 = 60; see below). That none of these options is used (except in the bicolon in Isaiah, where, however, the original form is still preserved, even if now discontinuous) tends to confirm the claim that the form we have found underlying each of the four passages is a fixed traditional saying. This is not to deny that one might expect to find very similar expressions in other societies in which a comparably high value is placed on the birth of a son.

The variant forms of the personal reference in the four passages cited fit successive stages in the spread of the news of a new birth. Jer 20:15 presents us with the initial announcement brought from the delivery room to the father. The quotation from *Aqht*, with which this section began, would correspond to the exclamation of the father on receiving the news, and Isa 9:5 to that of the larger family or community who claimed or acknowledged the child as in some sense theirs. Ruth 4:17 would reflect the version used by those who spread the news further abroad, referring normally to the father in the third person by name (here to the grandmother because of the peculiar situation developed in the book of Ruth). In other words, the saying *yld bn l* . . . "a son has been born to . . ." would pass through different transpositions as the announcement was made first to the father (*lk*) and other members of the family, who then claim it for themselves (*ly, ln*), until finally the word was passed around more widely in the community, the primary beneficiary of the birth being then referred to in the third person (*l*PN). While the announcement to the father would have been primary, it will be convenient to refer to the phrase in any of its variants as a birth announcement. (For this use of the term, more detailed discussion of the biblical passages, and discussion of some related passages, see Parker n.d. [forthcoming])

The primary form of the announcement—addressed to the father—is clearly recognizable in another Ugaritic context, transposed now to a mythological plane. Baal has copulated with a cow, and it is the offspring of this union to which Anat refers when she announces to Baal:

kibr lb'l [yl]d	for a bull [has been bo]rn to Baal
wrum lrkb 'rpt	a buffalo to the Rider of the Clouds
	1.10.3.36-37

(Traces of the *y* and the *l* in the last word of the first colon are still visible according to *KTU*.) Though Anat uses the polite third person to refer to Baal (and to meet the demands of versification), and his offspring cannot be called a son or boy, this is still recognizably the same saying. The nominal indirect object follows the subject, as in Ruth. Although, according to Wilson, we should expect the subject to be closer to the verb than the indirect object (Wilson 1982, 31), there are other clauses in which the same word order appears as in 1.10.3.36, e.g. 1.19.4.50-51; 1.23.52, 59.

The birth announcement is not a simple statement of fact.

The context of four of the five cases presented reveals that the saying is, as one might surmise, associated with joy. On receiving the news that he is to have a son, *bd!ni[l] pnm tšmḫ//w ʿl yṣhl pi[t]* "Danel's face shone happily//above, his brow glowed" 1.17.2.8-9. (For the meaning of the verbs cf. Ps 104:15.) Danel's following actions continue to express his joy: *yprq lṣb wyṣḥq//pʿn lhdm yṯpd* "he broke into a smile and laughed//set his foot on the footstool" 1.17.2.10-11. (For the general sense of the first verb v. Ullendorff 1977, 110-11; and compare with the first line: *rḥb py . . . //śmḥty* in 1 Sam 2:1). This description of the physical signs of Danel's joy is then echoed in his verbal expression of the same emotion mixed, in this case and perhaps often, with relief: *aṯbn ank wanḫn//wtnḫ birty npš/kyld bn ly* . . . " 'Now I can sit down and rest//and my soul can rest in my breast/For a son has been born to me . . .' " 1.17.2.12-14. The conjunction *k* "for" makes plain that the announced birth is the explicit reason for Danel's joy.

In Jer 20:15 the announcement to the father is immediately followed by a cognate infinitive absolute construction expressing the effect of the news on the father: *śmḥ śmḥhw* "giving him great joy." The context in which Isaiah speaks of the new royal birth is also one of general rejoicing:

hrbyth hgwy	You have multiplied the nation,
lw(Q) *hgdlth hśmḥh*	made its happiness great;
śmḥw lpnyk	thanks to you they are happy
kśmḥt bqṣyr	with the happiness of harvest.
kʾšr ygylw	with the happiness of
bḥlqm šll	dividing up spoil

Isa 9:2

The reasons for this rejoicing—introduced by the threefold repetition of the conjunction *ky* "for"—are that God has broken the oppressor's yoke (9:3), the bloody paraphernalia of the oppressor have been thrown onto the fire (9:4), and a son has been born to them (9:5). Finally, Anat's announcement to Baal of the birth of his calf is followed by the monocolon: *yšmḫ aliyn bʿl* "Aliyan Baal rejoiced" (1.10.3.38).

In each of these cases the literary context dwells sufficiently on the moment of the announcement that the joy and happiness of those to whom it is made is clearly and sometimes amply expressed. The birth announcement is therefore more of an exclamation than a bland statement and is probably best translated with an exclamation point following.

The question may be raised whether it is mere coincidence

that all the preserved cases speak of a son and none of a daughter. Although the number of cases is small, it seems likely that they are representative, and that news of the birth of a daughter was not so formally and joyfully proclaimed. The Ancient Near East in general placed a much higher value on sons than on daughters. Noteworthy is the reassurance that the female attendants give to two mothers-to-be dying in childbirth: "Don't worry, it's a son" (Gen 35:17; 1 Sam 4:20). Apparently the survival of the mother was a secondary consideration to the sex of the offspring! Until an example is found in which the birth of a daughter is announced, it will be best to consider the birth of a son as the occasion on which the birth announcement in the form we have described was used. (1.24.5 presents a tantalizing possibility of a counterexample, but the text is damaged, the different editions read it differently, and the context does not appear to support the placement of a birth announcement here.)

It is a long-debated question whether the announcement in Isa 9:5 follows the birth of the royal child, or is proleptic. It is quite clear that Danel's acknowledgement of the news of El's blessing in 1.17.2.14 is proleptic. In column 1 Baal reported Danel's childlessness to El and urged El to bless Danel. El did so, promising that Danel would have a son. Column 2 begins with the latter part of the speech in which this blessing is announced to Danel, who then expresses his delight at the news "because a son has been born to me." Only at the end of column 2 is there a reference to his counting the months of his wife's pregnancy. The birth of Aqhat must have taken place in the missing section of text following 1.17.2.46. Danel's use of the birth announcement is thus not a response to an actual birth, but to the announcement of a divine promise of a birth. For Danel this is as good as the fact (Van Selms 1954, 86).

But if Danel uses the first person version of the birth announcement in his acknowledgment of the actual announcement, and if in fact the announcement to the father is the primary form of the expression, it becomes probable that the second person version appeared in the preceding announcement to Danel (1.17.2. -8). The first part of the announcement speech is in fact missing; but the remains of the list of filial duties at the beginning of the preserved part of the column justify the restoration there of the beginning of that list. The usual restoration immediately before the list (e.g. Herdner 1963, 81, n.1) is a second person variant of the bicolon that precedes the list of filial duties in El's speech at the end of column 1:

wykn bnh [bbt	and he shall have a son in his house
šrš] bqrb hklh	offspring within his palace

1.17.1.42-43

This in turn corresponds to a bicolon in Baal's previous request that El bless Danel (1.17.1.25-26, where the verbs are jussive—"let him have etc."). While the speeches of Baal and El—request and response—appropriately share this bicolon, it seems less likely that the same bicolon would be used in the announcement to Danel and then be abruptly displaced in Danel's acknowledgment by the first person variant of the birth announcement. It is far more likely that the birth announcement is introduced in the speech which as a whole functions to announce the birth, and that this was then echoed in Danel's acknowledgment, just as the bicolon quoted earlier in the paragraph is introduced in Baal's appeal to El and then echoed in El's response (cf. Chap 2 C 2 b and c).

This supposition is reinforced by the fact that it is precisely the second person form of this bicolon that impinges on a related formulaic bicolon in the Baal tablets. That bicolon generally has the form:

. . . *bt lbʿl k(m) ilm*	. . . a house for Baal as for the gods
wḥẓr kbn aṯrt	a court as for the offspring of Asherah

The word *bt* may be preceded by *in* "there is no," or by forms of the verbs *ytn* "give" or *bny* "build." At one point (1.4.5.27-28) the words *ilm//bn aṯrt* (once *qdš*) of the eight other occurrences of this formulaic bicolon are replaced by the parallel pair *aḫ* + pron.sfx.//*ary* + pron.sfx. characteristic of *Aqht* (1.17.1.18-19; 20-21; 2.14-15). But none of those three passages could have been the immediate source of the influence, since they all have third or first person suffixes, while the Baal passage has second person suffixes. The intrusion of *aḫk//aryk* into *Bʿl* can only derive from a context in which the second person suffix was used with *aḫ//ary*, and the only such context would be in the announcement addressed to Danel in the lost beginning of 1.17.2. It therefore seems necessary to restore in that speech a second person transposition of the bicolon in which the birth announcement is embedded. This second person announcement to Danel of the birth of his son would have been the source of the borrowing of *aḫk//aryk* into the second person announcement to Baal of the building of his house. It is understandable that the poets should have confused some of the formulaic elements in the two passages, since not only the bicolon in question but the whole context has a similar structure in the two narratives. In both the announcement is based on a favorable divine response to a petition, and is therefore proleptic, being actually fulfilled only later.

In summary, there are several variants in Ugaritic and Hebrew literature of a stereotyped expression used on the occasion of a (male) birth. The primary form and use of this expression was probably to announce the birth to the father, in which case it used the second person suffix (Jer 20:15; restored at the beginning of *Aqht*, col. 2; the same situation is reflected in 1.10.3.36-37). But it was also used by the father or a larger group celebrating the birth (in which case it exhibits the first person singular or plural pronominal suffix: 1.17.2.14-15; Isa 9:5), and by those spreading the news to the community outside the social unit immediately involved (in which case it refers to the beneficiary of the birth in the third person: Ruth 4:17). The consistency of form and institutional setting and function in widely different literary contexts suggests that the authors were drawing on a stereotyped expression of ordinary life, common to Late Bronze Syria and first millennium Judah.

The basic form is adapted superficially to the constraints of each particular literary context in which it is used. Thus in the narrative context of Ruth it is Naomi rather than the father who is cited as the primary beneficiary of the birth. The more complex adaptation of the saying to Hebrew parallelistic verse in Isa. 9:6 was discussed above. In the case of *Aqht* it is adapted to Ugaritic poetic conventions without alteration by the addition of the comparative *km aḫy(/k)* "like my (/your) brothers" and the provision of a parallel colon composed of words corresponding to *bn* and *km aḫy(/k): wšrš km aryy(/k).*

C. The Vow

On his way to Udum to demand the lady Hurraya as his wife, Keret arrives at a sanctuary of the goddess Asherah. There he promises a gift to the goddess, if she will grant him success in his enterprise:

aṯrt ṣrm	O Asherah of Surra
wilt ṣdyn	and Goddess of Sidian:
hm ḥry bty iqḥ	If I take Hurraya into my house,
ašʿrb ǵlmt bḥẓry	bring the maid into my court;
ṯnh kspm atn	I will give her double in silver,
wṯlṯh ḫrṣm	her triple in gold

1.14.4.38-43

The vow consists of two major parts: an address to the deity, and a conditional promise. The address is comprised of divine names and titles. The promise is a conditional sentence, the protasis stating the condition—the desired object; the apodosis expressing the contingent promise—the gift to the deity.

Recently, Miller has identified a second example of a vow in Ugaritic (Miller 1988, 149-50). Text 1.119 prescribes on its reverse a prayer to be recited when the city is under siege (*kgr ʿz ṯġrkm qrd ḥmytkm* "When a strong (enemy) attacks your gates, a warrior your walls"—lines 26-27). Under such circumstances, the people are to pray to Baal (*ʿnkm lbʿl tšun* "you will raise your eyes to Baal"—27). The prayer reads as follows:

ybʿlm	O Baal:
[h]m tdy ʿz lṯġrny	[I]f you will drive the strong (enemy) from our gates,
qrd [l]ḥmytny	the warrior [from] our walls;
ibr ybʿl nšqdš	a bull, O Baal, we shall consecrate,
mdr bʿl nmlu	a vow, O Baal, we shall fulfil,
[d]kr bʿl nš[q]dš	a male [ani]mal, O Baal, we shall consecrate,
ḥtp bʿl [n]mlu	a sacrifice, O Baal, we shall fulfil,
ʿšrt bʿl n[ʿ]šr	a banquet, O Baal, we shall lay on,
qdš bʿl nʿl	we shall go up to the sanctuary of Baal,
ntbt b[t bʿl] ntlk	we shall walk the paths of the house of Baal.

1.119.28-34

(I follow here the text of Miller, benefitting as it does from the microscopic collation of Pardee—Miller 1988, 139-41. For the crucial restoration of *[h]m* in 1.28, Miller depends on Pardee's preference for *m* over Herdner's and KTU's *l*.) While Miller's identification of the vow here builds on previous analyses of the vow in *Krt* and in biblical literature, the consequent elucidation of the text is so convincing that we may here present it as evidence before turning to extra-ugaritic examples.

As in *Krt*, the vow consists of an address to the deity and a conditional promise. The address consists of the divine name/title *bʿl* preceded by the vocative particle *y*, and followed by enclitic *m*. The protasis, as in *Krt*, uses the conditional conjunction *hm* and a verb in the prefixing conjugation—here in the second person. The apodosis of both vows uses first person verbs in the prefixing conjugation. But while the condition of Keret's vow is the acquisition of a wife, in 1.119 it is the withdrawal of invading forces. Whereas in *Krt* the speaker promises to the deity a gift of an image of the desired person, in 1.119 the promise refers to offering ritual sacrifices, and to going to the god's sanctuary (to worship). In other words, the two vows are made in different circumstances and promise different expressions of gratitude—though both benefit the god's sanctuary. As we shall see, there are many different circumstances in which vows are made.

Two other formal features of 1.119 are worthy of note. First, this is a prescriptive text—it anticipates certain circumstances in which it prescribes the use of the quoted prayer. We have no direct knowledge about its actual use. Second, it takes poetic form. The protasis is a bicolon; the apodosis ends with a bicolon, which is preceded by five parallel cola, each consisting of a direct object, a vocative (*b'l*) and a first person plural verb in the prefixing conjugation. These five cola are grouped into a bicolon (with the verbs *nšqdš*//*nmlu*), followed by a second (parallel) bicolon (also with *nšqdš*//*nmlu*) extended by the addition of the fifth colon into a tricolon. Thus, although the initial address to the deity does not participate in this poetic structure, the vow of 1.119 shares something of the literary character of the vow in *Krt*.

While the ugaritic texts have so far yielded only these two vows, we are in the fortunate position of having several examples of vows in the Hittite archives and in Israelite narrative literature. The Hittite examples are closest, historically, geographically and in their social setting to those from Ugarit. They all date from the second quarter of the thirteenth century—roughly a century after our texts—and from Ugarit's closest and most influential neighbor. They appear in texts which appear to be a more direct record of actual vows made by particular individuals: a sequence of prayers by the queen Puduhepa to the sun-goddess of Arinna and her family; a collection of dream reports; a collection of vows, again by Puduhepa, to Ishtar of Lawazantiya (the object of a provincial cult of which Puduhepa's father was high priest); and an administrative record reporting a vow by Puduhepa and the objects given year by year in fulfillment of the vow. These provide a relatively direct testimony to the ways in which vows were expressed and what they requested and promised, at least in the central institutions of the Hittite empire.

In her prayer to the sun-goddess of Arinna and her family Puduhepa prays for the survival of the king, her husband. Turning to the goddess Lelwani, she makes the following vow:

> If thou, Lelwani, my lady, relayest the good (word) to the gods, grantest life to thy servant, Hattusilis, (and) givest him long years, months, (and) days, I will go (and) make for Lelwanis, my lady, a silver statue of Hattusilis—

> as tall as Hattusilis himself, with its head, its hands (and) its feet of gold . . .
>
> (KUB XXI 27 III 36-47; translation of A. Goetze in Pritchard 1969a, 394a)

The vows in the following prayers to members of the goddess' family are of the same form, but have as their condition solely the lesser deities' intercession with the sun-goddess and the storm-god on behalf of the queen's request. The text is sometimes damaged at the place where the promised gift is mentioned, but where preserved the text mentions an ornament and a golden shield.

While the king's health rather than the acquisition of a spouse is the final object of Puduhepa's vows, the gift promised in the first vow suggests how the object behind the poetic parallelism and hyperbole of *Krt* is to be conceived. The gift promised by a king in Syria as by a queen in Hatti would probably have been a statue of the person for whom he prayed, a statue plated with silver, and with its exposed parts—head, hands and feet—plated with gold. A contemporary figurine from Minet el-Beida, cast in bronze, has its body covered with silver and its head and headdress with gold. It also has a gold bracelet around one arm (Pritchard 1969b, no. 481 = Caquot and Sznycer 1980, Pl. IX d). Two figurines from Ras Shamra itself, dating from a few centuries earlier are made of silver and dressed in gold loincloths and torques (Pritchard 1969b, no 482 = Caquot and Sznycer 1980, Pl. VIII b). The largest of the three is .28 metres tall, so that they do not approach the scale proposed in Puduhepa's or Keret's vow. The first one in particular, however, suggests the kind of statue that both texts may have intended.

In form Puduhepa's vow corresponds broadly to the Ugaritic vows. It is a conditional sentence, promising a gift contingent on the granting of a request; and is addressed explicitly to a deity. In the Hittite vow the deity is mentioned after the initial conditional particle. Also noteworthy is the fact that the two clauses have a nicely balanced "If you . . ., then I . . ." (corresponding to the "if you . . ., then we . . ." of the second ugaritic vow). Both these features are typical, though not without exception in the Hittite vows.

The following three vows are recorded in the dream reports of the queen. In the second and third the goddess addressed is, for contextual reasons, not referred to by name or title. In the third the protasis (as in the *Krt* vow) does not use the second person subject.

> If you, goddess, my lady, will have made well again His Majesty, and not have him given over to the "Evil," I shall make a statue of gold for Hebat and I shall make her a rosette of gold.
>
> (KUB XV 1 I 1-11; trans. of H. G. Guterbock in Oppenheim 1956, 254, no. 30)

(Whether the statue promised here was to represent His Majesty or the goddess is not stated, but understood.) The next vow follows a deity's promise of long life for her husband (so that the explicit designation of the addressee is superfluous):

> If you do thus for me and my husband remains alive, I shall give to the deity three *harsialli*-containers, one with oil, one with honey, one with fruits.
>
> (*KUB* XV 1 III 8-16; Guterbock in Oppenheim 1956, 254-5, no. 31)

The following vow is made in response to repeated orders received in a dream to make a vow to the goddess Ningal, which again renders the designation of the addressee unnecessary:

> If [a disease] of His Majesty will pass quickly, I shall make for Ningal ten (?) oil-flasks of gold set with lapis-lazuli.
>
> (*KUB* XV 3 I 17-20; Guterbock in Oppenheim 1956, 255, no. 32)

The character of these vows is consistent with that described previously: a conditional sentence addressed to the deity, promising a gift in exchange for a favor.

All these Hittite vows are made by the queen for the health and survival of the king, her husband. The promised gift varies: a statue of the king, a statue of the goddess (or king?), certain precious containers.

The vows of Puduhepa to Ishtar of Lawazantiya are in a badly damaged state (*KUB* XLVIII 123; edition in R. Lebrun 1981, 95-107). But they too appear to correspond to the form identified above, and to be primarily for the king's health. What is interesting about the gifts promised is that they are usually accompanied by an indication of weight—an Ishtar in silver of one mina and an Ishtar in gold of twenty shekels, for example. Both the absolute quantities and the proportion of gold to silver in these vows provide further specifications for the kind of statue that a historical Keret might have promised, and confirm the poetic character of the language of the literary Keret's vow, with its conventional parallelism of two//three, silver//gold. Other statues and other objects are promised in these surviving fragments of vows. It is not always clear whom the statue is to represent, but it is usually of silver and gold of a certain weight. Occasionally, however, something is promised "of no matter what weight"—a telling disclosure of the desperation of the person making the vow.

The greatest commitment made by the queen appears in a vow preserved at the beginning of a document which records its annual fulfillment—annual because of the specific content of the vow:

> If you, oh goddess, my lady, preserve his majesty alive and well for many years, so that he walks before you, goddess, for many years;
>
> Then I, goddess, will (give) annually [. . .] the years of silver and the years of gold, the months of silver and gold, the days of [silver and the days] of gold, a cup of silver and a cup of gold, a head of his majesty of gold [. . . and] I will give you sheep annually—whether a hundred or fifty is of no matter.
>
> Otten and Soucek 1965, 16-17 (lines 3-9)

The form is consistent with the pattern we have seen before: "If you (divine names or titles) . . ., then I . . ." Puduhepa here promises silver and gold annually—corresponding evidently to the length of the king's life—as well as other objects. The subsequent account of the queen's gifts donated over the five succeeding years does not in fact correspond to what she has promised. It includes, for example, the regular gift of people to the temple—prisoners and deportees, but also young boys and girls. The dedication to temple service of slaves (including captives) is well attested; that of freeborn children less so (Mendelsohn 1949, 102-3; cf. Hannah's vow, discussed below).

In sum, the Hittite vows present us with the following general pattern. They consist of a conditional sentence with an address to the deity after the opening conditional particle. They usually have the form: If you . . . then I . . . All preserved examples are put in the mouth of the queen and are for the life and health of her husband, the king. The documents from which we know them are good evidence of the sanctuary's (priesthood's) interest in keeping track of such promises and ensuring their fulfillment (Oppenheim 1956, 193; Otten and Soucek 1965, 1). The gifts promised vary, but statues of silver and gold are frequent. Only in one case is the statue clearly of the person prayed for, and that case describes the limited use of gold on a silver statue. In other cases statues of the goddess are envisaged, the weight of a gold statue being specified as 20 sheqels and that of a silver statue as 1 mina (a ratio of 1:3). As suggested above, it is likely that a statue of the scale proposed by Keret would have been made of some other material, and then plated with silver, with some salient features plated with or made of gold—a form of construction known from ancient Syria, and attested specifically on a contemporary figurine from Ras Shamra's neighboring port town.

The vow in *Krt* concerns the acquisition of a wife for the king, as appropriate to the narrative context; but there is no reason to doubt that such a subject might figure in an actual vow. The form of the vow in *Krt* is probably adjusted to its present context since in the protasis it uses the language of the later marriage blessing (*√lqḥ bt//ǵlmt š√ ʿrb ḥẓr*; cf. 1.15.2.21-23), which does not permit the "If you . . ." that appears to be standard in the protasis of the Hittite vows, and is attested in the one other ugaritic vow. The appearance in the Hittite texts of vows in response to divine instructions given in dreams renders the more striking the absence of any reference to a vow in El's instructions during Keret's dream, and the intrusion of the vow in Keret's fulfillment of those instructions.

We owe our knowledge of the Hittite vows to the interests of the priests to whose deities the Hittite queen appealed, and to their administrative apparatus. From their content we know that they all have their roots in the queen's anxiety about the king's life. From their present contexts we know that the circumstances in which they found expression was in one case a prayer, in three other cases a memory of a dream. We have no further information concerning the circumstances in which these or the other vows were made.

The Israelite vows are somewhat remoter from Ugarit in time, dating from the following millennium; but they are written in a cognate language and, like Keret's vow, they all occur in narrative contexts, to which they are in varying degrees adapted (Richter 1967, 22-31; Parker 1979). These narrative contexts, while giving less direct information about the content of actual vows made by individuals in Israel, do reveal rather more about the circumstances in which the writers conceived of people making vows.

Five vows are preserved in Hebrew narrative literature. One is particularly close in form to that of Keret:

yhwh ṣb'wt	Oh Yahweh Sebaoth,
'm-r'h tr'h b'ny 'mtk	if you will only see the misery of your maid
wzkrtny wl'-tškḥ 't-'mtk	and remember me and not forget your maid
wntth l'mtk zr' 'nšym	and give your maid male offspring,
wnttyw lyhwh kl-ymy ḥyyw	then I will give him to Yahweh for his entire life
wmwrh l' -y'lh 'l-r'šw	and no razor shall touch his head

1 Sam 1:11

As in the two ugaritic vows, so here the vow begins with an invocation of the deity—divine name/title—and proceeds with a conditional sentence, introduced by *'m* (corresponding to Ugaritic *hm*) and using prefixing forms of the verb (or the equivalent perfect consecutives in the Hebrew) in both clauses. The Hebrew vow agrees with text 1.119 and the Hittite examples in using the second person in the protasis and the first in the apodosis. The context in 1 Samuel also provides a setting for the vow. As in *Krt* it is made in a sanctuary. Hannah had gone up with her family to "the house of Yahweh" in Shiloh, and utters this prayer "in the presence of Yahweh" (v. 12). This agreement between the two narratives is doubtless a reliable reflection of actual practice: the vow was made in the sanctuary to the deity of the sanctuary. As is implied by the records of royal vows in Hatti and as other biblical texts make clear, the fulfillment of the vow after the favorable response of the deity also took place in the sanctuary (Deut 12:5-6, 17-18, 26—Deuteronomy's insistence on the presentation of such gifts at the one sanctuary chosen by Yahweh presupposes that they had customarily been offered, not at other places in general, but at other sanctuaries). This is true in Hannah's case, even though, according to the story, Hannah had not told the priest that she had made a vow.

The votive gift was usually delivered immediately after the deity had done his or her part. So the Samuel passage contains a special explanation for the delay in the fulfillment of Hannah's promise—she had to wait until the child had been weaned: 1 Sam 1:21-24. Similarly, the Keret story notes immediately after his acquisition of the desired wife and her demonstration of the cardinal virtue of fertility that the goddess was offended as she remembered—and he did not—his vow: 1.15.3.22-30. Both Deuteronomy (23:22) and Ecclesiastes (5:3-4) warn against delay in the payment of a vow, the former in the context of various forms of stealing, the latter in the context of various forms of ill-considered speech. After the condition has been met, the vow becomes like a debt: the deity expects to be paid and will hold the defaulter accountable.

The vows of Keret and Hannah have in common a concern for the acquisition of a family. Keret had previously asked El for children (1.14.2.4-5 as restored by Ginsberg and most commentators since: *[tn b]nm aqny//[tn ṯa]rm amid* "grant that I may produce sons//grant that I might increase progeny"; but the remains of the second line appear to support the restoration: *[tn n]ʿrm amid* "grant that I might have many boys"—Seow 1984, 148, n.28). The fulfillment of that request depended on his acquisition of the bride promised by El, which thus becomes the object of his vow to Asherah. Hannah prays directly for a son. The vow of the childless woman praying for a son was common enough that a mother might address her male offspring as *br-ndry* (Prov. 31:2), that is, "son granted me by God in response to my vows."

Contrasting with Keret's vow and all the Hittite vows is Hannah's promise to give to the deity the very person whom she requests as the condition of her gift. Her fulfillment of her promise is of course the precondition for the larger historiographic narrative that follows. We shall return later to the question of whether individuals were actually given in fulfillment of vows in Israel. Whatever the answer to that question and whatever the date of composition of the early chapters of 1 Samuel, the comparison with *Krt* indicates that the basic form of Hannah's vow is consistent with that of the second millennium vows from Syria and Asia Minor. There is no reason therefore to think that the form used by ancient Israelites in general would have been any different from that used by their second millennium antecedents.

The other vows found in Hebrew prose narratives diverge from the generic form to a greater or lesser extent as they are modified by their contexts. They vary also in setting, in what they request and, like 1 Sam 1, in what they promise. Two further Hebrew vows read as follows:

ʾm-ntn ttn ʾt-hʿm hzh bydy	*ʾm-ntwn ttn ʾt-bny ʿmwn bydy*
whḥrmty ʾt-ʿryhm	*whyh hywṣʾ ʾšr yṣʾ mdlty byty*
	lqrʾty bšlwm mbny ʿmwn

	whyh lyhwh *wh'lythw 'wlh*
If only you will put this people in my power Then I will destroy their cities.	If only you will put the Ammonites in my power, Then whoever comes out of the doors of my house to meet me as I return victorious from the Ammonites Shall be Yahweh's, and I shall offer him up as a burnt offering.
Num 21:2	Jdg 11:30-31

(Jdg. 11:30-31 reads awkwardly at several points. *hywṣ'* and *'šr ys'* appear to be doublets. The major non-Semitic versions do not reflect both, which means that either the translators' Hebrew text had only one, or—more likely—that the translators realized that both expressions mean the same thing and need and could only be translated once—as in the preceding English translation. The use of *whyh* in two different ways is also stylistically awkward. Finally the last two clauses may be understood to be incompatible, denoting dedication to service in the sanctuary [as in 1 Sam 1 and Num 3:12] and sacrifice [as in Gen 22] respectively. For the most recent study of these and other problems in the narrative of Jephthah's vow, see Marcus 1986.)

The narrative introduction of both these vows refers to the deity: "And Israel/Jephthah made a vow to Yahweh as follows" (contrast 1 Sam. 1:11). For this reason the first part of the vow is omitted: the deity is not addressed by name (cf. the same situation in some of the vows in the Hittite dream reports). In both texts the protasis uses the second person as in 1 Samuel and 1.119 and as normally in the Hittite vows. The imperfect verb form of the protasis is preceded by an infinitive absolute as in 1 Sam 1:11. The apodoses vary. Num 21:2 uses the first person singular perfect consecutive like 1 Sam 1:11. Jdg 11:31 concludes with the same form, but here this is preceded by two clauses introduced by *whyh* (third person perfect consecutive). The first introduces a relative clause that identifies the person who then becomes the subject of the second clause and the object of the concluding verb. Granting that the precise present form of the apodosis is problematic (see the notes above on the text), one is still compelled to acknowledge that the basic form of the vow is here adapted in order to introduce the object of the promise, who is as yet unknown and can only be referred to by circumlocution.

These last two vows have a setting different from all those previously considered. Jephthah's vow is made between two references to his marching against the Ammonites (Jdg 11:29, 32), the second of which introduces his defeat of them. In Num 21:1-3 Israel's vow occurs immediately after reference to a battle with the Canaanites to whom it had lost numerous captives, and is followed immediately by reference to its defeat of the Canaanites. Although neither context gives a specific setting for the vow, it appears that the composers envisaged it as being made on a military campaign immediately before battle. It is unnecessary to propose, as have some commentators, that Jephthah's vow was in fact made at a sanctuary, or even that the text of the vow should be moved elsewhere to make that explicit. The presence of cultic functionaries (priests, prophets) on military campaigns, well attested in Israelite historiographic literature, provides for the proper observance of religious acts and utterance of religious pronouncements during military expeditions without benefit of a sanctuary.

Here, too, the fulfillment of the vow follows immediately after the meeting of the condition. In Num 21:1-3 the fulfillment of condition and promise is a single course of action: the Israelites' victory in battle leads directly into their destruction of the enemy's cities. In Jephthah's case the peculiar nature of the promise means that it cannot be fulfilled until he gets home. And there is a special reason for further delay: his daughter requests a grace period of two months in which to bewail her virginity (12:37-39)—which Jephthah grants, before finally fulfilling his promise to Yahweh. Even if verses 37-40 derive from an originally independent unit (Richter 1966, 503-17), their present combination with the preceding material recognizes the necessity of a special disposition permitting a delay in the fulfilling of the vow.

Both these vows request military victory, using the expression *'m-nt(w)n ttn . . . bydy* "If only you will put . . . into my power." In Num 21:2 Israel's promise corresponds to its condition in a way analogous to the relation of promise and condition in Hannah's vow. Both Hannah and Israel promise to give up to God what God is to give as the condition of the promise. Israel here promises to destroy the cities of the defeated enemy. Since the verb used is *ḥrm*, this destruction should be seen as a kind of gift to Yahweh.

The two clauses at the end of Jdg. 11:31 both involve Jephthah in making a gift of a person to Yahweh, since a burnt offering is also a gift to Yahweh. This more personal kind of vow may have been no rarer than Hannah's, so far as it concerned dedication to a sanctuary; but must have been very early and very rare—if indeed it was not purely fictitious—so far as it concerned human sacrifice (cf. Gen 22, 2 Kgs 3:27). It is the outcome—the fact that it is Jephthah's own daughter who meets the conditions—that makes this vow memorable and pregnant with pathos, providing for the composer the situation for the powerful narrative of Jdg 11:34-39, and the explanation for the memorialization described in Jdg 11:40.

Although the vows of Num. 21:2 and Jdg. 11:30-31—especially the latter—appear in a form somewhat altered by their present literary settings, they still share with those previously considered the same basic structure. But they have a different setting and a different concern. While the Hittite vows were concerned with the life and health of the king and were made in the sanctuary by the queen, heavily dependent on his welfare; and the vows of Keret and Hannah were concerned with getting a family and were made in a sanctuary by individuals accountable to their ancestors and living kin; the present two are concerned with gaining a military victory, and imply a commitment on the field of battle by the military leader with responsibilities to his tribe or nation.

The two remaining vows in the Bible are found in 2 Sam. 15:8 and Gen. 28:20-22. In the former Absalom requests of King David permission to go to fulfil in Hebron "the vow I made to Yahweh" while in Geshur. He quotes the vow in verse 8b:

> *ʾm-h(!)šyb yšybny yhwh yrwšlm*
> *wʿbdty ʾt-yhwh*
> If only Yahweh will return me to Jerusalem,
> Then I will serve Yahweh.

As in the preceding two cases, the initial address is omitted, the deity in question having been just mentioned by the speaker (verse 7). The deity is referred to in the third person in the protasis of the conditional sentence: "If DN . . ." This is perhaps to be explained by the fact that the vow is quoted in a speech addressed to David. In that context the use of the second person would be ambiguous. As in the preceding Hebrew example the verb appears in the prefixing conjugation following a cognate infinitive absolute (emendation of Kethib *yšyb*, Qere *yāšôb* to *hāšēb*). The apodosis begins with a first person singular perfect consecutive. Again the deity is referred to in the third person.

The condition is Yahweh's bringing Absalom back to Jerusalem. Absalom's promise is to serve Yahweh.

While the point of Absalom's request is that he be granted permission to go to Hebron, Hebron is not in fact mentioned in the vow as quoted. Taken on its own, the vow would imply that Jerusalem is the place where it is to be fulfilled. However, Hebron may have been omitted as unnecessary after Absalom's opening statement to the king: "Let me go and fulfil my vow . . . in Hebron" (15:7). It is understandable that the promise to serve God should be fulfilled in Hebron, as that was Absalom's birthplace (2 Sam 3:2-3).

More striking, in view of what has already been said about the fulfillment of vows, is the delay of several years between God's fulfillment of the condition of the vow and Absalom's present proposal to fulfil his promise. Here it is necessary to remember the larger narrative context. The request for permission to fulfil his vow is in fact Absalom's pretext for getting excused from Jerusalem to go to Hebron to pursue his seditious purposes. The delay in fulfillment does not arouse David's curiosity or suspicions. Absalom is portrayed as pursuing skillfully and methodically a strategy leading toward insurrection, to all of which David is sublimely oblivious. Absalom may well have concocted the vow for the specific purpose of moving on to the next stage of his strategy. The author is at once presenting the cunning of Absalom and the innocence of David. That David accepts Absalom's request unquestioningly is testimony to the conventional character of the substance and circumstances of the vow.

Its conventional character is confirmed by the substance and circumstances of the last Hebrew vow, found in Gen. 28:20-22:

'm-yhyh 'lhym ʿmdy
  wšmrny bdrk hzh 'šr 'nky hwlk
  wntn-ly lḥm l'kl wbgd llbš
  wšbty bšlwm 'l-byt 'by
whyh yhwh ly l'lhym
  wh'bn hz't 'šr-śmty mṣbh yhyh byt 'lhym
  wkl 'šr ttn-ly ʿśr ʿśrnw lk

If God will be with me
  and guard me on this journey which I am making
  and give me food to eat and clothing to wear
  so that I return alive and well to my father's house,
Then Yahweh shall be my God
  and this stone which I have made into a stela shall be a house of God

and of all that you give me I will be sure to return a
tenth to you

After his dream at Bethel Jacob made a vow. The initial address is omitted. The protasis begins with the conditional particle *'m* and a verb in the prefixing conjugation (followed by perfect consecutives). The verbs are in the third person (with the deity as subject) up to the last which is in the first person. The absence of an initial address may be explained by the content of the vow: Jacob does not yet know the deity, and will only acknowledge him when he has met the conditions of the vow. In the apodosis a perfect consecutive is followed by two imperfects. The third verb is in the first person, and the deity is referred to in the second. But the first two are in the third person, and the deity is the subject of the first: "Yahweh shall be my god" (though the sense is: "I shall acknowledge Yahweh as my god"). While the passage is still clearly recognizable as a vow, its form diverges more than that of any other from the common pattern.

While Absalom's and Jacob's vows clearly belong to the same type of utterance as all the other vows discussed previously, these two again are distinct from the others in their concern and setting. The condition of Jacob's vow is the deity's care for the subject during his exile (protection, provision of food and clothing), so that the subject returns home *běšālôm* "safe and sound." Apart from the references to food and clothing the protasis is closely related to God's promise in verse 15a, which uses the *hip'il* of *šwb*—like 2 Sam. 15:8. (*šwb bšlm* is also a concern of Jephthah's vow: Jdg. 11:31.) The vows of both Absalom and Jacob arise from their concern with returning safely from exile. If that condition is met, both promise to serve the deity. Of the two promises Jacob's is again the more detailed: adoption of the deity, establishment of a cultic center, and provision for regular contributions to the cult. These details may well be tied to actual cultic practices at Bethel (Westermann 1981, 558-61). The promise of cultic service is reminiscent of text 1.119, and is, of course, reflected frequently in the psalms.

The setting of Absalom's vow is not mentioned. We know only that he claims to have made it while he was in exile in Geshur, and that he proposes to fulfil it in Hebron. The context suggests that it was fictitious, concocted as an acceptable reason for leaving the court to go to Hebron. Discernment of the setting of Jacob's vow is complicated, like other aspects of this vow, by the complexity of the whole passage. According to the context the vow was made as Jacob was on his way to a distant country at what he has just recognized as and designated a holy place, and what is in fact, according to the same context, Bethel (verses 16-19). The relation of the vow to this context is, however, rather loose. God's response is conveyed through the account of Jacob's experiences, but also through God's speeches in 31:3, 13 and Jacob's in 32:10. Gen 35:1, 3, 7 may be understood as Jacob's fulfillment of his promise. But Jacob here acts on present divine instructions, and what he now accomplishes at Bethel is only loosely related to what he had promised. This is not the place to enter into a full discussion of that relation (but see Richter 1967; Westermann 1981, loc. cit.). What is clear is that Jacob's vow is of the same type as Absalom's, and that its present complex form is a function of the complex form and history of the larger context for which it was composed. This type of vow was used by one setting out on a journey to foreign parts or by an exile anxious to return safely home. Such would be willing to promise to serve the deity when they got back safely to their own (and their deity's) country. The motivation for vows of this type—an exile's longing for his homeland—is well illustrated in Sinuhe's prayer for his return to his native land ("The Story of Sinuhe" 157-164: Simpson 1973, 66 = Lichtheim 1973, 228-29).

L. R. Fisher has posited a closer relationship between Jacob's vow and that of Keret (Fisher 1975, 147-52). This is a claim that merits attention in this context. Fisher's comparison of the two is part of a larger comparison of the two cycles of narratives concerning Keret and Jacob. He connects the vow in both stories with a theme that is admittedly common to both stories—the expedition for a wife. However, there is not even any allusion to this theme in Jacob's vow, which, like Absalom's,, is preoccupied with safe return from abroad. Keret's vow is related directly to his marriage, but not to his journey. Jacob's, on the other hand, is related directly to his journey and has nothing to do with his marriage. Jacob in flight—Gen 27:41-45 (J)—makes his vow in response to a God-given dream. (The theme of the "expedition for a wife" in Gen. 27:46-28:5 [P] was introduced at a later stage in the tradition.) Keret, on his way to demand a wife from another king as part of a god-given mission, makes his vow spontaneously at an established shrine. In Genesis the vow explains the present cult at Bethel and identifies the god who introduced himself to Jacob with the God of Israel. In Keret the hero's failure to keep his vow after the success of his mission leads to his sickness. Thus the two vows are of different types and are used differently in the two contexts.

It is characteristic of the vow that it is used in situations of anxiety (cf. Jonah 1:16; Ps 66:14; Wendel 1931, 17). People may be so anxious, disturbed or desperate about their situation that they are willing to promise to sacrifice to the deity something really precious in return for relief. While many of the gifts promised by the Hittite queen may not have been a great sacrifice to her—and indeed her vows appear to have been so numerous as to be almost routine—those vows in which she promises something "of no matter what weight" and the vow of annual gifts for as long as the king might live reveal a real, personal desperation.

Similarly the vow of Jephthah—to sacrifice whoever . . .—expresses a degree of desperation beyond that of a material gift of fixed value (which is in fact never used in the vows quoted in Israelite narrative literature). What gives Jephthah's vow it's additional awesomeness is that, while one part of the apodosis suggests that the person is to be given to the service of God in the sanctuary, like Hannah's son, the last part suggests that the person is to be sacrificed to God, like the spoils of war in the other military vow. Here more than anywhere else we are compelled to ask whether we have to do with historical practice or literary effect. The investigation that would be necessary to produce a judicious answer to this question is beyond the scope of the present study. Whatever the answer, the question is, according to present evidence, raised only by the Israelite example. The Ugaritic vows, while poetic in form and, in the case of *Krt*, literary in context and use, conform in general substance to the actual vows of contemporary Hittite royalty.

The vow had certain religious and social and psychological features which deserve comment. The vow is a species of contract. While *do ut des* "I give that you may give" is a theory about the implicit meaning of sacrifice, *si dederis dabo* "If you give, I shall give" (Wendel) is the explicit form of the vow. This presupposes (like the *do ut des* theory of sacrifice) that those making vows have something to give the deity and that the deity can be influenced by gifts. If the deity responds favorably, not only those making the vow but also the sanctuary benefits. (The military vows in the Bible would be an exception to this statement.) If, however, those who make vows do not keep their side of the bargain, some penalty may be expected, perhaps levied by the sanctuary. Deut 23:22 designates the failure to fulfil a vow a sin, and warns that Yahweh himself will then seek what is owed him. *Krt* apparently illustrates such divine displeasure by noting that when Keret did not fulfil his vow to Asherah, she nevertheless remembered it; and his subsequent sickness is presumably of her doing. In the Jephthah narrative the possibility of non-fulfillment is implicit in the rejection of that idea both by Jephthah (Jdg 11:35) and by his daughter (Jdg 11:36). Presumably the penalty for non-fulfillment would be even more costly than the fulfillment of the vow—as apparently it is in *Krt*.

If the deity does not respond to the vow, neither the person making the vow nor the sanctuary loses anything. The individual has perhaps gained something: the alleviation of (personal) anxiety and of (social) shame, by putting into the deity's sphere some of the responsibility for changing the situation. By making the vow to the benefit of the sanctuary the individual also gains the interest and support of the sanctuary in exercising any means at its disposal to bring about the desired result. (Cf. the other outworkings of sacerdotal interest in the pentateuchal prescriptions and prohibitions concerning those who make vows, and Richter 1967, 32-39.)

Finally, the setting of the vow in the sanctuary before cultic personnel may explain an odd formal feature of the vow. When the deity is referred to in the protasis, direct address is normal. (The use of the third instead of the second person in the vows of Absalom and Jacob may be explained by their present narrative contexts.) When the deity is referred to in the apodosis, the third person is normal. (The exceptions here are in the prayer of Puduhepa, in which the deities are addressed in the second person throughout; and in the list of annual payments in fulfillment of a vow. In 1.119 the deity is addressed directly in the first five cola of the apodosis, but referred to in the third person in the last bicolon.) The shift to the third person for the actual promise probably implies a direct address to the personnel of the sanctuary, who serve not only as witnesses of the vow but also as its immediate beneficiaries on behalf of the deity. To state the matter in the opposite way: the presence of the cultic personnel as witnesses and eventual beneficiaries of the promise prompts the individual to address them directly at this point, and therefore to refer to the deity in the third person. The absence of any reference to the deity in the apodosis of Keret's vow is perhaps best explained by reference to the composers' euphonic sense.

At least five distinct species of vows have been preserved in the East Mediterranean cultural milieu, concerned with and conditional upon the good health and survival of the king (Hittite), the getting of a family (Ugaritic and Israelite), military victory (Israelite), deliverance from attack and siege (Ugaritic) and safe return from abroad (Israelite). What is promised in each

type is some kind of sacrifice or offering to the deity. In several there is a specific matching of what is requested and what is promised. In return for the preservation of the life of the king the queen promises a precious statue of him. In return for the successful winning of the desired bride the king promises a precious statue of her. In return for a son a childless woman promises the child granted her. In return for military victory the commander promises (the destruction of) the enemies' cities—what would normally be the victors' spoil. In return for safe arrival home the exile promises (cultic) service of the deity in their common homeland. Such a fit of condition and promise is not present in text 1.119, nor does it appear as a regular feature of the Hittite vows—a variety of precious objects is promised the deity in exchange for the king's good health. On the other hand, several of the Israelite vows promise not just an economic equivalent of some kind, but the thing itself: the spoils of victory granted to the defeated, the child granted to the barren woman. Actually the "thing itself" is not the ultimate desideratum. The army wants to remove the threat of the enemy; the woman wants to remove the shame of barrenness. If this primary need is met, they are prepared to give up the normal secondary benefits—the plundering of the enemy's goods, the various services a child performs for its parents. However, the contrast with the material gifts promised in the Ugaritic and Hittite vows remains. Is this feature of the Israelite vows a reflection of actual practice or a product of literary artistry? Whichever is the case, it suggests a difference in religious sensibility and moral outlook between Israelite literature on the one hand and the elite of Ugaritic and Hittite society on the other.

In conclusion, the vow, well attested in the Hittite archives of the Late Bronze Age, as well as, less directly, in first millennium Israel, has been adopted and adapted to their purposes by the composers of *Krt*. They have neatly conformed the basic structure of the vow to the parallelistic structure of their poetic narrative by making a typical bicolon of each of the vow's three parts: the address to the deity, the condition, and the promise. While the substance of Keret's vow is not precisely attested elsewhere, it is plausibly realistic, the condition being comparable with that in the vow of Hannah, and the promise with those of the vows of Puduhepa to Lelwani and Ishtar of Lawazantiya.

D. The Marriage Blessing

In the first tablet of *Krt* the eponymous hero has, at the direction of the god El, undertaken an expedition to Udum, the city of king *Pbl*, where he is to demand Hurraya as his wife. The two kings are negotiating through messengers when the first tablet of the work ends. The second tablet now lacks some forty lines at the beginning, after which comes a passage extolling the virtues of Hurraya and expressing the regrets of the Udumites. Perhaps this is the conclusion of a speech by *Pbl*, certainly one delivered on the occasion of the loss of Hurraya to Keret (1.15.1.1-7). Keret responds (1.15.1.8), but his speech is lost in the gap of some twenty lines at the beginning of the second column. As the text reappears, various gods are mentioned by name. Evidently they are assembling in Keret's house (1.15.2.8-11). Baal now calls upon El to bless Keret (1.15.2.12-16) and El raises his glass accordingly (1.15.2.16-20). The blessing is then quoted (1.15.2.21-3.16, with a gap of about fifteen lines at the beginning of column 3), after which the assembled gods bless Keret on their own account and depart (1.15.3.17-19). Hurraya promptly conceives and bears children (1.15.3.20-21).

Clearly the blessing is pronounced in a formal gathering after the contracting of a marriage (by Keret and the bride's father) and before its consummation. The occasion appears to be a wedding breakfast. El's blessing may be designated a marriage blessing. An analysis of its structure and purpose, and comparison with some similar biblical texts will confirm the appropriateness of this classification.

The blessing is addressed to the bridegroom, but its first subject is his bride, and she is mentioned only to introduce the subject of offspring:

aṯt [tq]ḥ ykrt	The woman you have taken, oh Keret,
aṯt tqḥ btk	the woman you have taken into your house
[ǵ]lmt tšʿrb ḥẓrk	the maid you have brought into your court
tld šbʿ bnm lk	will bear you seven sons
wṯmn tṯmnm lk	eight . . . (?) for you
tld yṣb ǵlm	She will bear the boy, Yassub
ynq ḥlb a[ṯ]rt	to drink the milk of Asherah
mṣṣ ṯd btlt [ʿnt]	to suck the breast of the maid Anat
mšnq[t]	who suckl[es]

(1.15.2.21-28)

Having spoken of the first son, El presumably went on to speak of the others in the fifteen or so lines missing from the beginning of the next column, because when the text resumes we have, after a refrain referring to Keret's greatness, a similar, though more succinct pattern for his female progeny: a general reference to Hurraya's conceiving and bearing daughters, an enumeration of these, and then the refrain again:

[mid rm] krt	Keret shall [be many, be great]
[btk rpi] arṣ	[among the dead rulers of] the Earth
[bpḫr] qbṣ dtn	[in the assembly of] the clan of Ditan
[wt]qrb wld [b]nt lk	[She] will conceive and bear you [dau]ghters
tld pǵt t[ ]t	She will bear the girl T[ ]t
tld pǵt [ ]	She will bear the girl [ ]
tld pǵ[t]	She will bear the girl[l]
tld p[ǵt]	She will bear the g[irl]
tld p[ǵt]	She will bear the g[irl]
tld p[ǵt]	She will bear the g[irl]
mid rm [krt]	[Keret] shall be many, be great
btk rpi ar[ṣ]	among the dead rulers of the Ear[th]
bpḫr qbṣ dt[n]	in the assembly of the clan of Dit[an]

(1.15.3.2-15)

The structure of the whole blessing may be presented schematically as follows:

Your bride will bear
(1) sons (a. summary statement
b. enumeration)
Keret will be great (refrain)
(2) daughters (a. summary statement
b. enumeration)
Keret will be great (refrain)

But this scheme ignores the last line of the speech: *ṣǵrthn abkrn* "To the youngest girl I will give first-born status" (1.15.3.16). However, the syntactic relation of this line with what precedes is odd: the suffix of the first word refers back to the feminine references *preceding* the second occurrence of the refrain. In content it jars with the rest of the blessing, which is concerned with the future greatness of the groom as realized in his anticipated offspring, and especially in the endowments of the first-born son; while this last line shifts the interest abruptly to the question of an irregular succession. Finally, it seem to stand outside the structure of the blessing as described above. It stands out as a conspicuous secondary addition to the blessing, presumably for the purposes of the larger narrative (see the discussion of the poem as a whole below). (For alternative treatments of this line see Gibson 1977, 16; Margalit 1976, 189-90.)

Clearly the purpose of the blessing as a whole is to assure the bridegroom of a fertile wife and a large family. This is achieved in what is preserved of the text by giving a traditionally ideal figure for the total number of sons, and by listing the daughters one by one. We may surmise that the text also gave a total for the number of daughters and listed the sons one by one—but 1.15.2.24-25 is obscure and the sequel to the statements about the first son is missing. That seven is a traditionally ideal number of sons is evident from several biblical passages. "The barren bears seven" in a hymn to Yahweh (1 Sam 2:5). Ruth is of greater service to Naomi than seven sons (Ruth 4:15). The destruction and desolation announced in a prophetic oracle is expressed in part by the losses of "she who had born seven (sons)," that is, of a woman who had achieved the height of human felicity and security (Jer 15:9; see Weiser 1960, 129). The express interest in these passages is in the mother's experience, but seven sons are of comparable significance for the father. The upright Job originally had seven sons (Job 1:2) and after his ordeal had seven again —or twice seven (*šib'ānā*, Job 42:13).

The blessing gives assurance of the fruitfulness of Keret's marriage also by referring to his greatness among, that is, in comparison with, his ancestors. The *rpu arṣ* are the now deified predecessors of the king, and *qbṣ dtn* appears to be a more specific designation of that ancestry. The two expressions appear again (the second in the form *qbṣ ddn*) in a pair of lines in the text of the funerary ritual 1.161, in which specific ancestors, categorized as *rpum qdmym* "ancient dead rulers" are named as well as two recent kings. Babylonian scribes include Ditanu among the ancestors of the kings of the Old Babylonian dynasty, and the same name, in the form Didanu, appears in the Assyrian king list among the antecedent "kings who lived in tents" (see Finkelstein 1966). It is not surprising that the scribes of Ugarit also claim this ancient tribal name for the ancestry of Keret (see further Astour 1973, 36-37).

There are several features of this lengthy, formal speech that we can immediately identify as appropriate to its present literary context, but not for the marriage blessing as it would have been used in ordinary social life. Its setting in *Krt* is a mythic-epic world in which the gods, led by the high god, El, constitute the community that pronounces the blessing. Since El is in this poem the "father" of Keret and Keret his "son," we might expect that the bridegroom's father would be the one to pronounce the blessing, and his family or clan the community that echoes it (Van Selms 1954, 38-39). Again, while El can make a simple prediction in the indicative: "The woman . . . will bear . . ."; the human community's blessing would be in the form of a wish in the jussive: "May the woman . . . bear . . ." or, invoking the deity: "May El grant that the woman . . . might bear . . ."—while El can simply promise what will be by his own divine authority, the human community may well invoke the deity in order to bring the divine favor to bear upon the marriage. While the wise El can spell out details of the number, names, and endowments of Keret's future children, the human community's wish can only be expressed in general terms—and might not presume to hope for the ideal seven sons. Finally, the poetic form of El's blessing might not carry over into an actual human marriage.

Adjusting our expectations accordingly, we may look for other versions of the marriage blessing in ancient Near Eastern literature. Several versions are in fact preserved in the Hebrew Bible.

Immediately after Boaz has promised to marry Ruth, and his commitment has been witnessed (Ruth 4:10-11a), a blessing is pronounced on him (vss. 11b-12). This is followed by a brief notice of Ruth's becoming his wife, conceiving and bearing a son (vs. 13). Here too we have a blessing pronounced between the contracting and the consummation of a marriage.

The blessing reads as follows:

ytn yhwh 't-h'šh hb'h 'l-bytk
  krḥl wkl'h
  'šr bnw štyhm 't-byt yśr'l
w'śh-ḥyl b'prth
  wqr'-šm bbyt lḥm
wyhy bytk
  kbyt prṣ
  'šr-yldh tmr lyhwdh
    mn-hzr' 'šr ytn yhwh lk mn-hn'rh hz't

May Yahweh make the woman who is joining your family
  like Rachel and like Leah
  who together built up the family of Israel,
So that you may produce abundant progeny in Ephrathah
  and leave a big family name in Bethlehem
And so that your family
  may be like the family of Perez
  whom Tamar bore to Judah
    through the offspring Yahweh may grant you
      through this maid

(For the philological foundations upon which this translation is based see Parker 1976, 23-4, esp. the footnotes. In addition to bibliography given there see Rummel 1981, 321-32; Brichto 1973, 22 and 25-6; Labuschagne 1967, who is followed by

Campbell 1975, 153-54. Campbell also follows Labuschagne in seeing the emphasis on fertility as a counter to Boaz' age. Neither compares other marriage blessings. Note Sasson's objection to their suggestion: Sasson 1979, 155. The slightly awkward last clause finds an almost identical counterpart in the independent clause of Eli's blessing on Elkanah and Hannah during their annual pilgrimage to Shiloh. While this is designated a blessing, it is pronounced, unlike all the reflexes of the marriage blessing, by a priest, and it expresses the priest's wish that they might have a child of their own in place of the one (Samuel) whom they had dedicated to Yahweh's service in the temple. "Then Eli would bless Elkanah and his wife, and say: *yśm yhwh lk zrʿ mn h'šh hz't* . . . 'May Yahweh grant you offspring by this woman . . .' "—1 Sam 2:20. cf. Gen 4:25 in which Eve declares after the birth of her third child: *št-ly 'lhym zrʿ* . . . "God has granted me offspring . . .")

While the blessing in Ruth is not strictly poetic (and neither is its context), it is clearly a formal utterance, carefully constructed in three parts treating of three successive subjects: Boaz' bride, himself, and his family. The middle part consists of two simple parallel clauses, but the first and third parts involve two elaborate and partially parallel comparisons—of Boaz' bride and hoped-for progeny with those of ancestors noted for their descendants. The point of each comparison is to introduce a model of prolific or noble offspring.

As anticipated above, the human community here invokes the deity as the one to give effect to their wishes, saying: "May Yahweh make the woman . . ." rather than "May the woman . . ." As in *Krt*, while the blessing is addressed to the bridegroom, the first object of blessing is the bride, and she is introduced only to raise the real subject of their progeny. Also as in *Krt* the bridegroom is introduced in a subordinate clause dependent upon "the woman." Here too the purpose of the blessing is to assure the bridegroom of a fertile wife and numerous offspring. In this case, however, that is achieved not by a listing of the children to be, but by the fuller citation of precedents—of legendary ancestors who have produced whole nations or dynastic lines. As Keret was to be great among his ancestors, so Ruth is to be on a par with Rachel and Leah, who produced the nation Israel for the man Israel, and Boaz' descendants are to be on the same plane as those of Perez, ancestor of the kings of Judah. (For the various associations of the particular names and their possible use in actual marriage blessings see Parker 1976, 25 and 29-30.)

In Ruth the blessing is pronounced by the elders (LXX) and, according to the MT, all the people at the gate immediately after the legal witnessing of the preceding events concerning the marriage of Ruth. There are strong reasons to suspect that this does not correspond to a real-life situation. First, the story is about an extraordinary set of circumstances. Second, it is characteristic of the book of Ruth that the action is developed in a limited sequence of scenes. The events within each scene are bound together by their common location. Since no other events take place at a wedding breakfast, the blessing, if it is to be quoted, must be incorporated into another scene. Third, the action of the preceding scene is already completed by the formal witnessing of the legal transaction that is worked out in that scene: Boaz calls upon the assembled company to serve as witnesses to what he has undertaken (*ʿdym ʾtm hywm ky* . . . "you are witnesses today that . . ." 9a), and they accept that role (*ʿdym* "we are witnesses" 11a). In the same way Joshua calls upon the people to serve as witnesses against themselves regarding what they have undertaken (*ʿdym ʾtm bkm ky* . . . "you are witnesses against yourselves that . . ."), and they respond: *ʿdym* "we are witnesses" (Josh 24:22); and Samuel calls upon Israel to accept Yahweh and his anointed ruler as witness to its acknowledgment that Samuel has done nothing wrong (*ʿd yhwh bkm . . . hywm hzh ky* . . . "Yahweh is witness against you . . . this day that . . ."), and they respond: *ʿd* "he is witness" (1 Sam 12:5). (On these legal formulae see Boecker 1964, 161-2.) In both Josh 24:22 and 1 Sam 12:5 the word of acceptance: *ʿd/ʿdym* "he is witness"/"we are witnesses" is a complete speech. (The identical sequence in the three passages is a strong argument against McCarter's claim that the text in 1 Sam 12:5-6 is conflated and that the second *ʿd* begins Samuel's next speech "Yahweh is witness . . ." [McCarter 1980, 210]. The people's acceptance of Yahweh's role as witness is necessary *before* verse 6, which begins a new section of text, quite different from the preceding [cf. Stoebe 1973, 232-33].)

The composers of Ruth have incorporated the blessing into the preceding scene by appending it to the word with which the witnesses accept their responsibility as witnesses, thus creating a speech which at once confirms the preceding action and invokes divine blessing upon its outcome. The blessing is no more a part of the preceding action than verse 13, to which it is in some ways more closely related: verses 13 ff. are the counterpart of 1.15.3.20-25 of *Krt*, each reporting immediately and succinctly the fulfillment of the preceding blessing.

For all its mythic-epic cast *Krt* suggests a more realistic occasion for the marriage blessing. The bridegroom hosts a banquet, at which a prominent person, perhaps the bridegroom's father, pronounces the marriage blessing which the generality of guests echo. We know from Gen 29:22; Judg 14:10 and Tobit 7:15 that in Israel a wedding involved a feast, generally given by the bridegroom's family (de Vaux 1965, 34). It is probable that this was the setting of the Israelite marriage blessing.

Rummel's objection to the preceding identification of these two texts on the grounds that the larger narrative contexts show that both texts are part of a traditional narrative sequence in which they function as responses to the childlessness of the protagonist (Rummel 1981, 321-32) ignores their specific institutional occasion in the texts, namely a marriage. It also fails to explain the peculiar insistence on the size of the family, as distinct from a single child, which would quite adequately remove the stigma of childlessness. On this distinction—and the concomitant distinction between the marriage blessing and the promise of a child to a childless couple—see the analysis and interpretation of promise narratives in Genesis in Westermann 1980, which plausibly suggests that the marriage blessing is the background of the divine promise of numerous descendants. In the case of Keret the divine response to his childlessness comes in text 1.14. Text 1.15 begins with the conclusion of a marriage.

Traces of the marriage blessing as described are to be found elsewhere in the Bible. In Gen 28:1-2 Isaac summons Jacob and blesses him, giving him instructions not to take a wife from among the Canaanites, but to go to Paddan-Aram and get himself a wife there from among his mother's family. The taking of a wife is accordingly here stated not in a dependent clause referring to a present circumstance, as in Ruth and *Krt*, but as a command: *wqḥ-lk . . . 'šh*. But a person cannot command more than marriage—after that one depends on God. So Isaac continues:

> And may El Shaddai bless you:
> make you fruitful and numerous
> so that you become an array of peoples
> Gen 28:3

This is followed by the wish that God might give Jacob and his descendants the blessing of Abraham (v. 4a); but that is then defined as the promise of the land (4b).

In this case Isaac is anticipating Jacob's marriage in a distant land far from his father. Accordingly, he blesses his son now.

But since the marriage has not been contracted and the bride is unknown, he cannot refer to her directly. The bridegroom-to-be therefore appears not only as the addressee but also as the object of the blessing. Nevertheless the blessing's theme—the number of the bridegroom's descendants—and its purpose—to assure him of numerous progeny—are those of the marriage blessings already discussed. As in Ruth the deity is invoked as the bestower of the blessing. Whether the reference to the blessing of Abraham can also be claimed as the citation of an ancestor as a model of such fruitfulness, as in the other marriage blessings, is rendered doubtful by the present definition of "the blessing of Abraham" in what follows as the possession of the land. That granted, the occasion, the form, the topic and the purpose of this pronouncement encourage us to see it as a truncated version of the marriage blessing more elaborately developed in Ruth and *Keret*.

Another truncated version appears in Gen. 24:60. Here Abraham's servant, representing his master in Aram-Naharaim, has contracted on Abraham's behalf for Rebecca to become the wife of his master's son, Isaac. Rebecca is now to leave her family and return with Abraham's servant to Canaan for her union with Isaac. Her family's situation is similar to that of Isaac above: they know that they will not be present at the wedding feast to join in the blessing then, so they dismiss her with their own blessing now:

> You are our sister—become thousands of ten thousands
> and may your offspring possess the gateway of their enemies
>
> Gen 24:60

The setting—between the contracting and the consummation of a marriage—again invites us to see here a version of the marriage blessing. But the situation demands an address to the *bride* by *her* family, so that the form is quite different. It begins with a vocative followed by an imperative and lacks any reference to the deity. What remains constant is the preoccupation with a vast number of descendants, and the objective—to assure a numerous and in this case explicitly powerful progeny.

Westermann classifies this utterance as a blessing on the departing (*Abschiedssegen*), uttered on the occasion of the departure of a member of the family. He recognizes the first line as originating in the marriage blessing, but refers the second line to the wish for military victory before a battle (in the original German—the English version simply has "a political wish" Westermann 1985, 390). But the second line is also concerned explicitly with progeny, and the overcoming of enemies is probably implicit in the greatness wished on descendants. The same line follows immediately the assurance of multitudinous descendants in the divine blessing—here a sworn promise—of Gen 22:17. Thus while the second line is not essential to the marriage blessing, it is entirely consistent and compatible with it, and may be accepted as a legitimate extension of what we have already seen.

A further example is perhaps embedded in Psalm 45. Here there is no narrative context to describe the institutional setting, which has rather to be inferred from the content of the song. Psalm 45 includes an address to the king, and an address to a young woman who is to "forget [her] people and [her] father's family" (v. 11; Eng. 10). Her beauty is desired by the king, who is now her "lord" (v. 12; Eng. 11). She is presented with gifts. On the basis of such features, the psalm is generally thought to celebrate a royal wedding (see e.g. Kraus 1960, 332-8; Weiser 1950, 233-60). While the precise occasion is unknown, the psalm clearly implies a public recognition and celebration of a royal wedding, rather than the restricted family or village community occasion that the previously treated texts have suggested. There follows in verse 17 (Eng. 16) a blessing:

tḥt 'btk yhyw bnyk	May your sons take the place of (i.e. be the equal of) your ancestors,
tšytmw lśrym bkl-h'rṣ	May you make them rulers over the whole land

The blessing addresses the bridegroom directly, neither invoking the deity nor referring to the bride, but introducing immediately the subject of multiple offspring, and citing as the model for their desired number and status the ancestors of the king. It is reasonable to conclude that this line of the psalm reflects the marriage blessing.

I have previously (Parker 1976, 30) mooted that the blessings in *Krt* and Ruth might be specifically *royal* marriage blessings, since one is addressed to a king and the other to the ancestor of a king. The marriage blessing of Psalm 45 is addressed explicitly to a king. It occurs in a song composed precisely for a royal wedding and used publicly on such occasions. Since, further, this is the one marriage blessing other than Boaz' or Keret's in which the bridegroom's ancestors are cited as models for his progeny, there are perhaps more grounds for claiming that feature as a peculiarity of *royal* marriage blessings than I realized previously. Admittedly this is a much briefer and more general blessing than those in Ruth and *Krt*—no names are mentioned, the bride is not even referred to. However, the psalm does not, like the narratives, address the one marriage of particular individuals, but was doubtless intended for use in the wedding ceremonies of successive kings, so that it would be quite inappropriate for it to be too specific in its personal references. Further, the psalm itself is not a blessing. The blessing contained in this one verse would be simply an allusion to, a distillation of the marriage blessing as expressed at some other stage in the ceremonies. All of this argues for the authenticity of the verse, and against the claim that it is the gloss of a later editor (*pace* Briggs 1908, 383, 390).

There are, as is well known, many other blessings, especially in Genesis, which exhibit one or another of the features here identified as components of the marriage blessing. The preceding study perhaps provides further support for the view of Westermann (1980, 149-55) that the marriage blessing is the ultimate source of both the blessing, and the promise, of numerous descendants, both in the patriarchal narratives and elsewhere. Thus, for example,the blessing of many offspring and power over enemies in Gen 24:60 would be the model for the divine promise of the same in 22:17. It may be true that the concern for numerous offspring is "a preoccupation at many times of life among many societies," which happens to find "particularly forceful expression on such occasions as a wedding," as I wrote in 1976. But it may also be the case that the fullest formal expression of that concern, which occurs on the occasion of a wedding, is the basis of its expression on other occasions and for other purposes. Thus when Jacob blesses Ephraim and Manasseh, he does so indirectly by announcing that the Israelites will pronounce as a blessing:

yśmk ʾlhym kʾprym wkmnšh	May God make you like Ephraim and Manasseh
	Gen 48:20

He thus blesses his two grandsons by composing a blessing for future generations which cites the former as the model ancestors of the latter. To put it another way, the authors use what we may take to be a later marriage blessing (invoking Ephraim and Manasseh as ancestral models) as the basis of their construction of the "original" blessing of those ancestors.

The same kind of blessing is anticipated in the promise to Abraham: "All the families of the earth shall bless themselves by you" (Gen 12:3b; cf. 18:18; 28:14; on the translation of the *nipʿal* see the discussions in Albrektson 1967, 79-80; Westermann 1985, 151-52). The sense of this promise is that in the future all humanity will say (especially at weddings?): "May you become (*or* may God make you) as fruitful as Abraham." The same kind of blessing is envisaged in the wishes for the king in Ps 72:17 (the *hitpaʿel* here and in the following references is interchangeable with the *nipʿal* previously). In Gen 22:18 and 26:4 it is explicitly by the patriarch's "seed" (*zrʿ*), i.e. descendants, that people will bless themselves. This recalls the "family" (*byt*) of Perez in Ruth 4:12 and the "clan" (*qbṣ*) of Ditanu in *Krt*. All three words in these contexts emphasize the progeny of the ancestor as the model of the felicity wished on the bridegroom in the marriage blessing.

While the traces of the marriage blessing in Hebrew literature are often partial and faint, allusive rather than explicit, *Krt* presents us with a singularly long, poetic elaboration of the blessing in a narrative and mythological setting, the elements of which are a rather direct reflex of its standard social setting.

The preceding two chapters have explored the composers' use of several formal poetic and narrative conventions and of a few non-narrative speech forms in the composition of *Krt* and *Aqht*. Another major element in the composers' repertory was the traditional tale. The following two chapters will trace the course of each narrative, recognizing as appropriate their use of the conventions and speech forms already identified, as well as of other cultural beliefs, literary motifs or social customs, but exploring particularly their use of traditional tales, identified on the basis of comparisons drawing on the larger body of ancient near eastern narrative literature. Each chapter will also note the most salient rhetorical structures peculiar to each narrative, and will conclude with an attempt at a general characterization and interpretation of the work as we have it.

Chapter 3

ANALYSIS AND INTERPRETATION OF *AQHT*

As is now well known, the three tablets of *Aqht* were found in a room of the high priest's house, which was situated between the two temples on the acropolis of the tell of Ras Shamra. All three tablets were inscribed by the same hand, that of Ilimilku, the resident master of the scribe's craft, who has left his colophon on the left edge of the first tablet (Herdner 1963, Pl. XXX and Dressler 1983, 45, n.5). While the first tablet was inscribed with six columns, the second and third had only four each—thus about 800 lines total. The order of the three tablets (1.17, 1.18, and 1.19) is now universally accepted. However, a significant proportion of the whole is missing. First, as appears from an analysis of the narrative, the story as we have it is truncated: the last column of the third tablet records only the beginning of a narrative section which must have continued on a subsequent tablet. Second, there are sizable gaps in that portion of the story which the three tablets cover: in both the first and second tablets the two middle columns are completely lost.

Caquot has recently suggested that there may be a tablet missing between 1.18 and 1.19 (Caquot 1985, 108). However, even granting his interpretation of the difficult first section of 1.19.1, it does not seem necessary to suppose any very large number of lines missing between the last preserved traces of 1.18.4 and the first line of 1.19.1. Indeed, the movement and balance of the narrative seems to demand a fairly direct route from the murder of Aqhat in 1.18.4 to its effect on the vegetation and Danel and his daughter in 1.19.1.19ff.

Within the scope of this analysis of *Aqht* I shall indicate in passing many of those smaller components and devices already discussed in chapters 1 and 2; but will concentrate on the larger structures: those discrete units of narrative—tales, episodes and motifs—out of which this, and other, longer narratives are composed. The poem's own internal indicators of literary form provide the basic evidence for identifying these simpler, discrete narrative units within the more complex, larger narrative. Comparison of these units with other narratives or sections of narrative in ancient Near Eastern literature will disclose their generic characteristics, and the more widespread existence and use of such generic material. Where a text is incomplete or damaged, such comparison may achieve no more than suggest an outline of what might have happened where the text is lacking. Where the texts are complete and relatively well understood, comparison may not only allow identification of the generic form, but also cast light on common features that had previously been obscure in one text or the other, and bring into relief the individual characteristics and aims of each example. In any case I shall raise the question of function in relation to environment, and especially that of the function, purpose, and effects of the individual section of *Aqht*.

I shall conclude by making some tentative remarks about the poem as a whole. Where do earlier interpretations of the poem stand in relation to the analysis undertaken here? Does the analysis disclose a consistent interest running through all the episodes in which the evidence is sufficient to permit the isolation of distinctive features? Any consistent thrust uniting those peculiarities may be treated as an important clue to the theme of the whole—pending wider attestation and investigation of the identified traditional material, recognition of other traditional narrative material in the preserved part of the poem, or discovery of further material clearly belonging to the same poem or of other copies of what we already have. Finally, I shall raise the question of the purpose of the whole poem in relation to its environment.

A. The Birth of Aqhat

The first few lines of tablet 17 are missing, so that we do not have the opening of the poem. The preserved text begins with the formulaic full introduction of Danel (1.17.1.1-2; cf. 2.27-29; 5.4-5, 13-15, 33-35; 1.19.1.19-21). This introduces his performance of an incubation rite, in which he partakes of, or offers up food and drink, lays down his garments, and lies down and passes the night (in the sanctuary) (1.17.1.2-5). Such a ritual is described more directly in the Hittite *Ritual against Impotence*: "They will spread out a bed for him in front of the table and they will also spread out the headdress or the shirt that had been lying on the rations [some of which had previously been fed to the 'sacrificer']. The sacrificer will lie down, (to see) whether he will experience the bodily presence of the deity in his dream" (translation of Goetze in Pritchard 1969a, 350). A narrative account of an incubation is found in the much later Egyptian tale of *Setne Khamwas and Si-osire*: "He went to the temple of Khmun, [made his] offerings and libations before Thoth . . . made a prayer before him . . . lay down in the temple. That night he dreamed a dream in which the mysterious form of the great god Thoth spoke to him" (Lichtheim 1980, 146). The widely known ritual actions described in *Aqht* contrast with *Krt*'s account of the king's going to bed and crying himself to sleep (1.14.1; see the fuller discussion in chap. 4 A).

This account of an incubation is extended through the framework of a seven-day sequence (5-15; see Chap 1 D) and finally reported to be effective on the seventh day (15-16: *mk bšbʿ ymm*//*wyqrb bʿl bḥnth* "then on the seventh day//Baal drew near in his compassion"). The word *ḥnt* is a hapax legomenon in Ugaritic. Cognates suggest "supplication" as another possible meaning that suits the context, and many translators have adopted this. However, they are divided over whether it is in response to Danel's supplication that Baal approaches Danel (cf. El's approach to Keret in response to the latter's tears: *wyqrb bšal krt* "and he approached Keret, asking:" 1.14.1.37-38), or with his own supplication that Baal approaches El. The preceding context seems to demand the former, the succeeding context—a speech to El—the latter. Clearly the immediate response to Danel's ritual activity is Baal's intercession with El on Danel's behalf. Later Baal or some messenger reports to Danel the results of the intercession (at the beginning of 1.17.2). *Aqht* makes no reference to a dream. Rather mythological scenes and communications seem to replace the dream we would expect in an incubation. Here the contrast with *Krt* is in the opposite direction: El appears to Keret and converses with him in a dream, as in the standard incubation account.

Quite possibly 1.17.1.15-16 was ambiguous in Ugaritic, as in my translation above, and may have occurred at two successive stages in an earlier, longer version of the narrative: first, to introduce Baal's response to Danel, in which he would have learned of Danel's plight (as El learned of Keret's in 1.14.1.2), and second (as now, apparently) to introduce his intercession with El on Danel's behalf. The more abbreviated version that has been preserved would be the result either of deliberate foreshortening or of haplography.

Baal's speech to El (1.17.1.16-33) immediately follows the colon referring to his "approach." It consists of three parts: first, an account of Danel's plight (16-22), which includes a reprise of the first bicolon describing his incubation (21-22); second, an appeal for blessing (23-26), including the general appeal for blessing (23-25; cf. 1.15.2.14-16) and the specific wish for the suppliant to have a son (25-26; cf. 42-43); and third, a list of the duties performed by a son (26-33; see Eissfeldt 1966; Koch 1967; Avishur 1978; Healey 1979). There follows a narrative introduction to El's blessing (34-36; cf. 1.15.2.16-20; Jackson and Dressler 1975; Dijkstra and de Moor 1975, 177; Pardee 1977; Parker 1979-80, 19-22; Margalit 1981, 82-84, arguing for the longer form proposed by Pardee). The blessing itself follows (36-). This consists of a general blessing (36-38; cf. 1.19.4.36-39), specific instructions for Danel (38-41), the announcement that he will have a son (42-43; cf. 25-26), and the list of filial duties (44-). The preserved part of the column ends in the middle of the list.

The letters and words of the first lines preserved in the second column are clearly the remains of the same list, though with the third person suffixes of col. 1 replaced by second person singular suffixes (1.17.2.1-8). Someone is announcing El's blessing to Danel. The missing lines at the end of col. 1 and the beginning of col. 2 must have contained the latter part of the list as spoken by El, a reference to Baal's coming from El to Danel (or possibly to the sending of some messenger to him), and the beginning of the list as spoken by whoever announces El's blessing. This announcement may have begun with a version of the earlier part of El's speech, including perhaps specific instructions (cf. 1.17.1.38-41), and probably the announcement that a son would be born to Danel as to his peers (see chap. 2 B and cf. 1.17.2.14-15). The birth announcement here serves as a divine promise.

Danel responds to the announcement in language commonly used describing the reaction to good news (1.17.2.8-11; cf. 1.4.4.28-30; 1.6.3.14-16). The longest version of this topos is discussed in chap. 1 B. The briefest version—the formulaic line *šmḫ* DN—is more frequent: 1.4.2.28, 5.35-36, 6.35-36; 1.5.2.20; 1.10.3.37, the latter appearing in a similar context to the present one, namely following the announcement of a birth. The next two lines (11-12) introduce Danel's speech (12-23), which consists of a statement of his relief (12-14); the reason for this—the birth of a son like his kin (14-15); and the duties of such a son, now with first person singular suffixes (16-23).

Up to this point there is a symmetry in the narrative. The movement is from Danel through Baal to El and from El back through Baal (?) to Danel. The expression of Danel's need leads to El's blessing, and the blessing leads back to the relief of Danel's need. The section is further bound together by the recurrence of the list of filial duties in each of the four speeches.

The divine word already assures Danel that his need has been met. He now returns home (1.17.2.26-27; cf. 1.19.4.8-9). Hospitality to the Katharat follows, framed by reference to their arrival (26-27) and departure (39-40). After their arrival the full introduction of Danel recurs (27-29), and the brief notice of his hospitality (29-31) is repeated in a seven-day framework (32-39), which issues in the departure of the Katharat (39-40). The numerical framework (see chap. 1 D 5) is used to extend the activity into a neatly framed episode, which by its repetitiveness slows down the progress of the action and postpones the account of the birth of Aqhat (contrast the birth of Keret's many children in two lines immediately following El's promise of such children in his blessing of Keret's marriage, and the departure of the gods—1.15.3.20-21). As the text deteriorates toward the end of the column, words such as *'rš* "bed," *yrḫ* "month," and numerals make clear that Danel now acts upon El's blessing, going to bed with his wife, who conceives; and counting the months of her pregnancy, until his promised son is born.

Many interpreters place the conception and birth at different points in these first two columns of *Aqht*. What is here (and in Gibson 1977 and Del Olmo Lete 1981) understood to be El's blessing of the sexual embrace of Danel and his wife (1.17.1.38-41), is taken by others to be a description of the actual conception of the desired son (Dijkstra and de Moor 1977, 178-79; Margalit 1983a, 75). As described above, the pattern of the text thus far suggests that El's speech continues to the end of col. 1 and that Danel learns of El's blessing only at the beginning of col. 2. It is only then that he goes home, and hence that coition and conception become a possibility.

Caquot and Sznycer assume that the son has been born (without any mention of the fact by the poet) prior to the visit of the Katharat, which they understand to mark the actual birth and the following seven-day period (Caquot and Sznycer 1974, 405 and 425, n. f). This compels them to attribute the numerals at the end of col. 2 to Danel's counting the months of his new son's age. But the counting of months is never associated with a child's growth. On the other hand, it appears frequently to mark the passage of the period of gestation, e.g. in several narratives preserved in the Hittite capital of Hattusa (Hoffner 1968; Siegolová 1971, 32), some of which are related to the present Ugaritic passage in Irvin 1978, 138. In a special case, the "birth" of the first human, an Akkadian text refers to the counting of months in the line *[wašb]at Nintu [ima]nnu arḫi* "Nintu [sa]t, [cou]nting months" (*Atra-Ḫasis* I 278), which is remarkably similar to *yṯb dnil [s]pr yrḫh* "Danel sat, [co]unting his/her months" (1.17.2.43—this comparison is made by Dijkstra and de Moor 1975, 180). Counting of months appears in the contexts of animals' pregnancy in Job 39:2 (Del Olmo Lete 1985, 89). It seems best, therefore, to interpret the entertainment of the Katharat as a rite to ensure conception, and to understand the remains at the end of col. 2 as referring to the coition and resulting pregnancy, followed, in the ensuing gap, by the birth of Aqhat.

Thus this section of the poem would have a central core, consisting of an appeal to the gods and the divine answer; but also a more extended form in which the hero acts upon the divine answer, following the cultic and natural procedures necessary for the fulfillment of the blessing. That final fulfillment would have come with the birth of the desired son around the end of col. 2. The tension set up by the opening incubation scene expressing Danel's need is relaxed in a series of stages: first, by Baal's intercession on his behalf, then by El's blessing, then by the announcement to Danel himself, then by the favorable visit of the Katharat and Danel's proper treatment of them, and finally by the conception and birth of Aqhat.

The course of this section of the poem is a familiar one in ancient Near Eastern literature. Its main structural elements are as follows: 1) the introduction of the hero as childless; 2) the appeal to the god; 3) the god's favorable response; (4) conception and birth. The essence of this structure is distilled at the beginning of the Egyptian tale of *The Doomed Prince* (already compared with *Aqht* by Irvin 1978, 86). This version is short enough to quite in its entirety:

> It is said, there once was a king to whom no son had been born. [After a time his majesty] begged a son for himself from the gods of his domain, and they decreed that one should be born to him. That night he slept with his wife and she [became] pregnant. When she had completed the months of childbearing, a son was born (Lichtheim 1976, 200; cf. Wente in Simpson 1973, 85-86).

The preserved part of the Hurrian tale of *Appu* (Siegolová 1971) uses the same basic structure. 1) Appu is portrayed as childless (Vs. I:16-37). 2) He presents a white lamb to the Sun-god (I:38-40), 3) who turns himself into a youth, approaches Appu, and asks him what he is lacking (I:41-45). After Appu has told him (II:1-4), the Sun-god tells him to sleep with his wife, assuring him that the gods will give him a son (II:4-9). 4) Appu now goes home (II:10) and (after a damaged passage concerning the Storm-god's reception of the returning Sun-god) presumably slept with his wife (in what is now a gap in the text), who became pregnant (III:7). Nine months pass and a son is born in the tenth (III:7-9).

Beside these four essential elements, *Appu* also shares with *Aqht* an interesting detail. The hero's initial childlessness sets him apart from his community. As the elders of his town sit before him at meals:

> one gives his son bread and meat,
> the other gives his son a drink;
> but Appu has no-one to whom to give bread
> (Vs. I 19-21)

This recalls the characterization of Danel's plight in Baal's speech to El—"he has no son as do his brothers//no offspring as do his peers"—and Danel's expression of relief on hearing of El's blessing: "for a son has been born to me as to my brothers//an offspring as to my peers." This expression of the isolation, and presumably inferiority, occasioned by lack of a son will have been an authentic reflection of common social experience, and not a mere literary convention.

The first chapter of 1 Samuel presents us with another version of the same basic narrative structure. 1) Hannah is introduced as barren. 2) In the sanctuary at Shiloh she expresses her need through a standard cultic form, in this case a vow (1:11; see chap. 2 C). 3) The priest of Shiloh blesses her (1:17), and Yahweh "remembers" her when she goes to bed with her husband (1:19). 4) She conceives and bears a son (1:20).

Here the deity can scarcely be said to be one of the characters in the story, being represented in the action by the priest. The reference in v. 19 serves rather as a reminder of who is ultimately responsible for the outcome of the characters' actions. The biblical narrative strips the story of mythology, and substitutes realistic detail, as in 1:13. It is again characteristic of many of the biblical stories that the central character is the childless *woman*—whereas all the ancient Near Eastern treatments of the subject focus on the man. But as in *Aqht* and *Appu* the plight of the childless person is made the sharper by a comparative reference. In this case Hannah's barrenness is rendered the more unbearable by contrast with the children born to her husband's other wife (1:2) and that wife's attitude (1:6).

Finally, as we shall see in chap. 5, the same structure has been adapted to the larger and more complex narrative with which *Krt* opens. Here the larger interests of the narrative produce a version which lacks a formal appeal, whether ritual or verbal, to the god; in which the god's directions address only the acquisition of a wife, not conception or birth; and in which the final outcome is children in general, not a son in particular. The pattern we have been discussing is, however, still discernible in the shaping of this narrative. 1) Keret is childless. 2) He cries himself to sleep, which 3) prompts El to appear to him in a dream, and ask him what he wants. 2) When Keret tells him, 3) El gives him instructions on how to get a wife. 4) Keret executes El's instructions. The marriage immediately issues in children.

All four stories, from four different literatures, share with *Aqht* the same generic features: the protagonist's lack of a son and appeal to the deity; the deity's response and its consequence: conception and birth. Other briefer references to the same sequence of events are to be found in Gen. 25:21, 25-26a (with the motif of conflict between two brothers, as in *Appu*), and 30:1a (including the motif of deprivation in relation to counterparts), 22-23a, both cases exemplifying the biblical focus on the woman. All the examples mentioned suggest that the underlying narrative structure represents a standard interpretation of a birth to a childless couple following an appeal to the deity. It is possible that stories developed around this interpretation of experience had an independent existence in the communities of ancient East Mediterranean societies. Their purpose would have been to give hope to the childless by showing that the gods have granted offspring to those who have turned to them. They are to be contrasted with those narratives in the Bible in which the childless couple is approached by divine initiative. Such stories, issuing in the birth of e.g. Isaac, Samson, John the Baptist, use many of the same elements, but for a different purpose: to introduce one who will be a significant divine agent. While Samuel is certainly such an agent, his mission is initiated not by the birth story but by the later call narrative (1 Sam. 3:2-18). What distinguishes virtually all the biblical birth narratives, whether employing the appeal to the deity or the divine initiative, is the centrality of the woman's (future mother's) role, as contrasted with that of the man's (future father's) in the other ancient Near Eastern texts.

In all the literary versions preserved, the story is found at the beginning of a much larger and more complex narrative. In *The Doomed Prince* it quickly introduces the hero whose real story begins with the subsequent pronouncement of his fate by the

Hathors. It appears to be no more here than a conventional prologue, introducing the main character. In *Appu* too it appears to be a quite conventional introduction of the two main characters. In fact, the divine aid is here a mixed blessing, as the gods did not use the "good way" for the first birth. Hence the name of the first child: Bad. Since the child named Bad is born first, in direct consequence of Appu's prayer and the Sun-god's promise, and yet the proemium of the story speaks of the destruction of bad people, the role of divine favor in the births must be seen simply as part of the traditional apparatus used to introduce characters as the children of a childless couple who sought divine aid. In 1 Samuel, while the basic structure is used to introduce the hero, the specific petition—the vow—is used to explain how Samuel came to be living in the temple (where he later received his divine call) from his childhood.

In *Krt* the generic pattern has been integrated with other materials, and the resulting complex narrative serves not so much to introduce the hero—Keret himself is the hero of the larger narrative—as to show how El reversed the king's wretched state through Keret's careful execution of El's detailed instructions. Keret's obedience results in his producing a large number of children. Only later and gradually are some of these distinguished. (See chap. 4.)

What distinguishes *Aqht* from these other cases is the carefully patterned cycle of speeches, including the list of filial duties repeated four times as a refrain; and the repetitive accounts of ritual acts: incubation and the cult of the Katharat. The story seems to move through a sequence of stages, each carefully framed, each giving place to its successor at a very leisurely pace, each in consequence seeming to invite pleasurable contemplation. As it moves graciously from scene to scene, from speech to speech, it gives not a hint of the tensions and conflict to follow. It uses the traditional narrative structure we have been discussing to present Danel as a model of meticulous piety, enjoying the gracious favor of the gods; and to introduce Aqhat as one whose birth was the result of that same careful piety and divine favor. This presentation of both characters will be reinforced in the next (preserved) section. When subsequently the gods turn against Aqhat, our image of him will be the more rudely shattered, and the piety of Danel the more harshly tested.

B. The Bow of Aqhat

Between the end of the text preserved in col. 2 and the beginning of that preserved in col. 5 there is a gap of some one hundred and fifty lines: about ten lines at the end of col. 2, two entire columns, and then about twelve lines at the beginning of col. 5. Since the story of Aqhat's birth must conclude in the first lines of this lacuna, some new episode must have been introduced around the beginning of col. 3. It is unlikely that there was any extensive account of how Aqhat grew up (similarly Xella 1976, 67). It is characteristic of ancient Near Eastern narratives that, following the account of the circumstances of the birth of the hero, there are only passing references to his growth to manhood. Judging by such cases as *The Doomed Prince* (Pap. Harris 500) Verso 4 = Lichtheim, 1976, 200; *The Sargon Legend* 1-11; *Appu* III-IV 2; Gen 25:24-27; Exod 2:1-11; 1 Sam 1-2; we may safely suppose that no more than a verse or two would have referred to Aqhat's growth to young manhood. The gap in the text may have been occupied by some episode of which we can see no trace in the surviving text. However, in view of the centrality of the death of Aqhat in everything that follows, and the role of the bow in precipitating his death, it seems more likely that cols. 3-4 contained a lengthy account of the origins of the bow, the delivery of which in col. 5 would have concluded the second major component of the larger poem. As I shall argue below, a separate narrative component starts around the beginning of col. 6, so that col. 5 is more likely to be the conclusion of what precedes than the first part of the sequel.

The text of col. 5 begins with the conclusion of a speech, evidently by the craftsman god, Kothar, in which he announces that he will take the bow *ṯmn* "there" (1.17.5.2-3; cf. the fulfillment of his intention *hlk*//*hl* "here" in lines 12-13). Perhaps, as many have supposed, the bow had been requested by Danel, who may have gone, or sent his son, in search of the materials mentioned in 1.17.6.20-23. In those lines Aqhat suggests that, if Anat wants a bow like Aqhat's, she present the listed materials to Kothar. If those same materials had in fact been acquired by Danel or his son in the lost portion of text before col. 5, these would then have been presented to Kothar, whose construction of the bow may have been described. At least some such developments (with which one might compare the preparations for and building of the palace for Baal in 1.4.5-6) would have led to Kothar's completion of the bow. They would lead nicely into Kothar's announcement (at the beginning of col. 5) of his intention to deliver the bow.

The bulk of col. 5 is a discrete episode concerning Kothar's visit to Danel. It is introduced immediately after the end of

Kothar's speech by what is usually the climactic line of a seven-day framework, but here is a mere gesture referring to the passage of time (see chap. 1 D 5). The text proceeds by means of a number of formulaic cola (see chap. 1 B): the full introduction of the hero (4-5), the description of his judicial activity on the threshing floor at the city gate (6-8; cf. 1.19.1.21-25), and the interruption of that activity at his sight of Kothar approaching with the bow (9-13).

The recurrence of the full introduction of the hero at this point (13-15) introduces the action proper. Danel addresses his wife, bidding her prepare a meal for the visitor and give him food, drink and honor (15-21). Her execution of his instructions (23-31) is interrupted by Kothar's presentation of the bow to Danel immediately on his arrival (25-28). This occurs after she has prepared the meal, but before she has served and honored him. The episode then concludes with Kothar's departure (31-33).

This episode recalls the visitation of Abraham by the three strangers in Gen 18:1-16 (as first observed by Good 1958, 72, n.4; the comparison was exploited in Xella 1978). Abraham is here portrayed resting at the door of his tent during the heat of the day. Three men suddenly appear before him. He eagerly greets them and prevails upon them to stay and enjoy his hospitality. He then instructs his wife to bake for them, while he himself fetches some meat, which he has a servant prepare. When the food is ready he serves it, and stands by while his guests eat. In a postprandial conversation the visitors promise him a divine gift—a son. After further conversation between the visitors and Abraham's wife, the visitors depart.

Another version of the same narrative structure appears in the next chapter, in which two of the same visitors come that evening to the gate of the city at which Lot is sitting. Like Abraham, Lot goes to meet them, prevails upon them to stay with him, and feeds them. His hospitality extends to protecting them from a mob. They reward him by warning him of the city's imminent destruction, and then depart, helping him to escape with them (Gen 19:1-16).

Both stories share a common structure: 1) the central character is portrayed at his normal activity for the time of day; 2) he is approached by strangers (actually divine envoys, but not initially recognized as such); 3) he offers them lavish hospitality; 4) the strangers reward their host; and 5) depart. The two Genesis stories are but adaptations of a widely found tale (cf. other adaptations in Ovid *Fasti* 5.493-536; *Meta*. 8.611-724; further examples in Gaster 1969, 156-57; S. Thompson 1955, V, Q45.1), which probably was circulated independently with the purpose of encouraging hospitality to strangers. In Genesis, though the basic structure has been preserved, this purpose has been overshadowed by the larger themes and purposes of the patriarchal narratives. (The emphasis on Lot's hospitality is nevertheless sufficiently strong to impress the author of 2 Peter with Lot's righteousness; see Alexander 1985.)

The same basic structure appears to lie behind two stories in the Elijah-Elisha literature of the books of Kings, though here it is handled rather more freely. In 2 Kgs 4:8-17 a woman presses her hospitality on Elisha, who then stops at her house regularly to benefit from this. She, recognizing that he is a holy man, furnishes a small room, which she reserves for him. Elisha, wishing to reward her, enquires what it is she most desires. He ascertains that she is childless and that her husband is an old man, and so promises her a son—which arrives as promised (cf. Abraham and Sarah). This story lacks the first and last elements of the traditional structure, and the woman probably realizes from the start that Elisha is a "man of God." Nevertheless, the story seems to draw on the same traditional tale as the two Genesis versions. Even though the woman recognizes her visitor early on as an *'yš 'lhym qdwš* "a holy (God-empowered) man" (v. 9), she does not anticipate by far the reward she finally receives (not even believing him when he first promises it to her—v. 16). Thus the tale preserves the traditional function of illustrating the possibility of unexpected rewards for hospitality, while adding that of teaching the power of the "man of God" and his word.

In 1 Kgs 17:10-16 a woman is gathering wood, when she is approached by Elijah, who asks her for hospitality. He announces in a divine oracle what her reward will be. She gives the hospitality as requested, and receives the promised reward. The relation of this story to those just discussed is vouched for by the appearance of the same structural elements (except the last) and by the underlying motif of hospitality rewarded. But here the significance of the third and fourth elements is changed: the stranger *requests* the hospitality, and announces the reward for it *before* receiving it. Like the last story, this one stresses the power of the prophet's word, but it also introduces the test of the woman's faith in his promise. It encourages respect for the former and emulation of the latter more than the practice of hospitality toward strangers—though the woman's hospitality does explain Elijah's survival during the drought. (A further dimension is added by the prefixing to the story of vv. 8-9, in which Yahweh gives Elijah instructions and predictions of which the following story becomes the execution and fulfillment.) In both these stories the interests of the prophetic narratives in Kings have prevailed over the original purpose of the traditional tale—without completely concealing or abandoning the essential elements of the latter.

While all the structural elements are present in the *Aqht* version, a number of modifications have here too obscured the original purpose. The identity of the visitor and purpose of the visit are known from the start—a significant difference from Gen 18:1-16 that Xella (1976, 67, and 1978) does not appear to recognize. Kothar announces that he will bring the bow, and Danel sees Kothar coming with the bow, before he gives directions for the visitor's entertainment. Further, Kothar presents his gift before Danatiya's hospitality, not after it. Thus even less than in 1 Kgs 17:9-16 can the visit be seen as a test of hospitality. The traditional materials have been completely adapted to the present narrative, in which they now serve as a simple transitional episode—admittedly very carefully constructed—describing Kothar's delivery of the promised bow (1.17.5.2-3). The careful construction, in continuity with that of cols. 1-2, spells out Danel's and Danatiya's precise observation of the proprieties suited to the occasion.

After Kothar's departure the full introduction of Danel reappears (1.17.5.33-35), introducing the next episode. As the text deteriorates, Danel apparently gives the bow to Aqhat, with a charge concerning the etiquette of the hunt, including such expressions as *ṣdk* "your game" (lines 37, 38); *bhklh* "in(to) his/her residence" (line 39). Thus the young Aqhat, like the young Esau, apparently became an *ʾyš ydʿ ṣyd ʾyš śdh* "a man skilled in hunting, a man of the open country" (Gen. 24:27). But the substance of Danel's commission and any response on the part of Aqhat is lost to us.

The general shape of this section of the poem, if indeed the substance of cols. 3 and 4 resembled the suggestions above, could be compared with the preparation of new armor for Achilles and its presentation to him (*Iliad* 18:368-19.23). There Thetis, Achilleus' divine mother, goes to Hephaistos and requests of him a shield, helmet, corselet and greaves. Hephaistos' design and manufacture of these is described in great detail. When they are completed, he gives them to Thetis, who goes back to Achilleus and presents them to him. Quite different in detail, the two narratives would share an interest in the divine origins of the hero's accoutrements, and issue in their presentation to the hero as the outcome of a divine visit.

C. The Murder of Aqhat

About ten lines are lacking at the end of col. 5 and another ten at the beginning of col. 6. The first preserved lines of col. 6 (lines 4-6) being formulaic, may be safely restored. They disclose that a meal is in progress, and the immediately following lines mention drinking vessels and wine. In line 10 the formula of recognition appears: *bnši ʿnh wtphn* "she (Anat, from the sequel) looks up and sees." The next few lines seem to describe Anat's reaction to the approach of Aqhat carrying his new bow. The bow is mentioned in line 13, perhaps as the object of the verb √*ṣby* "to desire" (*tṣb qšt*; Ginsberg 1945, 16, now followed by many others). There is scarcely enough space in the twenty lines missing between cols. 5 and 6 for the narrative to have described Aqhat's first hunt and a failure on his part to present his first game to the temple (cf. 1.17.5.37-39), as surmised by Gibson (1975, 65; 1977, 27; Caquot 1985, 109, n.1). Furthermore, the sequel, on the one hand, gives no hint of Aqhat's having committed such a cultic offense, and, on the other, displays Anat's strong desire for the bow. Aqhat's fate is adequately accounted for by this desire and his rejection of her offers (especially in light of the Gilgamesh passage compared below).

Anat now empties her cup on the ground (15-16), and addresses Aqhat (16-17). The ensuing dialogue consists of two pairs of speeches—each comprised of an offer by Anat and a rejection by Aqhat—and a final threat by Anat. Anat first offers Aqhat silver and gold in exchange for his bow (16-19). The divine offer of wealth is a commonplace, present also in Ishtar's offer to Gilgamesh (see below); implied in Keret's rejection of silver, gold, etc. in 1.14.2.51-2.3; and assumed in 1 Kgs 3:11, 13 (cf. chap. 4 A). Anat's *tn* "give" is countered by the *tn* "give" of Aqhat, who tells her to give the materials of which the bow is made to Kothar, who would make one for her (20-25). Anat then offers Aqhat immortality (26-33). The substantive escalation of her offer is supported by the formal repetition of her language—*irš . . . watnk*//*ašlḥk*—and its expansion into a tricolon in the second speech. Her second offer is also expanded with the claim that she will make Aqhat live as long as Baal (28-29), and that as Baal gives life and is celebrated for it, so she will give Aqhat life (*kbʿl kyḥwy . . . ap ank aḥwy aqht ǵzr* 30-33). Long life is also a standard divine offer and human, specifically royal, desideratum. It is what Yahweh expects Solomon to ask for (1

Kgs 3:11) and what Yahweh gives Solomon in 1 Kgs 3:14; what the cultic community says the king asked for and God granted in Ps 21:5 (cf. also *The Report of Wenamun* 2,57-58—Lichtheim 1976, 228; Wente in Simpson 1973, 153). She does not in this speech reiterate the condition: Aqhat's yielding his bow to her. Aqhat's second speech is a much more direct rejection of Anat (34-40/41). He rebukes her as a liar; quotes what appear to be proverbial questions concerning the fate of humankind; and answers these by directly contradicting the suggestion that immortality can be conferred on mortals and by asserting his own mortality. (The assertion of universal human mortality is another commonplace: see, e.g., the second harpist's song from the tomb of Neferhotep [New Kingdom]—Lichtheim 1976, 116; *Gilgamesh* III iv 6-8; X iii 3-5; Josh 23:14a; Job 30:12; Qoh 2:14-16; 3:19-20; 9:1-3; Ovid *Meta*. 10.32-35.) Finally he declares that bows and hunting are man's affairs and not woman's. Anat now drops her winning tone, and utters a threat (42-45).

A cluster of formulaic lines now conveys Anat to the residence of El (46-51; see chap. 1 B). There follows a dialog between the two deities (1.17.6.51-18.1.20). Only the beginning of Anat's first speech is preserved at the end of tablet 17, but it is introduced as a slander on Aqhat (*tlšn aqht ǵzr* 1.17.6.51). The ten to twelve lines missing from the end of tablet 17 and the first five at the beginning of tablet 18 must have been occupied by Anat's first speech and El's first response, because in 1.18.1.6 appears the word *tʿn* "she spoke up," which must introduce Anat's second speech. This is badly preserved, though the remains of lines 6-12 recall 1.3.5.19-25. Perhaps Anat threatens to destroy the palace with which El is so pleased (Margalit 1983a, 92). Certainly in lines 11-12 she threatens El's person (as she does in 1.3.5.24-25 and proposes to do in 1.3.5.2-3), and then ironically suggests that Aqhat will protect him from her (12-14). In his second speech (16-20) El acknowledges Anat's character (as he does in 1.3.5.27-28), bids her do what is on her mind, and pronounces the fate of those who would oppose her.

Further formulaic lines bring Anat back to Aqhat, as she begins her strategy for dealing with the uncooperative and insolent youth. But it is appropriate at this point to introduce a comparison with a section of another major work of ancient Near Eastern literature.

The dialogue between Anat and Aqhat, the goddess' journey to El and her conversation with him have a rather close homology in the sixth tablet of the Gilgamesh Epic. Ishtar, aroused by the sight of the newly washed and dressed Gilgamesh (1-6), accosts him, proposing that they become lovers, and offering him rich gifts, greatness and prosperity (7-21). Gilgamesh rejects the offer, asking what he is to give in return, graphically asserting that Ishtar is a treacherous object on which to rely, and citing the fate of the various lovers she has betrayed—to which he would be added (24-78). Ishtar then hurries off to Anu (79-82). She complains that Gilgamesh has insulted her (83-85). Anu responds that she got what she deserved (89-91). (This suggests the purport of El's missing reply to Anat's first speech.) Ishtar then makes her demand—the gift of a monster to destroy Gilgamesh—and threatens Anu with the release of the dead (94-100). Anu warns her that a drought will ensue (103-106), but Ishtar claims she is ready for such an eventuality (109-113). Anu then cedes the Bull of Heaven to her (117ff.).

The structure and motifs are very similar: 1) first dialog: a goddess is excited by the hero or his appurtenances, tries to entice him to yield what she desires, but is rebuffed. "Ishtar and Anath are both angered by the way in which a mortal hero contemptuously exposes a specious offer of glory" (Considine 1969, 90). 2) She hurries off to the high god. 3) Second dialog: (a) she maligns the hero, and gets an unsympathetic response; (b) she threatens the high god directly, thus finally gaining his authorization to have her revenge on the hero.

While the divergence of the two versions at this point betrays the particular larger literary purposes of their present contexts, their common structure so far suggests that both draw on a common tradition. (The differences in wording, style and content are sufficient to eliminate the possibility that either text is directly dependent on the other, even though the composers of *Aqht* may have had some knowledge of the Gilgamesh Epic.) The purpose of the generic story would have been to warn men against male presumption and female power. The latter knows no bounds, even in the divine sphere (where a goddess can exercise power over the high god).

Gilgamesh uses the traditional narrative material to depict another of the death-defying exploits of Gilgamesh and Enkidu—in fact, their last, so that tablet 6 becomes the turning point in the epic. *Aqht*'s use of the tradition is distinctive in both form and content. In *Gilgamesh* the encounter between goddess and hero consists of two long speeches—one proposal and one rejection. In *Aqht* it extends through five speeches that gradually develop the conflict between them: the goddess first offers wealth, then immortality; Aqhat rejects her offers, first indirectly by telling how to get a bow made for herself, and then directly by denouncing her as a liar and cheat; and finally Anat departs with a threat. Aqhat is not, like Gilgamesh, immediately scornful of the goddess, but is rather gradually provoked by her increasingly outrageous claims. The distinctive content of the *Aqht* version lies in Anat's aspiration to possess the bow, an implement used in a male role, and her threat of direct personal violence against El; and in Aqhat's detailed account of the composition of the bow and his assertion of the reality of death and of the normativeness of standard sex roles.

In the following passages the verbal correspondences between *Aqht* and *B'l* suggest a relationship that must be investigated alongside any comparison with *Gilgamesh* 6. The correspondences are found in 1.17.6.42-3 and 1.3.4.54-55; 1.17.6.46-49 and 1.3.5.4-8; 1.18.1.6-12 and 1.3.5.19-25; and 1.18.1.16-17 and 1.3.5.27-28. In 1.18.4.7-8 and 16-17 Anat uses language similar to that of the first pair of correspondences, which suggests that these are four instances of a more widely used transposable formula. The second pair are but two examples of a widely attested cluster of formulaic lines. Thus neither of the first two pairs of correspondences can be regarded as indicative of a specific, significant relationship between the two Ugaritic contexts. The other correspondences may have been more common than we now see—may, for example, have been part of the mythological language characteristic of Anat and her relationship to El. It is remarkable that this language does not recur anywhere else among the various visits that gods and goddesses pay to El; and that Anat's threats and El's acknowledgement of her character appear to fit their context in *B'l* much less satisfactorily than their present position in *Aqht*. On the other hand, their location and function in *Aqht* are strikingly analogous to the location and function of the corresponding material in *Gilgamesh*. While the Akkadian and the Ugaritic text each uses its own language and reflects its own culture, the structural similarities between the two are more significant for the relationship between the two narratives than are the verbal correspondences between the two Ugaritic texts. The latter are thus better explained as illustrating the degree to which particular cola and clusters of cola have become formulaic in Ugaritic poetry.

Similarly, Ishtar's threat to release the dead in *Gilgamesh* 6 is found again in *Nergal and Ereshkigal* (STT I, 28, V, 11-12 and 26-27) and in the *Descent of Ishtar* (CT 15, 45, 19-20). However, the threat is not used in the Sumerian antecedent of *Gilgamesh* 6. Tigay has observed that it is less plausible in (the Akkadian)

Gilgamesh 6 than in the contexts of *Nergal and Ereshkigal* or *The Descent of Ishtar*. He suggests that it had its origin in the latter and was borrowed from there into *Gilgamesh*, *Gilgamesh* and *The Descent* having several items in common (Tigay 1982, 173-74). The use of the same language in all three texts is testimony to the extent to which it had become a formulaic resource for the composers of such poems—as, I have argued, is true of the language shared by *Aqht* and *B'l*.

The comparison with Gilgamesh 6:1-119 supports the claim made above that 1.17.6 begins a new section of the poem. Each section is joined to the preceding material in a similar way. Gilgamesh's washing and dressing in the first lines of tablet 6 conclude his defeat of Huwawa in tablet 5, but then also make him the object of Ishtar's desire and so initiate the next episode in his and Enkidu's exploits. Similarly Aqhat's sporting of his newly-acquired bow concludes the section concerned with its fashioning and delivery, but then also makes it the object of Anat's desire, so initiating the next section of *Aqht*.

Ishtar's revenge takes quite a different course from that of Anat, so that comparison of the two sequels to the section just discussed will not be fruitful. In *Aqht* the sequel brings Anat with a few formulaic cola back to Aqhat (1.18.1.19/20-22) whom she addresses (22-23). Of the following dialogue only parts of the first lines of Anat's opening speech are preserved. Apparently she is conciliatory (on line 24 see Dressler 1979b; Xella 1984), referring to his going on a hunt (*tlk bṣd* 27), offering to teach him (*almdk* 29; cf. Yahweh as instructor in the use of the bow for war in Ps 18:35 = 2 Sam 22:35), and referring to the place *Ablm*. With these remains the text breaks off. Approximately 20 lines are missing at the end of col. 1, cols. 2 and 3 are missing entirely, and then a further 20 lines are lost from the beginning of col. 4. When the text resumes in col. 4, Anat is close to consummating her revenge upon Aqhat. Presumably the entire extent of this gap, then, was occupied with her preparations for revenge. As we shall see, the questions raised by the broken speeches in the first third of the preserved part of col. 4 seem to presuppose such a lengthy development.

The preserved part of col. 4 begins after a few fragments of lines with familiar formulae conveying Anat to *Yṭpn*, whom she immediately addresses (1.18.4.5-7). The following lines are incomplete until lines 17 ff. which are restored on the basis of their transposition in lines 28 ff. Nevertheless it is clear that Anat's initial speech (7-11) is followed by a speech by *Yṭpn* (12-

15, introduced in 11), which in turn is followed by a second speech by Anat (16-27, introduced in 16).

In her first speech Anat refers first to *Ablm*, and then to the moon:

ik al yḥdṯ yrḫ	How will the moon (not) be renewed?
b[ ]bqrn ymnh	In [ ] in its right horn
banšt[ ]qdqdh	In the waning (?) [of] its head
	1.18.4.9-11

(For the best recent analysis of these lines see Dietrich and Loretz 1985.) *Ablm* is of course the *qrt zbl yrḫ* "Town of Prince Moon." Is Anat suggesting that the renewal of the moon is threatened by Aqhat and his bow? Or is she reassuring *Yṭpn* that the moon will be renewed, that Yarikh will not react unfavorably to having Aqhat dispatched in the territory of his town? The latter suggestion has the merit of treating the speech as a unit. (For other suggestions see Kapelrud 1969, 76; Gibson 1977, 25; Margalit 1983a, 99.) In *Yṭpn*'s reply he refers to Anat's striking Aqhat for his bow (*at . . . tmḫṣh*). Clearly he knows what is being proposed, without having to be told so in this conversation. Is this a statement of approval ("you may strike him"), or is he insisting that *she* do the deed ("*you* strike him)? Or is he demurring ("will you strike him?")? He concludes by saying that the lad has laid food. Was he responsible for seeing that Aqhat kept the assignment at *Ablm*?

The damage to these lines leaves many questions unanswered. But since we know from the sequel that Anat proceeded immediately to use *Yṭpn* to kill Aqhat near *Ablm*, where she was proposing that Aqhat and she go in 1.18.1.27-31, we may presume that most of the missing material between cols. 1 and 4 was concerned with her preparations for that coup. Perhaps first, in a lengthy dialogue involving some thrusting and parrying comparable to that in 1.17.6, she would have persuaded Aqhat to go to *Ablm*. Then she would have set about acquiring an assistant. She may have tried unsuccessfully to persuade others to assist her before turning to *Yṭpn* (cf. *Inanna's Descent*, 179 ff.); or, since the dialogue with *Yṭpn* in the preserved part of col. 4 suggests that he was by then already familiar with the situation, and that she was dealing with objections he had raised or conditions he had laid down, the missing section may have included an initial proposal to *Yṭpn* and some subsequent investigation or actions designed to overcome his objections or meet his conditions. She may, for example, have cleared her plan with Yarikh (as she had previously in a general way with El). One or the other of them may have arranged for

Aqhat to sit down to the meal in which he is engaged when Aqhat and *Yṭpn* finally strike.

In any case, Anat now tells *Yṭpn* how she will use him in the murder of Aqhat. She will carry him like a bird of prey (*km nšr*), fly among a flock of birds of prey, and release him over Aqhat, whom he will strike on the head (√*hlm . . . qdqd*) while he dines. Aqhat's blood will drain from him and his life depart. Any allusions to falconry here are probably no more than that (Caquot and Sznycer 1974, 439, n. a; the more ambitious proposal by Watson 1977, adopted by Gibson 1977, has been well criticized by Pardee 1980, p. 289 and Margalit 1983a, 100-101). The weapons made by Kothar and used by Baal against Yamm are also said to be *km nšr* "like a bird of prey" in Baal's hand, and the second weapon strikes Yamm also on the head—√*hlm qdqd* 1.2.4.21-22, 23-24. The simile may have been even more common. What is unique here is the use of Anat's avian characteristics for the accomplishment of the murder. It is likely that Xella is correct in seeing Anat portrayed as a hunter, with scabbard for weapon and pouch for game (Xella 1976, 71-72, 87).

Anat's instructions and predictions of 1.18.4.17-26 appear in transposed form in 27-37. In the remains of the last lines of the column we find Anat weeping (*wtbk* 39). Her further actions in the aftermath of the murder appear to be recounted in the first nineteen lines of 1.19. These seem to treat of the finality of Aqhat's death and the loss of the bow. Unfortunately most of these lines are extremely difficult to construe with confidence. Even where they are complete the versification, syntax and lexicon are often quite debatable. (For the best recent treatment see Caquot 1985; earlier: Caquot and Sznycer 1974, 441-43; Dijkstra and de Moor 1975, 197-200.)

Anat's use of *Yṭpn* to dispose of her enemy is comparable with Inara's use of a mortal to dispose of the serpent in a Hittite story associated with the *purulli* festival of the Storm-God of Heaven, and preserved in the words of a priest of the Storm-God of Nerik (for text and translation see now Beckman 1982). Like other Hittite myths of Hattian origin this text is preserved in connection with a ritual. It is unusually succinct and compact, reading more like a summary of a myth than a real literary composition (cf. Hoffner 1975, 136). In this lapidary account, Inara prepares a rich banquet. She then goes to a certain town where she meets a mortal, and proposes that he help her in her enterprise. The mortal agrees, on condition that he first sleep with her. She concedes, and then takes him back to the banquet and hides him. Dressing herself up she then invites the serpent to join her at her banquet. The serpent and its brood emerge from their hole and consume everything. They are now unable to return into their hole, and so the mortal emerges and trusses up the helpless creature (sects. 5-11). In another version of this story either he or the goddess may have killed the serpent, but the story is now framed by references to the Storm-God, who at the beginning is defeated by the serpent and then invites all the gods to Inara's feast (sects. 3-4), and who at the end reappears to kill his already captured enemy in the presence of all the other gods (sect. 12). This frame, by glorifying the Storm-God and relating the events of the inner core story to his cult, gives the story its present function (and conforms it more closely to the combat myth; see the exposition by Fontenrose 1980, esp. 121-25), but it is clear that the essentials of the plot are contained within the core. It is Inara who plots and accomplishes the defeat of the serpent, with the aid of the mortal; and in the sequel (sects. 13-16), a separate folk-tale motif, they alone are the actors—there is no further mention of the Storm-God.

In both the Hittite tale just recounted and in *Aqht* 1) a goddess meets a mortal and 2) by some means prevails upon him to assist her. 3) It is arranged for the victim to partake of a meal. 4) The goddess places the helper so that when she is ready he can overcome the victim. We can only speculate whether *Yṭpn*, like the mortal in the Hittite story, bargained for sexual favors in exchange for his assistance; whether Anat, like Inaras, used her sexual charms to attract her victim to the banquet; and whether Aqhat had, like the serpent, succumbed to drink by the time the goddess' henchman fell on him—the relevant portions of the Ugaritic text are missing or too damaged. The comparison does tend to confirm the general outline of 1.18.1.19/20-1.18.4.37, as described above, as well as the existence of an earlier Hattian story in which Inara was the central deity, and not merely the agent of the storm-god.

The poor state of 1.18 does not permit confident claims about the particular characteristics or interests of this section of *Aqht*, except that portion that describes the manner of Aqhat's murder. Here the text is complete, both where Anat lays out her plan in detail before *Yṭpn*, and where, by a standard transposition, the two of them carry it out. The plan and its execution have Anat in the role of a bird above Aqhat, releasing *Yṭpn* down upon him. This seems to be a direct reversal of Aqhat's activity as a huntsman, in which he would release an arrow up at a bird.

The scope and general structure of this whole section (1.17.6-

1.19.1) recall two other narratives, that may be compared at this point.

The more elaborate, but unfortunately fragmentary myth of Elkunirsha (see Hoffner 1965; 1975, 141-2), also preserved in Hittite, but doubtless of West Semitic origin, appears to use several of the same narrative elements in the same order as in this section of *Aqht*. Thus Asherah makes a proposal to Baal, is rejected, and threatens him (cf. 1.17.6). Later Asherah bargains with El for permission to punish Baal. El replies: "Baal I hand over to you. Treat him as you please" (cf. 1.18.1). (There is a doublet of this last episode immediately preceding it: Baal reports the initial incident to El, who directs him to humble Asherah, which he does.) Asherah proceeds to harm Baal in some way, but another goddess (Anat?) has overheard the conversation between El and Asherah, and warns Baal not to eat Asherah's food or drink her wine. Here again, as in *Aqht* (1.18.4) and *Illuyanka*, the goddess' offering of a meal is an essential part of her plan for revenge. The fragmentary state of this story does not allow detailed comparison. It is at least obvious that the Elkunirsha myth has some complications that are not present in any of the other stories we have considered (the hero resorts to the high god and is authorized to punish the demanding goddess; the goddess' revenge may be frustrated by another goddess who is helping the hero). But it is equally clear that the Elkunirsha story moves through similar stages to *Aqht*: 1) the hero is accosted by a goddess, spurns her proposal, and is threatened by her; 2) the goddess goes to the high god and gets permission to punish the hero; 3) the goddess provides the hero with food and drink and harms him in some way.

There is one other ancient narrative which, while exhibiting several mutations or displacements (see Fontenrose 1980, 6-9) in comparison with the narratives examined above, is still worth comparing both because it is roughly coextensive with this entire section of *Aqht*, and because it has something in the hero's possession as the object of desire and ends with the accomplishment of the hero's murder. I refer to the story of Naboth's vineyard, in which a "parallel" to *Aqht* was seen by Ginsberg (1945, 3), but has not been further investigated. The obvious differences between the two stories may be summarized as follows. The deities of the mythological setting in *Aqht* become the king and queen of the historical setting in 1 Kgs 21 (as the mortals of the earthly setting of *Aqht* become the gods of *Elkunirsha*). In *Aqht* it is the goddess, in 1 Kgs 21 the king, who desires the hero's property. Consistent with this reversal of roles, in *Aqht* the goddess bullies the high god into permitting her to take what she desires by violence, while in 1 Kgs 21 the queen comforts the king by offering to get him what he wants. In the more independent story of 1 Kgs 21, the queen acquires possession of the desired object, and presents it to the king. In *Aqht*, though the damage to the text prevents certainty, it seems that the goddess does not acquire the desired object.

Behind these surface displacements the two stories reveal a common underlying narrative structure, that brings 1.17.6-1.19.1 closer to 1 Kgs 21 than to the *Epic of Gilgamesh, Illuyanka* or even *Elkunirsha*. 1) A deity/monarch desires something of the hero's, makes an offer for it, but is rejected (first dialogue). 2) He/she goes off, disturbed, to the high god's dwelling/monarch's palace. In a second dialogue, the goddess/queen by threats or words of comfort gets authorization to dispose of the obstacle to the desired object. 3) By means of outside assistance she then accomplishes the murder of the hero.

The divergent course of the endings of *Aqht* C and *Gilgamesh* 6 reflects the greater integration of the basic traditional narrative structure into those larger works. 1 Kgs 21:1-16 exemplifies the greater degree of integrity retained by the narratives of the books of Kings. At the same time it illustrates the mutations and dislocations that such a narrative structure can undergo, and the difference in dress in which it can appear in different cultures.

These comparisons provide further confirmation of the preceding analysis of 1.17.6-1.18.4 as a single discrete section, illustrating a more widespread traditional narrative structure, adapted and incorporated into the larger, complex poem. They also sharpen the picture of *Aqht* as of a genre distinct from both *Elkunirsha*, in which the actors are all gods, and 1 Kgs 21 in which the actors are all people. In both those cases, the relative equality of the actors makes for a view of life limited to human actions and reactions—those of the extended family in Elkunirsha, those of the political sphere in 1 Kgs 21. *Aqht*, like *Gilgamesh* and *Illuyankas*, presents us with a rare individual, coming face to face with the powers of the gods. But whereas in *Gilgamesh* the hero, defined as partly divine, is able to maintain his personal defiance of the gods (though not his friend's), and is limited ultimately only by his own mortality; and in *Illuyankas* the mortal hero, ambitious and clever in his dealings with the gods, is ultimately defeated by his own humanity; in *Aqht* the mortal hero, endowed with rare gifts and wisdom, is able to defy the gods for only a brief space, and is ultimately at the mercy of powers beyond his control.

D. Mourning—the acts of Aqhat's father

Lines 1.19.1.19-4.22/28 consist largely of a succession of ritual acts and pronouncements undertaken by Danel. The first group (1.19.1.19-2.25) follows his recognition of a natural calamity, but precedes his realization that Aqhat has been killed. A middle section, badly damaged, introduces messengers who announce the fate of Aqhat (1.19.2.26 to the broken end of the column). There follows a second group of ritual acts and pronouncements in which Danel deals directly with the loss of Aqhat (1.19.2.56-4.22/28). Throughout this section the plot seems to the modern reader to be practically at a standstill. Only with Pughat's request that she be blessed for a mission of vengeance (1.19.4.32-35) does the narrative pick up again.

It is clear that 1.19.1.19 marks the beginning of a new section of the poem (Caquot 1985). The preceding lines of the column still speak of Anat (line 5), Aqhat (12) and the bow (4, 14, 16); while lines 19-25, though damaged, clearly introduce Danel again, not only with the common formulaic bicolon, but also with the two bicola that depict him sitting for his usual juridical role on the threshing floor at the gate (cf. 1.17.5.4-8).

The following two lines are almost completely missing, but apparently his daughter Pughat is now with him, for, in the formulaic colon, "she raised her eyes and saw" the vegetation withering (30-31) and the birds of prey hovering over her father's house (32-33—as in similar language they had hovered over Aqhat in 1.18.4.19-21 and 30-31).

The condition of the vegetation is a consequence of the misdeed done, as in Jer 12:4:

ʿd-mty tʾbl hʾrṣ	For how long will the land be dry
wʿśb kl-hśdh yybš	and the vegetation of the whole countryside wither?
mrʿt yšby-bh	Because of the wrongdoing of its inhabitants
spth bhmwt wʿwp	beasts and birds have ceased

(cf. Hos 4:2-3). Offences against nature lead nature to take offence. As reflected in the biblical passages, drought leads to the disappearance of animals as well as plants. The birds of prey are the one group that benefits in these circumstances, and in *Aqht* they, as we know, are closely bound up with the murder of the hero. Danel and Pughat, however, see only these natural effects of the murder without knowing the cause. Similarly according too 2 Sam 21:2 David did not recognize the connection between a three-year drought and the murder of the Gibeonites by Saul, until he enquired of Yahweh the reason for the drought.

At these sights Pughat weeps, and, after a reference to the tearing of his clothes, Danel begins to speak. Since neither Danel nor Pughat is aware that Aqhat has been killed, these responses cannot be interpreted as acts of mourning for Aqhat. Rather they are the appropriate reaction to the natural calamity that father and daughter see before them. (Cf. the second occurrence of the bicolon referring to the tearing of Danel's clothes, discussed in the next paragraph.)

Danel's speech is not introduced by one of the standard formulae, but—following the formulaic designation of Danel, *apnk dnil mt rpi* "then Danel, the man of Rapi'u"—by the verb *yṣly*. In all the cognate languages this verb means "to pray." In the Ras Shamra vocabulary lists, however, the Ugaritic noun *ṣily(at)u* corresponds to Akk. *ar]āru* "curse." On the other hand 1.119.17 appears to have the (Ugaritic) noun *ṣlt* meaning "prayer," though the text is, according to Herdner, "very uncertain." The uncertainties continue: the first part of Danel's speech is notoriously difficult. Commentators are not only divided as to whether it is a curse or a prayer, but even as to where it begins and ends (for some examples of diverse treatments other than the standard translations see de Moor 1974; Mustafa 1975, 103-4; Margalit 1982, 418-23). Everything in the context (see recently Margalit 1982, 420-21) and in comparable situations elsewhere in ancient Near Eastern literature argues for its being a prayer, and that now appears to be the dominant view, which is accepted here. Danel adjure the clouds to give rain. The following repetition of the bicolon referring to the tearing of his garments (1.19.1.46-8) is this time introduced by, *k*, probably best interpreted as the conjunction *k* "for," so that the bicolon is here the last clause of Danel's speech, intended to motivate the elements to produce rain. As such it would be a transposition of the corresponding lines 36-37—a response to his previous activity, broadly comparable to Pughat's later response to another ritual activity of Danel (see below and chap. 1 D 3).

Danel now directs Pughat to prepare his riding beast, which she does, and then lifts him onto the animal (1.19.2.1-5; 5-11; v. Chap. 1 C 1 a). Duly mounted, Danel proceeds on a tour of the cultivated fields, kissing what vegetation there is, and expressing the wish that it may sprout up and be gathered in by Aqhat (12-18). As the audience waits for Danel to learn of Aqhat's fate, the tension is increased by the irony of Danel's reference to Aqhat as the one to harvest the revived vegetation, and by the careful repetition of the passage with minimal changes (19-25; v. chap. 1 D 4).

All these acts and words are directed toward bringing the drought to an end. But since the actors do not know the cause of the drought their efforts are futile. At this juncture, Pughat looks up and sees two messengers on their way (26-28). This begins a passage (1.19.2.27-44) which, though damaged, clearly recounts how the messengers conveyed to Danel and Pughat the fact and the manner of Aqhat's death (42-44 taking up the language of 1.18.4.24-26 and 36-37; restorations of the less formulaic preceding lines have been proposed by Dijkstra and de Moor 1975, 206-8; and Margalit 1983b). Danel's response is now conveyed through the formulaic cluster describing the reaction to bad news (44-47). Since this cluster is usually used when the messengers are first sighted (see chap. 2 B), its postponement here until after the delivery of the message maintains the suspense of an audience identifying with Danel. The last traces of the column invite the restoration of the formulaic introduction of a speech (*yšu gh] wyṣ[ḥ* "he raised his voice and cried" 47-48).

When the text resumes in 1.19.2.56, a new activity is beginning. In the missing lines (48-55) there was most probably a brief lament and perhaps a description of acts of grief. Lament and acts of grief—always in the reverse order, however—follow the news or discovery of death elsewhere: in 1.5.6.11-22 and 23-25; 1.5.6.31-6.1.5 and 6-8 (El's and Anat's reaction to the discovery of Baal's death); in Gen 37: 34 and 35 (Jacob's reaction to news of Joseph's death); and even in a historically and culturally more remote text such as Ovid *Meta*. 4.545-56 and 551-52 (the reactions of Ino's Phoenician attendants to the discovery of her death). (In all of these the lament includes the resolve to follow the deceased into the grave.) The same sequence—acts of grief, then lament—appears in David's reaction to the news of the death of Saul and Jonathan (2 Sam 1: 11-13 and 17-27) and of Abner (2 Sam 3: 31-32 and 33-34).

The rest of the poem, so far as it is preserved, is concerned with the bereaved family's responsibilities to their murdered kin. The lengthy next episode is a description of a series of actions that are repeated three times (1.19.2.56-3.14; 3.14-28; 3.28-45), the third of which is successful (v. chap. 1 D 2). Seeing the hovering birds of prey, Danel calls on Baal to break their wings (those of their mother and their father in the second and third accounts respectively), so that he can inspect their viscera for traces of Aqhat's remains, and, if he finds them, weep over them and bury them. Each time Baal immediately obliges. (The almost contemporary version of the Akkadian tale of Adapa has a similar motif, though without divine agency: "'Let me break your wing.' No sooner were the words out of his mouth than its wing was broken"—EA 356:3-5; Watson 1976b, 372.) In the first two versions Danel finds nothing and calls upon Baal to restore the birds. In the final version he finds Aqhat's remains, removes them, weeps over them and buries them, not now placing them in the grave associated with the underworld gods, as proposed each time in his initial appeals to Baal (*aštn bḫrt ilm arṣ* cf. 1.5.5.5-6 transposed in 1.6.1.17-18)—the language is now clearly quite different, though the precise text is uncertain (Virolleaud's copy, transcription, Herdner and Dietrich, Loretz and Sanmartin all read differently; see recently Margalit 1981 and Dressler 1984b).

The passage concludes with what is this time a conditional curse: May Baal break the wings of the birds of prey if they fly over my son's grave and disturb his sleep. Such a curse may have been in common use, being entirely consistent with the culture's general beliefs and the specific concerns of those who have just buried their dead. It might indeed have suggested the entire preceding narrative, in which the unconditional conjuration of Baal to break the birds' wings is the basis for his actual breakage of them and the whole succeeding account of Danel's search for Aqhat's remains. In its present position the final conditional curse plays a striking aesthetic role. It begins by reiterating the opening words of Danel in the first of the three preceding series of actions (and by the same token reversing Danel's final words calling for the restoration of the birds' wings). As the audience might begin to wonder how much longer this is going to go on for, the protasis is added, the call for breakage thus being converted into a conditional sentence giving closure to the whole episode.

The next episode is another cycle of three series of actions. Though the colon which introduces the episode is another conundrum, the structure and meaning of the rest of the episode is here transparent (see chap. 1 D 2). Danel progresses to a named place, his speech is introduced, he curses the place, concluding with a "forever and ever," and then wields his staff. Danel curses three places, all close to where Aqhat was struck down (*d ʿlk mḫṣ aqht ǵzr*). The first two place-names are not otherwise mentioned in the poem; the third is *Ablm*, which we know from 1.18 to be the site of Danel's murder. The triple repetition thus again exhibits two failures followed by a success.

Danel's actions here presuppose the same situation as does Deut 21:1-9, particularly in its earliest form (see Zevit 1976), namely that, in the absence of the culprit, a town was accounted guilty of a crime committed in its vicinity. Danel by his curses brings on the guilty town its appropriate punishment. The innocent town would defend itself from such imprecations by an oath of innocence, prayer for exoneration, and/or appropriate rituals (cf. Deut 21:1-9; in laws and in judgments the authorities also hold such towns guilty, administering fines instead of curses, but also accepting oaths of innocence—see, e.g. CH §§ (23 and) 24; and the judgment in MRS 16 95 RS 20.22 44-55).

After cursing *Ablm* Danel returns home, and in a passage reminiscent of the cult of the Katharat in 1.17.2 receives mourners (1.19.4.8-22; v. chap. 1 D). They come and weep for Aqhat for seven years, then Danel bids them depart. The numerical sequence which shapes the visit of the Katharat is here replaced by a series of preposition phrases ("from days to months, from months to years, up to seven years") between the two statements of the bicolon that describes their activity. Following the climactic "then in the seventh year" a tricolon introduces Danel's speech, also a tricolon, in which he dismisses them in language virtually identical with that of the tricolon in which they arrive. The superimposition of this chiastic structure on the traditional numerical sequence is peculiarly suited to such an episode which ends not with a climax but with a return to the starting point:

A Introduction of Danel as subject—he goes home (bicolon)
B The mourners come in (tricolon)
C They weep (bicolon)
D For seven years (three short cola of two words each)
C_1 They weep (bicolon)
"Then in the seventh year" (climactic monocolon)
A_1 Introduction of Danel as subject—he speaks (tricolon)
B_1 Dismissing the mourners (tricolon)

The mourners are similar to the *mqwnnwt* and *ḥkmwt* summoned to come and wail in Jer 9:16-18. These were women skilled in matters relating to mourning and able to make tears flow from people's eyes (cf. the male *ywd'y-nhy*—men skilled in matters of mourning—in Amos 5:16-17; both passages use the image of a general mourning as a poetic conceit to enforce the prophet's message that the people are doomed to die.) The seven-year period of mourning is found in the Elkunirsha myth.

On hearing that 77//88 of her sons have been killed, Ashertu "appointed wailing-women and began to wail for seven years" (translation of Goetze in Pritchard 1969, 519). The weeping period for Jacob in Egypt was seventy days (Gen 50:3b); but this was later succeeded by seven days in the Jordan valley (Gen 50:10). The inhabitants of Jabesh Gilead fasted for seven days after burying Saul (1 Sam 31:13). Seven days was probably the common custom, hyperbolically extended to seventy in Gen 50:3b, to seven years in *Elkunirsha* and *Aqht*.

Immediately after his dismissal of the mourners Danel offers up a sacrifice and incense, to which Pughat responds with her request for his blessing on her mission of vengeance. Some commentators take Danel's sacrifice to mark the end of the period of mourning (e.g. Caquot 1979; Del Olmo Lete 1981, 351). Pughat's speech, in which she speaks both of this sacrifice and of her proposed mission, would then serve to connect the present section with the next section. But there is nothing in the tricolon that speaks of Danel's sacrifice and burning of incense (if *dǵṯ* is correctly so interpreted) that compels us to associate such acts either with his mourning for the dead or with the following mission of vengeance. (Incense is never used among sacrifices to the dead in Mesopotamia before the Neo-Babylonian period, according to Bayliss 1973, 123-24. It is not specifically associated with death or with revenge in any of the texts reviewed in Nielsen 1986.) Consequently, a judgment about the juncture between sections D and E must be based on literary criteria. But these are also not clear at this point. The relation between the cola describing Danel's activity and those reporting Pughat's response is not exactly what one would expect (cf. chap. 1 C 3). Further, between the tricolon describing Danel's sacrifice and the transposition of the same at the beginning of Pughat's speech are three damaged lines in which only a reference to *[mṣ]ltm mrqdm* "cymbals, dancers" is certain.

In view of the close connection of Pughat's speech and Danel's sacrifice, the sacrifice is here treated as the beginning of the next section. This is lightly supported by the absence of references to sacrifice or incense in comparable literary treatments of reactions to a death, and by further considerations to be stated in the discussion of section E.

The preceding section has comprised little narrative in the usual sense of that term. The only advance in the plot is that Danel and his daughter have learned that Aqhat has been murdered, and have carried out their normal social duties in such a situation: (lament and acts of grief?), retrieval and burial of the remains, cursing of those held responsible, mourning. Such acts are familiar from other literature. In *B1* the announcement of Baal's death (1.5.6.8-10) leads directly into El's acts of grief (11-22) and lament (22-25; cf. above on 1.19.2.48-55), and Anat's retrieval and burial of the remains (1.5.6.25-6.1.18) and revenge on the killer (1.6.2.30-37). In 2 Sam. 3 the announcement of the killing of Abner precipitates David's curse on the killer (v. 29), acts of grief and mourning (31), burial of the deceased (32a), continued weeping (32b-4) and a lament (33-34). In 2 Sam. 1 acts of grief (v. 11) are followed by mourning (12), revenge (15), a curse on the killer (16), and a lament (2:19-27). (While the same elements recur, the order of such acts, in literature at least, is not fixed.) Nowhere else in Ancient Near Eastern literature, however, do the composers dwell at such length on the description of such universally expected and understood acts. Clearly this extended sequence of scenes, each one carefully elaborated and patterned, must play an important role in the purposes of the composers and the reception of the audience. It must accordingly have a significant part in any serious attempt to interpret the poem as a whole.

Unfortunately, there is to my knowledge no comparable treatment of the subject elsewhere in ancient Near Easter narrative. And given the lack of descriptions of comparable rituals elsewhere in cultic literature, it is impossible to be very precise (beyond identifying the fantastic elements) in speaking of the particular *literary* interpretation here given to normal *cultic* activity. Despite this lack of materials for comparative study, it is certainly possible to emphasize the clear aesthetic interests of this section, from its careful construction and play with repetition and variation, to its use of irony and suspense, particularly in the material preceding the arrival of the messengers with the news of Aqhat's murder.

It seems equally clear that the uniquely full and precise exposition and repetition of Danel's activities and pronouncements, both before and after the arrival of the messengers, portrays the man, more even than in the first section of the poem, as a model of piety, carrying out meticulously and persistently all the duties and responsibilities of a patriarch in his situation. In this his daughter plays a supportive role, first recognizing the disaster that had overtaken nature in col. 1 and then dutifully preparing Danel's beast and helping him onto it in col. 2. This gives a slight intimation of the major role of family piety that she will play in the next section.

This section is clearly integrated with the preceding section by the use of the birds of prey, through which Anat had accomplished the murder. They now convey to Danel and his daughter the extent of the drought, serve as the object of the curse protecting Aqhat's grave, and figure especially in the elaborate account of Danel's efforts to recover Aqhat's remains.

E. Revenge—the acts of Aqhat's sister

The question of the demarcation between section D and section E may be irrelevant. In the social life implied by the poem revenge on the killer was one more of the duties of the surviving family. It may be that for poets and audiences the breaking of the news to Danel was a more significant break in the structure of the narrative than the present shift from mourning to revenge. On the other hand, as literature the poem now shows a marked shift from episodes carefully and patiently constructed with abundant use of repetition, to a succession of brief acts and speeches that move the action forward rapidly with a minimum of repetition, indeed with the appearance sometimes of a deliberate avoidance of repetition when the conventions would almost seem to require it. In any case, as we shall see, comparative evidence favors treating this particular section as at least derived from an independent narrative structure.

Danel performs a sacrifice, offering up incense to his god (1.19.4.22-25). According to the broken passage in 25-27 the ceremony included dances. A speech by Pughat is introduced by a formulaic monocolon (28). She refers first to his sacrifice (29-31), in language transposed from 22-25, then asks for his blessing, proposing to kill Aqhat's killer (32-35). The request for a blessing—*ltbrkn alk brkt//tmrn alk nmrt* "just bless me, and I will go off blessed//consecrate me and I will go off consecrated"—expresses, in only slightly different language, that faith in the effectiveness of the addressee's blessing that we find in the Moabite king Balak in his message to the diviner Balaam: *'t 'šr-tbrk mbrk (w'šr t'r yw'r)* "whoever you bless is blessed (and whoever you curse is cursed)" (Num 22:6). Faith in the power of the father's blessing in *Aqht* is replaced by that of the professional in the story in Numbers. It is preserved, however, in Isaac's words to Esau, in which he refers to his prior blessing of Jacob: *w 'brkhw gm brwk yhyh* "and I blessed him, and blessed he shall be" (Gen 27:33).

The formulaic monocolon that introduced Pughat's speech now introduces Danel's response (1.19.4.35-36). He confers upon her a general blessing (36-39 cf. 1.17.1.36-38), and the specific commission to avenge the death of Aqhat (39-40, transposed from the proposal of 34-35).

Pughat now prepares for her mission by attending first to her toilet (40-43) and then to her wardrobe (44-46). In her toilet she washes and ruddles herself (40-42), as Keret did in preparing for his campaign (1.14.2.9; 3.52; the ruddled shields and persons of warriors are referred to in Nah 2:4—Margalit 1981, 146). The damaged remains of 42-43 correspond to 1.3.3.1-2 and 1.3.4.45-46 (in passages describing the toilet of Anat, also incompletely preserved). In dressing herself she first dons a hero's garment, then puts a knife into her sheath, and over all slips a woman's garment (in a rare chiastic quadricolon: a b b^1a^1). In another rare "quadricolon" (a b a^1b^1) Pughat proceeds to the tents of *Yṭpn* (46-50). In a monocolon unique among introductions to speech, word of her arrival is brought to *Yṭpn* (50-51). He is told that *agrtn* has entered his camp (51-52). He gives instructions that she be given wine to drink (53-54). These are promptly executed (54-56). His subsequent speech, introduced in 56-57, is unfortunately damaged and incomplete (57-). Lines 58-59 are almost completely preserved, and may mean: "the hand that struck down Aqhat shall strike down/has struck down/may it strike down thousands of foes." Though the individual words of line 61 are well-known, they are not all unambiguous, and the syntax and versification is certainly ambiguous. What is clear is that the drinking continues (*tšqy* twice).

Plainly Pughat acquires her father's blessing for a mission of vengeance. She prepares to kill the killer of her brother by equipping herself as a warrior, but over the warrior's accoutrements she dresses as a woman. She proceeds to *Yṭpn*'s camp. Does Pughat know who *Yṭpn* is? At least when he speaks so knowingly about the killer of Aqhat, she must realise that he is her man. Comparative evidence (see below) tends to support the assumption that she knew who and where her target was. Does *Yṭpn* know who Pughat is? This question is more difficult. His entourage refer to her as *agrtn*, which could mean "she who hires us" (cf. Akk. *āgirtu*) or "she whom we hire" (cf. Akk. *agirtu*). Many commentators prefer the former interpretation, on the assumption that Pughat has disguised herself as Anat, and that Anat had hired *Yṭpn* to kill Aqhat. Although the preserved part of 1.18 does not indicate how *Yṭpn* was engaged to serve as Anat's hatchet man, a commercial arrangement seems inappropriate for the mythological setting. Further, there is nothing in the description of Pughat's toilet and dressing to suggest that she is making herself look like Anat (the use in line 43 of a formulaic colon also used with Anat proves nothing). Yet the word *agrtn*, used by *Yṭpn*'s comrades, marks their recognition both of some characteristic in her and of some relationship to them. If the meaning were "she whom we hire," the reference could be to a prostitute. The point of Pughat's toilet and dress, apart from the hiding of the weapon, might be to present herself precisely in that role. But the text itself does not permit of firm conclusions to any of these questions.

The conclusion of this section is suggested not only by the comparative evidence to be investigated shortly, but also by the world-view which appears to inform the poem. As was stated earlier, the illegitimate shedding of blood is an offence against nature, with consequences in nature ("bloodshed pollutes the land" Num 35:33a; cf. Jer 12:4, quoted above in section D, and Hos 4:2-3). The vegetation dies immediately after the murder of Aqhat; Israel suffers a drought because of the murder of the Gibeonites by Saul (2 Sam 21:1). Such consequences can only be stopped by the killing of those guilty of the crime ("the land cannot receive absolution from the bloodshed, except by the shedding of the blood of the one who shed blood" Num 35:33b). So the drought ceased, when those who bore the guilt of Saul's crime were killed (2 Sam 21:8-10). The drought which afflicts Danel's land can only be relieved by the killing of the one who killed Aqhat.

Assuming that the poem as a whole would have concluded with the establishment or restoration of order as understood by the culture—and such a conclusion appears to be almost universal in ancient literary works—and recognizing the preceding understanding of the relations among murder, natural catastrophe and revenge, it is legitimate to conclude that *Yṭpn* was killed before the end of the poem. The manner of his death is suggested both by 1.19.4 and by the following comparative evidence.

The last section of *Aqht* is regularly compared with the story of Judith in the apocryphal book of that name. *Judith* merits a closer look, not only because it tends to confirm our expectations of the ending of Pughat's adventure, but also because it corresponds to the structure of the preserved part of the latter more closely than has been noted. The book begins with a broad focus on the West (chaps. 1-4), which is narrowed first to Israel (4-7), and finally to the individual heroine, Judith (8-13). The first seven chapters provide a historical setting for the story and introduce Judean themes. But the heart of the book begins with the introduction of Judith in chapter 8, and continues with a narrative focussing on the actions of the two protagonists through chapter 13. These six chapters comprise a quite distinct narrative, and it is precisely this narrative that is comparable with 1.19.4.22- . The structural correspondences between the two narratives argue for an ancient traditional source or model for the story of Judith.

Seeing the threat the invader poses to her people, Judith promises that God will deliver Israel by her, and prays to God to that effect (8:32-9:14)—a promise and prayer that correspond to Pughat's proposal and request for blessing. Judith then attends to her toilet and wardrobe (10:1-5), journeys to her destination (10:6-10), and is introduced to her victim by his attendants (10:11-18)—the sequence is exactly that of 1.19.4. After some developments peculiar to the more elaborate narrative of Judith, the victim, the general Holophernes, prevails upon the heroine to come and drink with him (12:10-20). Again the correspondence is precise: Pughat too is offered drink, and drinks, before any reference is made to *Yṭpn*'s bibulosity. It is on the basis of such a precise structural correspondence of the two narratives that one may reasonably conclude that Pughat went on, like Judith (13:1-8), to wait until her host was overcome by an excess of alcohol, and then to kill him.

The occasion for Judith's venture also bears comparison with that which prompts Pughat's proposal. Judith responds to the cultic self-humiliation of her people as they cry to God about their plight (4:9-12, 14-15), just as Pughat responds to the mourning and sacrifice of her family as they bewail their plight. (Judith is actually introduced in mourning garb [8:5], but that relates to her mourning for her late husband, not to the crisis which she now turns to address. Of course, it may derive ultimately from an element in the form of the traditional tale on which the author of *Judith* has built.) Second, Judith utters her prayer at the time the evening incense is offered (9:1; cf. Exod 30:8; Ps 141:2; Nielsen 1986, 52, 53, 80), and it is precisely an offering of incense that Danel is making when Pughat asks for his blessing. The connection between the initiation of the mission of vengeance and the offering up of incense in both narratives tends to suggest that Danel's sacrifice initiates this section rather than concluding the preceding section (cf. D above). (Xella is alone in interpreting the sacrifice as an act of propitiation by Danel to the gods responsible for Aqhat's death, performed even as he blesses Pughat's mission of vengeance—Xella 1976, 74-75). On the other hand, the link with the state of mourning depicted in the preceding section of both poems tends to confirm the close narrative connection between the end of the preceding section of *Aqht* and the beginning of this.

Judith won acceptance as a *bona fide* visitor in Holophernes' camp by pretending to be a traitor to her people; but she finally ensured that she would be left alone with him by exploiting her physical charms (Jdt 12:10-13:2). We have already suggested that one object of Pughat's toilet was to appear seductive to her victim—one interpretation of the term *agrtn* would be consistent with that suggestion. Such susceptibility to a woman's charms and to alcohol is also seen in the serpent on which the goddess Inara seeks revenge on the storm-god's behalf in the present form of the Hittite tale, *Illuyanka*, discussed in C above. Though the role of host and guest are here reversed—she is the hostess—Inara dresses herself up to be attractive to the serpent, and plies him with drink. He is then easily overcome and killed.

But Pughat's scheme also includes the concealment beneath her woman's garb of weapons to which she will have immediate access when the occasion to use them finally presents itself. Pughat's ruse is comparable with that of Ehud. He too concealed a sword under his clothing (Judg 3:16), and then, like Judith, gained admittance to the enemy's private suite, contrived to be left alone with him, killed him and made his escape (17-26). In *Illuyanka* Inara also has a secret weapon: the mortal whom she keeps hidden until the time to strike.

Another motif used in this section of the poem, if indeed we are correct in our hypothesis about the outcome of Pughat's escapade, is the shameful fate of a warrior who is killed by a woman—a fate shared by Holophernes, Sisera (Judg 5:26-27, 4:21) and (almost) Abimelech (Judg 9:53-54, where the shame of such a fate is explicit; cf. in later classical literature, Ovid *Meta*. 12.608-11).

These comparisons all tend to confirm what an internal analysis of 1.19.4 suggests: that *Yṭpn* was overcome with drink, and that Pughat then drew her concealed weapon and killed him, now seen to correspond with traditional narrative motifs. (Xella is alone in thinking that Pughat and *Yṭpn* were reconciled during their symposium—Xella 1976, 75.)

Beside the obvious contrast in setting between *Aqht* and *Judith*, there is also a contrast between the national, monotheistic piety of the Jewish lady, who trusts her life to God in a bold and clever plan to save God's people from a foreign invader; and the familial piety of the daughter and sister, who asks her father's blessing for an errand of vengeance for a murdered brother. In other respects the pace of the action in these last forty lines of *Aqht* is so rapid that little can be said about the treatment of the motifs and structure pertaining to the particular character of the poem or purposes of the poets. We can note that the rapidity of the action here contrasts with its prolixity in the rest of the preserved parts of the poem.

F. The Interpretation of Aqht

Arguments for viewing the Rephaim texts (1.20, 21, and 22) as belonging to *Aqht* were first developed at length by Caquot 1960. Later Caquot and Sznycer (1974, 463, 466) and Dijkstra and de Moor (1975, 171-72) gave summary reasons for the same view. More recently, Caquot and Dijkstra have expressed themselves more cautiously (Caquot 1979; Dijkstra 1979); but some still urge that all six tablets should be viewed as part of the same work (Sapin 1983, 166-7, nn. 45-46). Other recent commentators have judged the Rephaim tablets to be independent of *Aqht* (Gibson 1977, 27, n. 2; Del Olmo Lete 1981, 411).

The preceding internal and comparative analysis of narrative structures has shown how, in accordance with the generally understood progress of the story, section C proceeded directly from tablet 1.17 to tablet 1.18; how, damaged and difficult as they are, the opening lines of 1.19 continue the subjects of the last column of 1.18; and how the remainder of 1.19 devolves from the action in 1.18.4. There is no comparable connection between the structure of the narrative, so far as it can be traced, in any of the so-called Rephaim tablets (1.20-22) and that in any of the *Aqht* tablets.

The mention of *dnil*//*mt hrnmy* in 1.20.1.7-8 is the strongest evidence for a connection between the two groups of tablets, but that need mean no more than that this well-known hero was mentioned in another poem. At most it may mean that there was another traditional story about Danel in circulation at Ugarit—as there was centuries later among the author and audience of the passages mentioning Danel in Ezekiel (14:14, 20; 28:3). (The recent debate among Dressler [1979a, 1984a], Day [1980], and Margalit [1980] over whether Ezekiel's Danel is the Danel of *Aqht* or a contemporary of Ezekiel mistakes the issue. There is every reason to think that Ezekiel had a character of traditional story in mind, like Noah and Job; but no reason to think that the traditional story was precisely the version we have in the Ugaritic *Aqht*. The *ṣdqh* of Ezekiel's Danel is an indication of the more Judean character that the story must have had in Ezekiel's circles. Cf. the Weidner Chronicle's moral and religious interpretation of the Sargon legend—Drews 1974,

392-93.) The Sumerian traditions about Enmerkar, Lugalbanda, and Gilgamesh provide a good example of the treatment of the same characters and similar themes in different poems.

The assumption that the Rephaim texts constituted the continuation or conclusion of *Aqht* was influenced by the mythological interpretation of the latter, which saw *Aqht* as another rendering of the Baal myth ("a doublet of the Baal myth" according to Fontenrose 1980, 138-42; cf. recently Dijkstra 1979, 208.) This demanded that Aqhat be revived. The Rephaim texts seemed to present dealings with the underworld and a celebration. Given the mention of Danel, what else could the subject be but the resurrection of Aqhat? But the widespread belief in the resurrection of Aqhat, still maintained by Gibson (1975, 68; 1977, 27) and Xella (1976, 74, 82) has been well criticized by Dressler (1979a) and Del Olmo Lete (1981, 362), and dismissed even by Dijkstra (1979, 208). Again, there is nothing in the preceding internal and comparative analysis of the narrative structures of *Aqht* to justify the assumption that Aqhat was restored to Danel.

The lack of structural connections between the analyzable narrative of *Aqht* and the largely fragmentary Rephaim poems argues strongly against any assumption—pending the discovery of further texts that would indicate otherwise—of a direct literary relationship. Accordingly any attempt to interpret *Aqht* must proceed on the evidence of the three tablets reviewed above. (For a review of earlier interpretations of *Aqht* v. Caquot and Sznycer 1974, 409-15; Caquot 1979.)

While the preceding study has focussed on the narrative character of the poem, many commentators have favored mythological interpretations. Such interpretations tend to be based on the general significance of narrative units, motifs or symbols. I argue that the interpretation of a particular poem or narrative must be based on the particular significance acquired by such elements in their present context and relationships within the work in question, i.e. the particular significance ascribed to them by the work's composers and audiences.

Several recent interpreters, both those seeking a mythological significance in the poem and those seeking connections with the monarchy of Ugarit and similar city-states, have made much of the bow (earlier Gaster 1961, 316-26; recently Liverani 1970, 866 and 868-69; Hillers 1973; Dressler 1975; Xella 1976). This is certainly a distinct feature of sections B and C. However, it is limited to those two sections, and is neither anticipated in section A nor heard of again in section D or E. Its significance for the poem as a whole is further put in perspective by contrast with the significance of Aqhat, whose participation in the action is also limited to the two sections, B and C, but who dominates the entire poem, even when he is not present. Thus A anticipates his birth almost from the first line, D and E are based entirely on the consequences of his murder and his family's concern for and duties to him. In this respect *Aqht* is reminiscent of *Julius Caesar*, but its title is even more obviously justified than that of Shakespeare's play (*pace* Sapin 1983, 166-67 and n.45). The bow, on the other hand, whatever its significance in the two sections in which it appears, is ignored in the rest of the poem, and thus cannot be of central importance for the interpretation of the poem as a whole. (Dijkstra considers the bow episode to have been added secondarily to give a mythological motivation for Aqhat's death—Dijkstra 1979, 208. For Gibson, the "patently fantastic and supernatural scenes" of 1.17.6-1.18.4 are also secondary—"a mere backcloth against which Danel's piety is put to the test," somewhat like the opening scenes of Job—Gibson 1975, 67.)

It may be thought that as a divine gift the bow is worthy of more attention. But divine bows were part of the mythological baggage the poets were heir to—Homer, refers to Pandaros' bow that was a gift of Apollo (*Iliad* 2.827), and items of armor worn by the Homeric heroes are frequently identified as made or given by the gods (*Iliad* 8:194-95; 18.83-85; 18.368-19.23; see further Xella 1976, 80). The composers of *Aqht* adopt this traditional trait, and use the divine origin of the bow to justify Anat's envy and Aqhat's presumption—and thus ultimately Aqhat's murder. The most important thing about the bow as used in this poem is the fact that it is a composite bow, a relatively new piece of technology, that allows Aqhat to display his modern analytic knowledge, when Anat makes her first offer for it.

The vultures are another prominent object in the poem, exploited as mythologically significant by Xella (1976). But their appearance too is limited to two (C and D) of the five sections of the poem as preserved. Even there their role is largely conventional. They consume Aqhat's corpse, and later serve as one of the indicators of drought and starvation for Danel and Aqhat. After Aqhat's burial they are the object of a curse, conditional upon their disturbance of his resting-place. These roles all reflect natural functions of birds of prey or natural attitudes of members of Danel's society toward them. Their most striking function is in 1.18.4 when, hovering over Aqhat before the murder, they are used as a screen or camouflage by Anat and *Yṭpn* for the actual murder. As suggested above, this may be an ironic reversal of the hunter's killing of birds with his arrows (cf. Xella 1976, 71-2, 87).

The longest appearance of the birds of prey—in Danel's search among them for his son's remains—is a consequence of the obvious fate of Aqhat's corpse, and seems to have been creatively elaborated in light of the subsequent conditional curse (see D above). Thus, while the birds of prey are associated with Aqhat's death in 1.18.4-19.3, much of this association is natural and necessary, and can hardly be acclaimed as highly significant for the poets or audiences. Whatever their significance in C and D, they cannot be taken to be an important clue to the meaning of the whole poem.

More comprehensive mythological interpretations have been proposed in recent years. The most distinctive (and neglected) interpretation is that of Xella (1976), who traces the nucleus of the poem back to an old hunting myth in which the young hunter dies for an offence against the *Potnia Thērōn*, the goddess protecting the animals. This has been subsequently reshaped and reinterpreted in an agrarian society by those responsible for agrarian ideology. (Fontenrose has since also related *Aqht* to the wide-spread myth of the hunter and the huntress, but does not distinguish the two major types—pristine and agrarian—exploited by Xella, claiming that the institutions of a hunting society were irrelevant for the cultivators and herders who made up the indigenous and immigrant populations of ancient Hellas. See Fontenrose 1981.) Hunting being now no longer necessary for survival, but a sport (so also Fontenrose 1981, 254), it was enjoyed particularly by royalty. Hence, it is the interests of the royal elite of an agrarian society that have shaped the present form of the myth.

Xella's method is a structural analysis combined with comparisons from the history of religions. This is illuminating in its own way, though it appears to depend on the assumption of the presence of certain features not actually attested in the poem. He claims that the basic structure of the myth would have changed little since its earliest appearance, though the central motifs would have been more substantially altered by the scribe-priests of the agrarian monarchy (1976, 64). He further claims that the poem is not linguistically or stylistically differentiated from the other Ugaritic poems. In these respects it is clear that Xella is not so interested in the particular character of the poem, or the purposes of those giving it precisely its present form, but rather in the general character of the underlying myth, and the function of that mythical structure for the cultured scribal elite and the monarchy it served.

Dijkstra has also undertaken a comparative mythological study, and on that basis presented an outline of a supposed earlier version, again closely related to the myth of the hunter and the huntress (Dijkstra 1979, 206; cf. Fontenrose 1981). The love theme, that is more prominent than in Xella's version, but consistent with Fontenrose's interpretation (Fontenrose 1981, 252-54), requires a separation of Anat and *Yṭpn*, and, at least as maintained for the present version, has been undermined by Dressler's argument about the language of 1.18.1.24 (1979b; cf. Xella 1984).

But these interpretations all focus on the alleged primeval mythical origins of the poem, which, while they may explain the origin of some of the contents of the poem, do not come to grips with the particular choice of narrative structure, poetic form, or language made by the composers of the present text.

It is undeniable that the murder of Aqhat is central to the whole poem (see below). But it is important to distinguish this death from the mysterious demise of the storm-god at the hands of the god of Death (Mot) in *B'l*. (The correlation of the death of Aqhat with the death of Baal has been recently restated by Fontenrose 1980 and Sapin 1983, 176). Admittedly Aqhat's death is recounted with mythological trappings: it is accomplished by a goddess through the fantastic use of a man as a bird. But such trappings do not require that we seek a mythological or ritual significance in the death. Ishtar's conflict with Gilgamesh in Gilgamesh 6 is also replete with mythological trappings, yet it is undisputed that that episode constitutes another daring exploit of the two heroes, whom it finally brings face to face with the reality of death. As in Gilgamesh, so here traditional mythological paraphernalia are used for larger literary purposes.

The emphasis here is on the fact of murder by an initially undiscovered assailant. The consequences of the murder of Aqhat are no more mythological than they are bureaucratic. They are, in fact, far less mythological than the sequel to the killing of the bull of heaven in *Gilgamesh*, since there follows there a meeting of the divine council (admittedly in a dream) and a direct address by Shamash to Enkidu, while in *Aqht* the gods make no further appearances as characters in the narrative, unless we consider the verse in which Baal acts upon Danel's appeal: "May Baal break the wings of the birds of prey." The rest of the preserved poem is devoted to the *social* consequences of the murder of Aqhat—first, to the social obligations imposed by its natural consequences, and then, after the fact of the murder is made plain, to the social obligations imposed on the family of the victim by the circumstances of the murder.

As it presents itself to us, the poem does not refer to, or require our reference to, a seasonal or fertility or astral myth or to royal ideology (Del Olmo Lete 1981, 357, 361)—or, I would add, to a hunting myth. We might again admit its *genesis* in a paradigmatic account of an encounter between god and man, which established the limits of human freedom in face of the arbitrary will of the gods (Del Olmo Lete 1981, 356)—such still seems to be a main thrust of section C (only). But finally, for the interpretation of the Ugaritic poem of *Aqht* as a whole, we must align ourselves with Del Olmo Lete, when, noting Gaster's observation that what we now have in the poem is a purely literary work, he remarks that it is this that should be the object of our interest (1981, 356).

Therefore, rather than seeking the general mythological significance of certain elements in the poem, let us review how the versions of traditional tales that we have found in *Aqht* have been combined to produce a single and unique whole. Section A, using a conventional introduction to stories about personages with remarkable fortunes, emphasizes the piety of Danel's life before the gods, and the gods' benevolence toward him; hence the peace and order of the world Aqhat enters. Section B, of which we have only the last column, reinforces the impression of Danel's (and now his wife's) piety and of the divine favor they enjoy, and at the same time serves to transfer the focus of interest to Aqhat, here endowed with a bow made by the god, Kothar.

But the divine gift immediately becomes the cause of a divine disturbance in Danel's idyllic world. With the beginning of section C and Anat's first sight of the bow, everything tends toward the murder of Aqhat near the end of the section. Provoked by the specious offers and irregular aspirations of Anat, Aqhat's knowledge and wisdom—his expert knowledge of the composition and use of the bow, his wise understanding of the universality of human mortality—swells into contumacy. He becomes guilty of hubris toward Anat (Del Olmo Lete 1981, 362-63)—though it must be stated that this is a matter of personal affront, not of the transgression of a general divine law (contrast *Gilgamesh* 7).

The rapid complication in 1.17.6 shatters the peace and harmony of the preceding scenes and portends the divine wrath to come. Anat, having failed to persuade Aqhat to yield the bow, violently persuades El to give her a free rein with the object of her malevolence. Her aggressiveness and violence, which appear both in her attitude toward El and in her treatment of Aqhat, are heightened by comparison with the role of Ishtar in *Gilgamesh* VI and even more with that of Inara in *Illuyanka*. The preparatory details of her scheme for disposing of Aqhat are no longer preserved, but she finally accomplishes that end by shooting *Yṭpn* at the hunter from among the birds of prey. The hunter is hunted down (v. Xella 1976, 87, 79). The offended goddess is avenged.

It is important to reiterate that there is no further play with the mythological side of this account of Aqhat's death. The gods make no further appearances as characters in the drama as preserved. But the fact of Aqhat's murder dominates everything else in the poem. Everything that follows concerns the social responses to the conditions precipitated by the murder and then to the circumstances of Aqhat's death itself. As Baal, El and Kothar had blessed and prospered the pious Danel in A and B, Anat provokes and then destroys the precocious Aqhat in C. But if the murder of Aqhat in C shatters the order and prosperity of Danel's world as seen in A and B, that order is restored and that world recreated gradually in D and E (cf. Xella 1976, 88), as Danel and his daughter carry out the appropriate and adequate responses to the murder (cf. Gibson 1975, 68; Del Olmo Lete 1981, 363).

To state this in more formal, critical terms: the first five columns of 1.17 constitute the exposition of the poem. The gift of the bow at the end of the fifth column introduces the complication of the next five columns (1.17.6-1.19.1), culminating in the crisis of 1.18.4. The unravelling of the consequences of that crisis, the denouement, follows in the next four columns (1.19.1-4 and beyond). Thus:

Exposition	A, B	1.17.1-5	five columns
Complication	C	1.17.6-1.18.4	five columns
Denouement	D, E	1.19.1-4 + ?	four columns + ?

Such an analysis demonstrates the integrity of the whole poem by concentrating on the movement, the progression of the narrative. By looking at the poem as a static structure, we can see that the unity of the whole is reinforced by patterns, repetitions and balances that, quite apart from the forward movement of the narrative, pull the originally distinct elements together and in particular hold the earlier and later parts of the whole in balance. We may exclude the more obvious narrative ironies, such as Anat's offer of life and Aqhat's assertion of his mortality in 1.17.6 followed by Anat's accomplishment of his death in 1.18; Anat's use of the eagles as camouflage for her and her hatchet man in 1.18.4 and Danel's use of the eagles to recover Aqhat's remains in 1.19.3.

More striking, because not deriving from the progression of the narrative, is Baal's request for El's blessing of Danel and El's conferral of the blessing in A, as balanced by Pughat's request for Danel's blessing of herself, and Danel's conferral of the blessing in E—the blessing of a son at the beginning of the poem balanced by the blessing of an act of revenge for the son's death toward the end. Similarly, Danel's return home after the successful incubation, and the subsequent visit of the Kotharat for rites associated with pregnancy and birth in A is balanced by his return home after the successful retrieval and disposal of Aqhat's remains, and the subsequent visit of the mourners for rites associated with death and mourning in D. In both these examples, the connection is made quite explicit by the use of common linguistic and poetic forms. There is a less explicit, but broader, balance between the duties of a son toward his father, repeated four times in the opening tale of Danel's appeal for a son, and the duties of the father toward his son described at such length in the later account of Danel's response to the news of Aqhat's murder.

There are several slight linguistic connections between 1.17.6 and later sections of the poem. Thus Anat, promising vengeance on Aqhat, says she will fell him beneath her feet (*ašqlk tḥt pʿny*); while Danel, seeking to recover Aqhat's remains, prays that Baal will do the same to the birds of prey (*tqln tḥt pʿny*). Aqhat, in rejecting Anat's offer of life and asserting universal human mortality, speaks of human "fate" (*uḫryt*); while Danel, cursing the cities held responsible for the murder in their vicinity, wields a staff which bears a similar name (*uḫry*).

There are several connections between sections C and E. In section C Aqhat's death is assured by his repudiation of Anat's request for the bow, which he insists is not a weapon for a woman. In section E vengeance for Aqhat's death appears to depend on Pughat's assuming male dress and weapons. There appears to be a conscious balance here between the role of Anat as murderer in C and Pughat as avenger in E. (Pughat and Anat are the poem's protagonist and antagonist, Anat being the dominant figure, according to Margalit 1983a, 67.) Anat's innate and blatant propensity to violence, which leads to the death of

Aqhat, is balanced by Pughat's assumed and concealed readiness for violence, which would have led to the death of Anat's agent, Aqhat's killer. Anat's successful scheme (now largely lost) in 1.18.1-4 is balanced by Pughat's (presumably successful) scheme in 1.19.4- . As Anat put Yutpan in her scabbard (*ḥbš*//*tʿrt*) as her weapon against Aqhat, so Pughat puts her knife (*ḫ*[ ]//*ḥrb*) in her scabbard (*nšg*//*tʿrt*) as her weapon against Yutpan.

It is apparent that the composers of *Aqht* have, by adopting, transforming and combining several different traditional narratives, produced a larger work of striking unity. What emerges as the distinct common theme that informs this new unity?

Many still wish to see in Danel and in his activities and experiences a reflection of the person, activities and experiences of the king (thus still Del Olmo Lete 1981, 358, n.95, 359-60). But, increasingly, voices have been raised against this reading of the text: Caquot and Sznycer 1974, 414; Gibson 1975, 66 (who more appropriately compares the patriarchs of Genesis, and pictures Danel as a village chief); Dressler 1979a, 152-54, who argues that the text does not allow the reading *mlk* "king" in 1.19.3.46.

Del Olmo Lete has also emphasized the importance in the poem of religious and social institutions and moral duties (1981, 358-60). Social roles and duties seem to receive supreme attention, judged by the number of such that are referred to, the extent to which they are described, and the frequency with which they are reinforced by repetition. Thus in section A the fourfold repetition of the six bicola on the duties of the model son, the repetitive accounts (within a numerical framework) of the incubation ritual and of the father-to-be's entertainment (cultic service) of the Kotharat; in section B the use of a traditional narrative structure exhibiting generous hospitality—here expressed first in the form of instructions and then transposed into their execution (even though the traditional function of the structure has been displaced by the simple narrative necessity to have Kothar visit Danel in order to deliver the bow to him). In section D the poets have produced the most elaborate account of such roles and duties, with abundant use of repetition, in the form of the succession of actions and speeches conscientiously performed by Danel. Finally in section E we are presented with the resolute and expeditious activity of the daughter of the family, undertaking the duty of vengeance.

All of this speaks specifically of *familial* piety—a piety built on the assumption of the solidarity and indispensability of the family, including its past and future members. For this piety, the greatest tragedy and the greatest challenge is the loss of a son (cf. Gen 22). Danel's pious family thus faces the worst life can bring. Yet the poem shows how that piety steadily, persistently, and apparently successfully copes with that worst.

Finally, we must raise the question: why was this work elevating traditional, family responsibilities recorded by the scribe laureate of Ugarit, and kept in the residence of the high priest of Ugarit? Is there not a conflict here between the institutions of the poem and those of the Ugaritic monarchy? Such a conflict is suggested by Margalit (1983a, 68). Others claim that the poem is, on the contrary, expressive of the ideology of the Ugaritic monarchy (Liverani 1970, 869; Xella 1976, 483; del Olmo Lete 1981, 358-60 and 356, n.88). Del Olmo Lete attempts to combine this view with his recognition of its broader interests by emphasizing the domestic character of second millennium royalty, citing the royal homes of the Odyssey. But the contrast between the world of Danel and that of the archaeology and archives of late bronze Ugarit remains—not to mention the world of *Krt*.

Is the poem, then, an indirect criticism of the more legal-rational aspects of the Ugaritic administration? Or was it used solely within the Ugaritic priesthood to reinforce its own faith in the power of sacred word and act? While it may have functioned in either or both of these ways, neither seems an adequate explanation of the poem's character or presence in the setting in which it was found. Was the main function of the poem purely aesthetic? Certainly there is ample evidence of the composers' interest in aesthetic form, and therefore, by definition, of an artistic motivation. "Why *should* men try to 're-create' their personal and social world?" asks Richard Hoggart. "One reason seems to be that men do it not so as to effect anything but, so to speak, for its own sake; because they feel wonder and awe about the nature and terms of their life; and because they feel amusement, irony and pride at man's attempt to cope" (Hoggart 1966, 247). While there may not be much ground for amusement in *Aqht*, the rest of this quotation seems quite pertinent to the poem, which may have been enjoyed as a satisfying portrayal of life in an idealised past era, a life with its own tragedies, but also with its own orderly and beautiful institutions that in the end prevailed. In the word of Caquot and Sznycer (1974, 413-4) and Del Olmo Lete (1981, 364) *Aqht* may have been a "classic" of ugaritic society.

If indeed its character gives it a universal value in the life of the community, it is impossible and unnecessary to define for its performance a precise institutional setting and occasion. Like the Homeric epics, *Gilgamesh* and the *chansons de geste* it could be performed at any time (Del Olmo Lete 1981, 364). Given its predominating artistic characteristics, the poem probably functioned in several ways—on different occasions and even for different groups on the same occasion (cf. Finnegan 1977, 241-43).

Chapter 4

ANALYSIS AND INTERPRETATION OF *KRT*

As in the case of *Aqht*, the tablets on which were inscribed the narrative about king Keret were found in the high priest's house, which was situated between the temples of Baal and Dagon. They appear to have been inscribed by the same hand; and again a colophon on the edge of one tablet, the third, refers to Ilimilku as the scribe (Herdner 1963, Pl. XXVI). All three tablets (1.14, 15 and 16) had six columns of text, and must have comprised together about a thousand lines. The first tablet is almost completely preserved or restorable, with only a few lines at the beginning and end of the first and last columns and a few lines in the middle of col. 5 completely unretrievable. The other two tablets are more severely damaged. Of the second tablet we now have only the last few lines of the first column and the first few lines of the last; a couple of dozen lines of the second and fifth columns (and those lines not complete); and of columns 3 and 4 the remains of about thirty lines each, of which few are complete. Of the third tablet we have the first and last columns virtually complete; remains of almost all the lines (but none complete) on the second and fifth columns; and about fifteen virtually complete lines of each of cols. 3 and 4.

The sequence of the three tablets is uncontested, and it appears that among recent commentators none except Gibson seriously reckons with the possibility that we are lacking a tablet between any two of the three we now have (Gibson 1977, 20). On the other hand, most conclude that the poem did not finish with the end of our third tablet (but contrast recently Gibson 1977, 20; Del Olmo Lete 1981, 243, 273). I have argued that an analysis of the narrative structure shows that a new section of narrative begins in the last column of the third tablet (Parker 1977, 167-69), and so join those who claim that our three tablets, like the three of *Aqht*, must have been followed by at least one more (see section D below).

The following analysis will proceed on the same basis as that of *Aqht* in the preceding chapter.

A. Keret's Acquisition of a Family

Only odd letters of the first few lines of the poem are preserved. 1.14.1.6-25 seems to constitute a prologue, giving the background situation for the actions that begin in line 26. Lines 6-25 begin with a general statement about the loss of Keret's family (6-11), and conclude with his contemplation of the same general conditions (21-25). Formally, the tricolon of 21-23 corresponds to the bicolon of 10-11; the *itbd* of 8 is taken up in the *yitbd* of 24 (see Del Olmo Lete 1981, 246 and Chap. 2 D 4). The middle part of this prologue—lines 12-21—is notoriously difficult in its details, but it is generally agreed that it specifies the various ways in which Keret lost his immediate relatives (on the sequence of numerals see Chap. 2 D 5). In any case, lines 21-25 present us with the demise of the entirety of Keret's family, and, by emphasizing his contemplation of this loss, lead us into the following account of his reaction to it, culminating in his dream and its theophany.

This prologue is, as has often been noted, reminiscent of the prose prologue of the book of Job. In particular, 1.14.12-21 recalls Job 1:13-22. The Job prologue opens with a description of Job's idyllic life (1:1-5). The scene then shifts to the divine court, where the *śāṭān* secures Yahweh's permission to remove from Job everything that he has (6-12). This is then accomplished in the repetitive account of the rapid succession of blows that deprive Job of all his household (13-22; his wife appears only in 2:9). In the context of the book of Job this loss is the first test of Job's faithfulness to Yahweh, and of course does not lead into narrative developments comparable to those of *Krt* (the later narrative of chap. 42 very quickly and easily reverses Job's calamity), but rather into the poetic exploration of undeserved suffering that is the primary purpose of the present book. But the prose framework is clearly of independent origin, and within it the scenes in heaven, which interpret Job's misfortunes as a test of his piety proposed by the *śāṭān* and accepted by God, are a secondary addition. In a still discernible earlier stage in the transmission of the story (Alt 1937; Horst 1969, 3-5; Leveque 1970, 123-28), Job, a man of exemplary piety (1:1-5), is suddenly overwhelmed by a rapid succession of disasters (1:13-22), which are accepted as from God both by Job (1:21) and the narrator (42:11). The prologue of *Krt* provides us with another version of the central motif of this story: the sudden loss of a man's entire family.

A similarly sudden, comprehensive calamity is described in the first person by the serpent in the Egyptian story from the

Middle Kingdom known as *The Tale of the Shipwrecked Sailor*. The serpent moralises to the shipwrecked sailor on the happiness one experiences in recounting a disaster once it is a thing of the past. It proceeds to recount a calamity it had experienced itself:

> I was here with my brothers and there were children with them. In all we were seventy-five serpents, children and brothers, without mentioning a little daughter whom I had obtained through prayer. Then a star fell, and they went up in flames through it. It so happened that I was not with them in the fire, I was not among them. I could have died for their sake when I found them as one heap of corpses. (Lichtheim 1973, 213; cf. Simpson 1973, 54)

Here there is no immediate narrative context. The episode is recounted in isolation for a moral purpose—to let the victim of the shipwreck see that others have suffered comparable catastrophes and survived to see better days. Yet the same narrative motif on a larger scale is the central focus of the larger narrative in which the serpent's tale is told. The serpent's speech is part of a longer autobiographical narrative by the sailor, who had begun by recounting how he had once been on a sailing expedition with the best sailors in Egypt, when they had been suddenly overwhelmed by a storm that sent the ship down with all hands. He himself had been the only survivor to reach the island where he had the encounter with the serpent. This longer narrative is used to serve the same purpose as the shorter: to provide comfort to another party, in this case, the official to whom it is addressed. Both the sailor's autobiographical account of his shipwreck and within it the serpent's autobiographical account of the loss of his family use the motif of the sudden and complete loss of one's immediate community.

A brief account of the destruction of a person's entire group—family, household, or crew—with that person remaining as sole survivor, was thus a motif common to Ugaritic, Hebrew and Egyptian literature. As an extreme case, it doubtless epitomized the smaller-scale experience of disaster which must have been familiar, if not personally, at least at second hand, to many people in the ancient world. It represented to people the worst they might have to face; and the treatment of the motif in literature might explore the meaning of such catastrophes (superficially in *The Shipwrecked Sailor*, more profoundly in Job), or depict the divine favor by which life might be rebuilt after such devastation (as in *Krt*).

The use of this motif in *Krt* serves to establish at the beginning of the poem the fact of Keret's lack of family. In the immediate context it serves to bring Keret to the state of grief that leads to the intervention of El. In other words, the fact that Keret is not simply starting without a family—as Danel starts without a son—but has just suffered the loss of his former family, motivates his behavior as described in the next several lines, which in turn motivates El's response. Beyond this the poets do not exploit the motif, for there is no further allusion to the dire blows rained upon the king in these early lines. However, his sudden losses here are balanced at the end of the first section of the poem by the promise and immediate production of an ideal family (1.15.2.21-3.25).

Immediately following the prologue, the narrative focusses on present action: Keret enters his chamber and weeps profusely (26-30). As he weeps, sleep overcomes him so that he lies down and falls asleep (31-35). In the next verse he is dreaming and El is coming down to him in his dream (35-37). (The use of the prepositional phrase [*bḥlmh*//*bḏhrth*] to refer to Keret's dreaming enables the poet to shift to El as the subject of these clauses, and so also of the following monocolon introducing El's enquiry of Keret [37-38]).

In these few verses the poets have created an unusually revealing account of Keret's mental state and its effects. In this respect, the contrast with *Aqht* is patent. There we are immediately introduced to Danel as engaged in a cultic act—incubation—appropriate to one who, we quickly learn, has no son like his peers. In *Krt* there is no explicit reference to a formal act of incubation (though many are content to classify his behavior as such), but a brief notice of a series of deaths that leaves Keret reeling, so that he retreats to his chamber, weeping helplessly, until he finally falls asleep. In the place of *Aqht*'s repetitive account of a ritual, *Krt* has a progressive account of personal anguish and grief. In place of *Aqht*'s objective, mythological account of intercession and blessing among the gods, *Krt* has a more psychological and realistic account of the sufferer's falling asleep obsessively preoccupied with a problem, and then dreaming of a divine response to the problem. This is much closer to several biblical passages which will be compared below.

The vision introduced in 1.35-37 takes the form of a dialogue consisting of an enquiry by El (1.38-), a response by Keret (1. -2.5), and then a lengthy speech in which El gives Keret instructions and predictions (2.7-3.49).

El approaches Keret with an enquiry (1.37-38). He asks why Keret is weeping (38-41), and whether he desires dominion comparable to El's (41-43). The first question, repeating the parallel pair √*bky*//√*dm*ʿ for the third time in fifteen lines, emphasizes the continuity of El's speech with the preceding, and the directness of El's response to Keret's condition.) At this point the text breaks off, so that we do not know how, or indeed whether, El's speech continued. The last nine lines of the column are missing; but the preserved part of the first three lines at the beginning of col. 2 reveals unmistakably the distinctive list of treasures that will recur several times in the negotiations between Keret and *Pbl* (see below, and above Chap. 2 D 1). We know that Keret must now be speaking, since the next bicolon uses 1 sg. verb forms, and the following monocolon introduces a second speech by El. The complete restoration of the refrain concerning royal treasures (in that form in which it constitutes a rejection of an offer) takes us back into the last line or two of col. 1. Again the question arises: did this mark the beginning of Keret's speech (as in all its later occurrences it marks the beginning of a speech), or was it preceded by other statements by Keret? I shall return to both questions. Keret's speech concludes with a wish that he might get sons (2.4-5; *qny*, like English "get," means both "acquire" and "beget").

To the two questions concerning the scope of these first two speeches a third must be added. Why did Keret reject royal wealth? Did El offer him such, following his mention of sovereign power? A deity is known to have offered wealth to a mortal on another occasion in these narratives: Anat first invited Aqhat to ask for silver//gold (see Chap. 4 C) in exchange for his bow—an offer which he then rejected indirectly by telling her how to get a bow for herself. El may have made a similar offer (with quite different motives) to Keret, which Keret then also turned down. That this is likely is suggested by further comparative evidence.

In the Hurrian tale of *Appu*, preserved in Hittite, the childless Appu makes a sacrifice to the sun-god, who, in the form of a young man approaches Appu and asks him what he lacks (I 38-45). Appu's reply is substantially the same as Keret's: "I have property. . . . I lack only one thing: son or daughter" (II 2-3). The sun-god then tells him what to do and assures him that the gods will give him a son (II 6-9). which they do (see Siegolová 1971).

In I Kgs 3 Solomon goes to Gibeon and offers up a great sacrifice. Yahweh then appears to him in a dream at night, and offers him anything he would like to ask for. Solomon makes the famous request for good judgment. (This much is briefly compared with *Krt* in Del Olmo Lete 1981, 249, n. 42.) God then says that, because Solomon has chosen this rather than long life, wealth, power over the lives of his enemies, he will both grant his request and also give him what he has not asked for: wealth, honor and long life. (The whole passage is compared with the corresponding section of *Krt* in Seow 1984.)

In all three stories the deity approaches the hero and invites him to state what he needs. In both *Appu* and 1 Kings the divine enquiry is open-ended. But Appu makes a point of rejecting wealth before making his actual request, and after Solomon's request Yahweh makes a point of saying to him that he had expected him to ask for wealth, power over his enemies, or long life. That wealth, power over enemies and long life were the traditional desires and therefore prayers of kings (and others) can easily be shown (in addition to the preceding texts see Pss 2:8-9; 21:5; and cf. the negative version of the divine offer in 2 Sam 24:12-13). In the preserved part of the initial exchange between El and Keret, the god suggests the second of these (dominion = power over enemies) and Keret rejects the first (wealth). Since the deity does not make an open-ended offer, as in *Appu* and I Kings, we can perhaps best explain the present text on the assumption that El's suggestion of godlike dominion was rejected by Keret, and that Keret's rejection of wealth was a response to an offer of wealth by El. In fact the present gap in the text would be neatly filled, if El's speech continued after line 43 with the wording of the refrain (in its transposition as an offer: *qḥ ksp wyrq* "take silver and gold"), which is four lines of text; if Keret's speech was then introduced in one line of text; and if in that speech Keret first rejected sovereign power in language corresponding to El's in 1.41-43, which is almost three lines of text. Keret would then appropriately move on to reject El's second offer in the next lines (52ff.).

It remains odd that El would have offered and Keret rejected the same things that *Pbl* would offer Keret and that El would advise him to reject. One suspects that an original text that might have referred to silver and gold has been contaminated and ultimately displaced by the later pervasive refrain. The closest model we have for such an original text is the offer of Anat in *Aqht*: *irš ksp watnk//ḫrṣ wašlḥk* "ask for silver and I will give it you//for gold and I will confer it upon you" (1.17.6.16-17). In any case, the text would have Keret rejecting an offer of wealth from El, and insisting on his need of a family, just as later, on El's instructions, he will reject *Pbl*'s offer of wealth and insist on his need of a family.

All three narratives of Keret, Appu and Solomon, share the motif of the surprise request. The deity asks what the hero lacks, expressly or tacitly expecting one of the traditional requests of wealth, power or long life. The hero expressly or tacitly rejects such options and requests something distinctive—though for both Keret and Appu that is progeny, which we know to be a common request in other literary contexts (see Chap. 4 A). The motif in any case serves to place special emphasis on the hero's request. In the particular case of *Krt*, the poets also use it to refer to El's supreme power (significant in the larger poem) and to foreshadow Keret's rejection of *Pbl*'s attempt to buy him off.

Having learned of Keret's real need, El now begins his lengthy second speech, which will conclude the theophany and dream. In this speech he gives Keret directions and predictions that will enable him to meet his need. The only clear, formal markers of structures larger than the verse in this lengthy section are the speeches toward the end and the occasional numerical sequence. Otherwise, we are dependent on discerning shifts of subject (cf. Del Olmo Lete 1981, 250).

El tells Keret to cease weeping (2.7-9)—the crucial first word is mostly missing, but in the context *bbk//bdm*ʿ "from weeping" is clear. Keret is to wash and ruddle himself, especially his arms (9-11), presumably in preparation for battle (cf. 1.19.4.40-42; Nah. 2:4 and Chap. 4 E). He is then to go in (12) and get materials for sacrifice: a sacrificial sheep//lamb, bread, bird, wine and honey (13-19). There he is to take to the roof of the wall-tower (20-22), and there perform a sacrifice to El in heaven (22-24), bringing down Baal with his sacrifice (25-26). He is then to descend from the roof (26-27). The purpose of the sacrifice is doubtless to gain the support of the gods for the expedition he is to mount.

Keret's next move is to be the preparation of food for the expedition (2.27-31). Appropriately provisioned, the army is to march out (32-34), innumerable and all-inclusive (2.34-3.1). The inclusion of the weakest members of the community is reflected in the call to prepare for war in Joel 4:10—"Let the feeble say: 'I am a warrior!' " The inclusion of specific groups unlikely to be effective in war contrasts with the exemptions envisaged in Deut. 20:5-8. The new husband specifically (1.14.2.47-50) is exempted from military service in Deut. 20:7 and 24:5. Such comparisons confirm our sense of the hyperbolic exhaustiveness of this levy.

The hyperbole and imagery used in the description of Keret's army is recalled in the briefer references to armies of overwhelming numbers in Jdg. 6:5; 7:12 (*kdy-'rbh lrb . . . 'yn mspr* "like locusts in number . . . innumerable"; cf. Jer. 46:23b), and to the larger horde of people following Holophernes' army in Jdt. 2:20—"a motley host like a swarm of locusts, countless as the dust of the earth" (NEB).

Numerical sequences are now used to express the time and distance covered by the army's march to *Udm*, and the period for which the city is besieged before its king commences negotiations. El directs Keret to proceed with his host for six days, until at sunrise on the seventh he arrives at *Udm* (1.14.3.2-5), which he is to beseige (6-7), driving from the fields, threshing floors and springs the women who gather fuel and water (7-10). For six days he and his army are to remain quiet (10-12), not using their missiles against the city (12-14). This is reminiscent of the six-day silence and military inactivity that Yahweh, then Joshua, enjoin on the troops besieging Jericho (Jos. 6; cf. Del Olmo Lete 1965). The expedition is in effect more like a triumphal, sacred procession than a military campaign (Del Olmo Lete 1981, 251).

On the seventh day king *Pbl* will be unable to sleep because of the noise of the city's animals, now presumably hungry and thirsty (15-19; cf. Job 6:5). He will send an embassy to Keret (19-21), thus opening up negotiations. The message (21-32) will begin with the standard designation of the sender (2.10.1; 2.11.3-4; 2.12.4-5; 2.13.3-4; 2.14.1; 2.16.1; etc.); will convey an offer of wealth and terms of peace; and will urge Keret to lift his siege of *Udm* and depart, on the grounds that the city has been given to its present ruler by El himself.

It was of course a common move for a besieged king to try to buy off the invader (see, e.g., 2 Kgs 12:18-19; 18:13-16). Here the proferred treasure consists of silver and gold, horses and chariots, and prisoners of war, male and female ("slaves for life"). This list corresponds rather closely, in the items mentioned and in their order of value, to the treasure acquired by the Egyptian monarchs of the eighteenth dynasty in their Asiatic campaigns. As one historian has summarized the records: "With the exception of large quantities of looted gold and silver treasure obtained in the sack of cities, . . . horses and chariots were perhaps the most valuable booty taken in these wars. . . . Enumerated with the horses, but second in importance, were the prisoners of war, male and female, who were driven back to slavery in Egypt" (Drower 1973, 478). As Drower notes, for the first kings of the dynasty a few horses and chariots were worth individual mention; by the fifteenth century the records refer to a hundred or so at a time. Where it was a question not of loot, but of gifts, one or two horses were still significant in the thirteenth century: Ammistamru II requested a gift of two fine horses from a member of the Hittite court—RS 20.184:8-12 (Nougayrol, Loroche, Virolleand, and Schaeffer 1968, 98); the delivery of one horse from Carchemish to the king of Ugarit is recorded in a legal record drawn up for the purpose——RS 16.180 (Nougayrol 1955, 41). In the century or two prior to the writing of our copy of *Krt* a gift of three horses as part of an offer to persuade an attacker to lift his siege of a city would not have appeared unreasonable.

These comparisons suggest the appropriateness and authenticity of this refrain in the context of the negotiations between the two kings. That in turn is consistent with the suggestion made above that the use of the refrain in the dialogue between El and Keret at the beginning of the dream is a secondary adaptation.

Many documents from Ugarit record donations of land and buildings by the kind of Ugarit to particular subjects, some such gifts to be held by the recipient in perpetuity (see Nougayrol 1955, *passim*). Doubtless it was a gift of this kind that the poets had in mind in expressing *Pbl*'s claim to rule and ownership of his city. Since it is El himself who is speaking here, and since he does not expressly deny *Pbl*'s claim, he is presumably tacitly endorsing it. This being the case, the claim should motivate Keret to respect the city.

To return to El's speech: as the next stage in the negotiations Keret is to send back an embassy to *Pbl* (32-33). His message (33-49) is to include a rejection of the offer of wealth (33-37), but not that of terms of peace. (If *šlmm šlmm* referred to something more concrete—peace offerings—we should expect to see the words included among those Keret repeats in his rejection of *Pbl*'s offer.) In fact, Keret is to make an alternative peace proposal: that *Pbl* give him his offspring, the beautiful Hurraya (38-40), characterised as having the beauty of the goddesses Anat and Athtart (41-42). (Particular emphasis is laid upon her eyes—43-45).

Keret is to go on to claim that El has given her to him in his dream (46-47), that she might bear offspring to Keret (48-49). There is a striking balance here between *Pbl*'s claim on his city—that it was given him by El—as motivation for Keret's raising his siege, and Keret's claim on Hurraya—that she has been given him by El—as motivation for *Pbl*'s giving him his daughter.

With this reply that Keret is to send to *Pbl*, El's speech and Keret's dream simultaneously end. The next bicolon has Keret awaking and realizing that this was a dream (52-54)—a standard feature at the end of ancient Near Eastern dream reports, in which it marks the recognition, not that the preceding experience was an illusion ("only a dream"), but rather that it was of special significance (a vehicle of a divine message).

El's speech has thus concluded with a prediction of what *Pbl* will offer Keret and what Keret is to demand. Keret is not informed whether *Pbl* will oblige, or, if he does, whether Hurraya will produce the desired offspring. The poets doubtless clipped short the account of the anticipated negotiations here just as deliberately as they extended them later in their account of the actual negotiations. To spell out the final resolution of the confrontation at this stage of the story would render the remainder tedious; whereas to extend the negotiations, as the poets do in 1.14.5-15.2, adds to the suspense before the final resolution.

Two more specific features of the last verses of El's speech may explain why the poets ended it here. First, their mention of El's gift of Hurraya and of her bearing of offspring to Keret hark back to Keret's initial appeal, and at the same time anticipate the conclusion of the story in 1.15.3.20-25 (noted in Del Olmo Lete 1981, 253). They thus function as a kind of fulcrum in the total structure of this first section of the poem. Second, the mention of the dream in the penultimate verse reminds El, Keret, poet, and audience that this *is* a dream; hence El stops speaking, Keret wakes up, and the audience looks for Keret to act on the basis of this theophany.

What follows immediately in 3.52ff. is an execution and fulfillment of the instructions and predictions in 2.9ff. At this point we need to recognize the basic structure that has shaped the first section of *Krt*, namely the dream theophany in which the deity responds to a person's need (with the following compare the discussion of incubation in ugaritic and Israelite literature in Del Olmo Lete 1984, 86-93). The elements of this traditional narrative form at its simplest are as follows: 1) the hero is in a plight; 2) the hero falls asleep and dreams; 3) the deity appears and announces to the hero the way out of his plight; 4) the hero awakes and proceeds to act upon the divine announcement, thus escaping from his plight.

The late Egyptian story of *Setne Khamwas and Si-Osire*, preserved in a copy of the Roman period, provides a succinct version of this. The Pharaoh has ordered the magician, Horus-son-of-Penashe, to protect him from the sorceries of the Nubians to which he has been subjected. Horus-son-of-Penashe takes various steps to accomplish this, including the following.

> He went to the temple of Khmun, [made his] offerings and his libations before Thoth . . . the great god. He made a prayer before him saying: ". . . Let me know how to save Pharaoh [from the sorceries of the] Nubians!" Horus-son-of-Penashe lay down in the temple. That night he dreamed a dream in which the mysterious form of the great god Thoth spoke to him . . . (—Thoth instructs him how to protect the Pharaoh). Horus-son-of-Penashe awoke from the dream in which he had seen these things. He understood that what had happened was the doing of the god. He acted according to every word that had been said to him in the dream. (Lichtheim 1980, 146-47)

This account refers specifically to a cultic incubation, that is, to certain ritual acts performed to induce the dream theophany. Other versions, like *Krt*, depict less formal means of establishing contact with the deity. A biblical example closer to *Krt* is found in 1 Kgs 19. This is one of the more developed and complex Elijah narratives, but the traditional structure with which we are concerned is still clearly distinguishable. Elijah is several times shown to be at the end of his tether (verses 2, 4, 10, 14). The divine response to his plight is delayed by two different narrative episodes (5b-6bα and 7-8), so that there are now three different references to his falling asleep (vv. 5a, 6b, 9a). Yahweh finally addresses him: "What are you doing here, Elijah?" (9b). Elijah replies by referring to his plight as the only surviving faithful Yahwist (9b-10). Yahweh now gives Elijah instructions (15-16), predictions (17), and reassurance that he is not alone in Israel (18). Elijah proceeds to execute the divine instructions. (The complex development of the Elijah-Elisha narratives results in a transformation and rearrangement of the instructions in their execution—the third charge is executed in vv. 19-21, the first two in 2 Kgs. 8-9).

This narrative has been secondarily expanded by the theophany episode in which Yahweh instructs Elijah to go out of the cave onto the mountain and witness a series of natural phenomena in which Yahweh will not be present, and then finally to hear a contrasting quietness. Elijah accordingly goes out of the cave (11-13a). Yahweh's initial question of 9b and Elijah's reply of 10 are then repeated (13b-14), in order to resume the flow of the preceding narrative (see Würthwein 1970). These verses—11-14—introduce theological reflection on the nature of God's self-manifestation, and then reiterate the preceding material in order to retain its close connection with what follows. This addition also makes the holy mountain, Horeb, the site of the theophany—part of an interest in inviting comparison between Elijah and Moses—thus also introducing the transitional vv. 7-8 (for the composition of the whole chapter see now Jones 1984).

The story in 1 Kgs. 19 is complex, and incorporates several distinct theological and historical interests, including especially the motif of miraculous feeding in the wilderness; the journey to Horeb, the mountain where God met Moses; and the reinterpretation of the nature theophany. The structure of one distinct narrative strand, however, is clearly the same as that outlined above: the hero's plight; his sleep; the divine address, including instructions and predictions; the hero's execution of the instructions.

In two respects, this narrative is closer to *Krt* than the Egyptian example. First, the prayer of verse 4 expresses the depth of the hero's despair, but there is no other indication of a cultic setting or ritual. Yahweh approaches Elijah, like El Keret, out of a compassionate interest in his suffering devotee, not in response to a formal incubation. Second, the encounter with the deity consists not just of instructions, but of a small conversation, as in *Appu* (discussed above): Yahweh first enquires after Elijah's problem; Elijah tells Yahweh his problem; and only then does Yahweh proceed to give him instructions.

Aqht, which begins with an incubation ritual, substitutes for the dream theophany a mythological scene in which Baal intercedes with El on behalf of the supplicant. But the first two columns of *Aqht* otherwise reflect a similar structure to that we have been considering: Danel, in a plight subsequently expressed in Baal's incession on his behalf, "spends the night" in a sanctuary; (in response to Baal's intercession) El announces instructions and predictions (which are conveyed to Danel); Danel executes the instructions, and thus is delivered from his plight. In the three Semitic texts, similar expressions mark the characteristic core of the narrative:

Krt	1 Kings	*Aqht*
wyšn . . . wyškb	*wyškb wyyšn* (5a) *wyškb* (6b)	*wyškb*
	wyln (9a)	*pyln*
wyqrb bšal krt	*whnh dbr-yhwh 'lyw wy'mr* (9b)	*wyqrb b'l*
mat krt	*mh-lk. . .'lyhw* (9b)	-------------

A further example of the same fundamental structure is found in the Hurrian tale of *Appu* (see Chap. 4 A). Appu, lacking a son, makes a sacrifice to the deity, who sees from heaven and approaches Appu in human form, giving him instructions and comforting him with a promise. Appu's presumed execution of the instructions (in a gap in the text) leads to the birth of the desired son. Here, an actual encounter with the god in human form is substituted for the dream theophany—there is no reference to falling asleep, dreaming or awaking. But despite this different type of communication between deity and human, the narrative is structured in the same sequence: a needy individual performs a religious rite (as in an incubation), is addressed by and receives instructions from the deity, executes these and thus meets his need. In *Appu*, as in *Krt* and *Aqht*, the hero's basic need is for progeny—specifically for a son in *Appu* and *Aqht*; for an entire family in *Krt*.

Two narratives about Hagar exhibit a comparable structure. In Gen 16 Sarai illtreats Hagar, who flees into the wilderness (5-6). Here an envoy of Yahweh finds her (7), enquires what she is doing there, and, on learning of her plight (8), instructs her to return to her mistress (10), and comforts her with a promise concerning the greatness of her future offspring (10 and 11-12). The present narrative assumes Hagar's execution of the envoy's instructions, as it jumps forward to the birth of Hagar's child and Abram's naming of it (15).

Here again there is no reference to a dream. Rather, the divine envoy, rather like the god in human form of *Appu*, comes face to face with Hagar in the wilderness. Yet the sequence of events is otherwise the same: the heroine's plight, the divine response with instructions and predictions. There is even a conversation as in *Krt*, *Appu* and 1 Kgs 19. The conversation is particularly like that of *Appu* and 1 Kgs 19: divine enquiry, statement of the sufferer's plight, divine instructions and comforting prediction. As noted, the author of the present version of Gen 16 found it unnecessary to make Hagar's execution of the instructions explicit.

In Gen 21 Hagar and her son are sent into the wilderness (14). They run out of water, so Hagar leaves the child under a bush, and, unwilling to watch it die, goes and sits some distance away, weeping (15-16). Then God hears the boy's voice and an envoy of God calls to Hagar "from heaven," in a single speech asking what is the matter, instructing her to take the boy again, and comforting her with a promise concerning the child's future (17-18). Then God "opened her eyes," and she saw a well and gave the boy a drink (19), thus implicitly (though without any verbal correspondence) executing the previous instructions.

This narrative follows the same basic pattern. Hagar's plight is developed with considerable pathos (cf. *Krt*). Again there is no reference to a dream, but the divine speech is framed with references to Hagar's weeping and God's opening her eyes (allusions to a dream-like state?). The speech contains the same elements as in *Appu*, 1 Kgs 19 and Gen 16.

Of all these narratives, *Krt* is probably closest to the human experience which lies behind them all; that is, it is the most revealing of the psychological and physiological basis of the dream theophany, given a culture in which dreams are understood to convey real messages from another world, and in which gods are expected to communicate with people through such media. This account of a spontaneously experienced dream theophany is transposed in the other narratives in one of two ways. On the one hand, *Setne Khamwas* represents the institutionalized form (incubation) of the dream theophany, in which it is induced by certain rituals performed in the sanctuary of the god (cf. the opening scene of *Aqht*). On the other hand, several of the cited narratives represent mythologized versions of the dream theophany, substituting for the dream various mythological or theological representations of the divine response to the person's plight—intercession and blessing among the gods (*Aqht*), an envoy of God speaking from heaven (Gen 21), an envoy of Yahweh meeting the person (Gen 16), a god looking down from heaven and then assuming human form and approaching the person (*Appu*). 1 Kgs 19 is the least susceptible to such precise differentiation, retaining one clear marker of a dream theophany (Elijah "spent the night there"—*wyln šm*), but not sustaining that frame of reference. *Krt*, on the other hand, is unambiguous and full in its representation of a spontaneous dream theophany.

Keret's execution of the instructions El gives him in the dream takes us back almost to the beginning of the action (2.9ff.), and constitutes the longest repeated passage in Ugaritic narrative poetry. From the point of view of narrator and audience, repetition and familiarity must be balanced with variation and novelty. Something of the plot must be kept in reserve for the audience to anticipate while it enjoys the transposition of instructions into execution, of events predicted into events fulfilled. On the several small variations between El's speech and the following account of its realization see Chap. 2 C 1 b. Some larger variations require comment here.

Keret dutifully follows the course of action laid out in the dream—sacrificing, provisioning, mustering, marching—until the third day of his journey to *Udm*. At that point the list of seven days is shortened by the intrusion, after the first and second, of "after sunrise on the third" (4.32-33). A new episode now appears. Keret comes to a shrine of the goddess, Asherah (34-36), and there he makes a conditional vow of a gift (36-38). He promises Asherah that if he is successful in bringing Hurraya home as his bride, he will give to the goddess an image of his prize in silver and gold (on the form and substance of the vow see Chap. 3 C). This raises the question in the mind of the audience, why, in a long narrative in which Keret is clearly acting out El's instructions to the letter, he should now initiate this unanticipated act with reference to another deity? It appears to raise questions about Keret's total dependence on El, and it adds an element of tension with respect to both deities. What will El make of this contract with Asherah? How will Keret please both El and Asherah?

The poets now use a unique numerical framework of four days, in order to bring Keret to his destination on the seventh day (see Chap 2 D 5). The siege of *Udm* proceeds as predicted, as far as the reference to *Pbl*'s inability to sleep because of the noise of the animals (1.14.5.7-12). Here appears the next major variation. Whereas in El's speech *Pbl* immediately sends an embassy to Keret, here he first addresses his wife (12-14). Of the following fifteen lines only the ends are preserved, so that it is impossible to make continuous sense of the passage. Does *Pbl* give his wife instructions?—in which case we should expect her execution of them to be reported in the same fifteen lines (v. Chap. 2 C 1 a). But speech continues through line 21 (*išlḥ*—1 sg. verb), and then a second speech is introduced in 22-23 (*gm* [ ]*yṣḥ* "he cries out . ."). Does *Pbl* seek his wife's advice (cf. Bernhardt 1955/56, 110)?—in which case we should expect her to reply to him. But the subject of the second speech is masculine. This could introduce *Pbl*'s address to the messengers, to whom he is speaking in 29-30, but then we would have to suppose that he made some introductory remarks to them before commissioning them. Perhaps the best interpretation of the evidence is to conclude that in the first speech *Pbl* simply expresses to his wife what he is thinking of doing in the situation; and that the second introduction of direct speech serves to mark a change of addressee as *Pbl* now makes some opening remarks to his messengers.

While the text is no better preserved from line 30 to the end of the column, it can safely be restored on the basis of El's prediction in 1.14.3.19-32—with two changes. The first change is the relocation of a particular verse. The bicolon 1.14.3.27-29, *Pbl*'s request that Keret remove himself from *Pbl*'s domicile, is now moved to the end of *Pbl*'s speech (1.14.5.44-45). Thus, while in El's version the speech concluded with the assertion that *Pbl*'s town was a gift of El—an appropriate climax in the mouth of El; that assertion is now followed by the appeal for Keret's departure—an appropriately practical conclusion in the mouth of *Pbl* himself. The choice of different verses for the conclusion of *Pbl*'s speech indicates the poets' alertness to what is most fitting in each context.

The second change is the extension of El's instructions to include the various stages involved in actually sending a message. El's version simply states that *Pbl* will send an embassy to Keret (1.14.3.19-21) and then quotes the message once. The present narrative version first has *Pbl* address the messengers, directing them to Keret, telling them to address Keret (1.14.5.29-32) and quoting the message; and second, again in formulaic language, has them depart, make their way to Keret, and address him (1.14.6. -2; again there seems to be a line or two unaccounted for here), before quoting the message a second time (1.14.6.3-15; also partially restored).

Similarly, whereas El tells Keret to send the embassy back to *pbl* (1.14.3.32-33) and cites the message once (33-49), the narrators now have Keret reply to the messengers (1.14.6.16) and give them the message (17-35, lacking the second bicolon concerned with Hurraya's eyes); and then has the messengers, in the same formulaic language as above, depart, make their way to *Pbl*, and address him (35-39). While *Pbl*'s speech, in both versions here, corresponds with the version in El's prediction, beginning *tḥm pbl mlk* "message of *Pbl*, the king," Keret's message, lacking an introduction in his directions to the messengers, is given a full introduction by the messengers in the form of the bicolon: *tḥm krt ṯʿ//hwt nʿmn*["message of Keret the Noble//word of the gracious [" (1.14.6.40-41). The rest of their speech is now lost. It must have continued in the first c. 18 lines of the missing beginning of the next tablet. As mentioned above, the protraction of the negotiations by the full use of formulae and epic repetition at this point—and in contrast to the treatment of the negotiations in El's speech—heightens the suspense by the delay of the climactic resolution.

Of the first column of 1.15 only the last eight lines are preserved, the last one of which introduces a speech by Keret. Presumably the negotiations between Keret and *Pbl* are still proceeding, since Keret's last speech to *Pbl*, as communicated by the messengers, clearly demands a response. Assuming that the first line of this tablet, as of the other two, read *lkrt*, and that the messengers' repetition of Keret's speech occupied eighteen lines, as in 1.14.6.17-35, the remaining missing lines may be restored as follows (cf. Ginsberg 1946, 21-22; Herdner 1963, 68, n. 1; Del Olmo Lete 1981, 257, 302):

line 20*: *wy'ny pbl mlk* "then king *Pbl* replied" (without accompanying formulae, cf. 1.14.6.16);

lines 21*-24*: the first four lines of *Pbl*'s reply;

lines 25*-31*: the remainder of *Pbl*'s reply (= the preserved lines 1-7);

lines 32*-36*: the formulaic account of the departure of the messengers (cf. 1.14.6. -3, 35-39);

lines 37*-40*: the first four lines of *Pbl*'s message (=lines 21*-24* above).

Lines 1-7 would then complete the delivery of *Pbl*'s message to Keret. Whatever the substance of the first four lines of that message, the preserved part speaks of the benefactions of Hurraya, and of the wailing of the *Udm*-ites for her, as she goes off to join Keret (as apparently implied by the *'m krt* of the obscure lines 3-4). In other words, Keret's request has been granted—immediately on its receipt, if the suggested restoration of the column is correct. *Pbl* had claimed immunity for his city in the name of El, so was presumably bound to acknowledge Keret's claim on his daughter made also in the name of El.

Pbl's speech contains the striking simile:

arḫ tẓǵ l'glh	the cow lows for its calf
bn ḫpṯ lumhthm	the freemen's sons for their mothers
ktnḥn udmm	so wail the *Udm*-ites (for Hurraya)
	(1.15.1.5-7)

In the same vein the Baal cycle has the simile: *klb arḫ l'glh//klb ṯat limrh//km lb 'nt aṯr b'l* "as the heart of the cow for its calf//as the heart of the ewe for its lamb//so is the heart of Anat after Baal" (1.6.2.6-9 = 28-30). The imagery is familiar already in Sumerian literature. A recently published text has a mother goddess seeking her offspring like a cow for its calf, a ewe for its lamb and a nanny-goat for its kid (BM 98396, esp.

lines 1-3, 8-9, 26-27; see Kramer 1982). Behind these literary passages lies the observation and sympathy of those engaged in animal husbandry—found again, for example, in the Middle English lyric poem "Sumer is icumen in" (lines 8-9): *Awe bleteth after lomb, Lhouth after calve cu* "The ewe bleats after the lamb, The cow lows after the calf."

Whatever Keret's response to *Pbl*'s message (introduced in 15.1.8, but otherwise lost), his speech must have rapidly concluded the negotiations, because after the missing first twenty lines of col. 2, he is already back in his palace with the bride he has claimed, and is receiving the congratulations of the gods. The first broken lines (1.15.2.2-7) mention several individual gods, then the whole divine assembly (*ʿdt ilm*). Following the formulaic introduction of Keret (1.15.2.8), two broken lines seem to refer to his reception of his guests (8-10). A summary reference to the arrival of all the gods (11; cf. 1.17.5.25-26 and see Chap. 2 E 1) leads into the introduction to a speech by Baal (12), in which he calls upon El to bless Keret (13-16; cf. 1.17.1.24-25 and see Chap. 2 E 3).

El now raises his cup (16-18; cf. 1.17.1.34-36 and see Chap. 2 E 4) and pronounces a blessing (1.15.2.21-3.16). This is a marriage blessing, discussed in detail in Chap. 3 D. In this context it is noteworthy that the initial reference to the bride (1.15.2.21-23) uses language very similar to that of the vow, and is probably the source of the latter (see Chap. 3 C). In any case, the resumption of the same language at this point in the present form of the poem emphasizes the fulfillment of the condition Keret had laid down for his making a gift to Asherah.

In the blessing El announces that the bride will bear seven//eight sons (23-25); and names the first (Yassub), who will be suckled by the goddesses Athirat and Anat (25-28). Rulers claim to have been suckled by a goddess as early as the presargonic royal inscriptions from Lagash. El thus establishes now that Yassub will be Keret's successor as king.

The fifteen lines missing from the beginning of the next column must have provided further information about Keret's sons. As the text reappears we can restore on the basis of 1.15.3.13-15 a tricolon that speaks of Keret's greatness in comparison with his legendary ancestors (2-4). A monocolon then announces Hurraya's conception and birth of daughters (5-6) which are listed one by one, for a total of six (7-12). The tricolon on Keret's greatness is reiterated (13-15). While everything to this point is modelled on the traditional marriage blessing, there is now added a first person statement by El that he will confer first-born status on the youngest daughter (16). As was argued above (Chap. 3 D; see already Parker 1976), this is a secondary addition, inserted not only into the blessing, but also into the narrative that concludes with the next few lines. (Recognizing the inappropriateness of such a transfer of first-born rights in this context, Gibson prefers to translate: "I will give the first born's blessing [even] to the youngest of them"—i.e. to all equally [Gibson 1977, 92 and n. 1]. But the transfer of the rights of the first-born do become an issue with the addition of the story beginning in 1.16.6, in which the first-born is cursed by his father.)

The gods reiterate El's blessing as they depart (cf. 1.17.5.31-33 and see Chap. 2 E 1), thus concluding the last major episode of this section of the poem. The poet now rapidly concludes the story with what appears to be an incipient numerical framework referring to the conception and birth of one son, two sons (20-21), and the achievement after seven years (22) of a total number of sons and daughters corresponding to the number "vowed" (23-25; on 20-25 see Chap. 2 D 5). Presumably the reference here is to the number promised (i.e. vowed) in his marriage blessing by El. In any case, the inconcinnity in the birth of the seven//eight sons and six daughters (of the blessing) in a period of seven years is reminiscent of the anomalous birth of thirty sons in one year to the queen of Kanesh, and of thirty daughters to her some time later in another year, as recounted in the few lines at the beginning of the Hittite story about the town of Zalpa (v. Otten 1973). (It also suggests the inappropriateness of seeking a realistic explanation of the numerals in 1.14.1.16-20—so Del Olmo Lete 1981, 260, n. 75.)

These lines conclude the story, in the sense that the problem raised at the beginning—Keret's need of a family—has now been met. Admittedly it has been met in stages, first by El's instructions and predictions in the dream theophany, second by Keret's successful pursuit of those directions and conclusion of negotiations with *Pbl* for his daughter, and third by El's reappearance and promise of children to the marriage, a promise which the narrators quickly assure the audience was promptly fulfilled.

The claim that this story may stand—and in this case originally stood—as an independent entity is based not only on its internal structure, but also on certain features which are peculiar to this section; on the comparative evidence for stories with similar beginnings and endings and with some similar scenes and episodes, always in the same order; and on the few unique verses which are explicable not in terms of their present context (with which they stand in some tension), but only as secondary additions serving to attach later narrative material to this original tale.

As I have pointed out elsewhere, there are several titles that are found only in this first section, and that mark it off from the rest of the poem as preserved (Parker 1977, 166-67). These include two titles of Keret: *n'mn ǵlm il* "the gracious one, the boy of El" (five times from 1.14.1.40-41 to 1.15.2.20); *'bd il* "servant of El" (three times from 1.14.3.49 to 1.14.6.34-35); and two titles of El: *ab adm* "father of humankind" (seven times from 1.14.1.37 to 1.14.6.32); and *ṯr ab(h/k) (il)* (four times from 1.14.41 to 1.14.4.6—and four times outside *krt*; contrast the alternative *ṯr il ab(h/y/k)* sixteen times in other texts and not once in *krt*). Since the rest of the poem is less well preserved than this first section, and since some of these occurrences are in repeated or transposed passages, it is possible that the observable distribution is misleading. However, in conjunction with the self-sufficient narrative structure of this section of the poem, and with the comparable narrative structures to be discussed immediately, the presence here of some distinct terms and formulae support the hypothesis that this first section of the poem once had an independent existence in a social (and literary) context different from that in which the subsequent narrative material was added.

In the course of tracing the structure and development of this first section of *Krt*, I have referred to comparable episodes and motifs in other ancient Near Eastern literature. The question must now be raised whether there are in that larger literary environment narratives which are comparable to this first section of the poem as a whole.

The narrative is initiated and concluded by brief accounts of the loss (1.14.1.6-25) and restoration (1.15.3.20-25) of family to Keret. The same narrative framework is used in two well-known biblical narratives, those of the books of Job and Ruth. As was mentioned above, Job loses all his children at one blow in Job 1:18-19. The text equally quickly restores them to him in Job 42:13. In Job's case the catastrophe at the beginning is extended to cover first his livestock and servants—1:14-17—after which the loss of his children is climactic. In the restoration at the end of the book, Yahweh blesses Job with twice as many livestock and sons, and with daughters unmatched for beauty (42:12-15). Both loss and restoration are presented as "acts of God," and serve as a frame within which the poet can explore freely the momentous issues which now occupy the intervening chapters. Neither loss nor restoration is developed into a discrete narrative episode, but rather is reported succinctly by a messenger or the narrator. They are not of narrative interest themselves, but serve solely to set up and then resolve the situation which the poet wishes to explore. The narrative body of the folk-tale which the author used as a source is almost completely displaced by the great poem.

Ruth also begins with the loss of family: Naomi loses her husband and then her only two sons in the first few lines of the story (Ruth 1:3-5). Again the story concludes with the restoration of a family to Naomi: specifically with the birth "to Naomi" of a son (4:13-17). In this case the restoration of family means the birth of a legitimate son to the widowed daughter-in-law—and that is the result of Naomi's and Ruth's acts (with the discrete guidance of Yahweh) through the body of the story. Here the interest of the authors is precisely in those acts which lead Naomi from childless widowhood to the confidence that she will have a "son" to care for her in her old age (Ruth 4:15). In comparison with the fulsome description of those acts and the leisurely pace of each scene, the deaths of Naomi's family at the beginning are reported in the most laconic form (1:3, 5), and the arrival and reception of the heir at the end are sketched as economically as the special circumstances and tone of the story allow (4:13-17).

The pertinence of these passages to the prologue and epilogue of the first section of *Krt* is patent. In all three cases the composers set their major literary work and interests in a frame which rapidly and tersely reports first the loss of the hero's (heroine's) family and finally the restoration of family to the hero (heroine). It seems unlikely that the biblical writers derived this device from *Krt*, or that the composers of *Krt* first created it. More likely is the hypothesis that this was a widespread pattern in ancient Near Eastern folk-tales.

We have already spoken of the skeleton which structures the body of this section of *Krt*, namely that of the dream theophany with divine instructions, in which a needy individual goes to sleep, in a dream is addressed by and receives instructions from the deity, and awakes to execute these and thus meet his or her need. This narrative structure, visible in the institutionalized form of an incubation in the story of *Setne Khamwas and Si-Osire* (cf. the formal cultic acts that induce the divine response in *Appu* and *Aqht*), was seen also to underlie the opening sections of narrative in *Aqht*, *Appu*, Gen 16 and 21, and 1 Kgs 19, in all of which (except possibly the last) the dream is displaced by various mythological or theological portrayals of divine communication with human beings.

Since it is in this first section of *Krt* (to which I shall refer as *Krt* A) and in *Aqht* A that the two poems have most in common, it is worth pausing to consider the contrasts between the two. The dominant interest in *Aqht* is in the ritual acts of the hero, the duties of the desired son, the formal preparations for the birth. *Krt* ignores such matters, and focusses instead on the hero's personal experience, his extraordinary expedition, and even more on the negotiations between the two kings, which occupy more than three of the nine columns over which this first section of the poem extends. *Aqht* is interested in the cultic and mythological context of its subject; *Krt* is more interested in the theological dimension of its subject: El's direction and blessing of the hero. The world of *Aqht* is that of the family, private and exclusive—we see nothing of Danel's social context in 1.17.1-2. In *Krt* the family question is public, and is developed in military, political and diplomatic moves. While the action in *Aqht* moves forward in a succession of formal, static, self-contained scenes, in *Krt* there is a more fluid narrative progression, as well as more graphic description of actions, scenes and situations. A similar contrast between different types of biblical narrative will be obvious.

In the broadest terms, the narrative of *Krt* A, as of Ruth and Job, moves from loss of family to acquisition of family; and that movement is structured by an expression of need that elicits divine instructions, the execution of which results in the meeting of the need, as in the Egyptian *Setne Khamwas*, the Hurrian *Appu*, the Hebrew 1 Kgs 19 and Gen 16 and 21, and the Ugaritic *Aqht* 1-2. If the loss and recovery of family may be referred to as the silhouette of the narrative, and the dream theophany with divine instructions as its skeleton, its more particular thematic structure may be termed its flesh and blood. It remains to define this more particular theme and structure in *Krt* A, and to consider several homologues in which it is also found.

Setting aside the dream theophany with its introduction and lengthy repetition of the later narrative account of Keret's expedition, the plot of this first section of the poem may be outlined as follows: need of family, journey to land of potential spouse, negotiations for spouse leading to conclusion of marriage agreement, marriage ceremony (blessing), and birth of offspring. Two biblical narratives share this subject and structure.

The first is found in Gen 24 (mentioned in this connection in

Eissfeldt 1944). Here, Isaac is not only childless but unmarried, so that his need of a wife is obvious from the start. Since Isaac must marry within the clan they have left (3-4) but not leave the promised land to which they have moved (5-7), and since the father is old (v. 1), the father commissions a servant to go to their ancestral homeland to seek a wife for Isaac (vv. 2-9). The servant undertakes the journey (v. 10), and with Yahweh's support identifies Rebeccah as the woman for Isaac (12-21). Most of the rest of the chapter is then occupied by the negotiations for the spouse, beginning with the servant's gifts to Rebeccah (22) and request for lodging (23), and continuing with Lagan's enthusiastic welcome (30-33), the servant's lengthy account of his mission (34-49), and Lagan's immediate granting of Rebeccah to Isaac (50-51). The actualization of the agreement is delayed by further negotiations as to the time of departure of the servant with Rebeccah (54b-58). Rebeccah herself finally closes the discussion (58). Since the wedding itself will be back in Canaan where Isaac is, the bride's family now pronounce their blessing on her (60)—the only reference to the wedding ceremony. The story concludes with the union of Rebeccah and Isaac (67), the birth of their children being treated in the context of other interests in 25:21-26.

The second example is found in the book of Ruth. Naomi, with no family but her also childless and widowed daughter-in-law, Ruth, journeys back to Bethlehem in her homeland. There negotiations take place which lead to the conclusion of a marriage agreement by which Boaz takes Ruth as his wife (Ruth 4:9-10). The marriage ceremony is again represented only by the marriage blessing (4:11b-12). Ruth immediately bears a son (4:13).

The story of Ruth is distinctive, especially in assigning the leading role to the two women. One consequence of this is that instead of the hero's demand of a spouse and conclusion of negotiations in his own behalf, as in *Krt* (a role that a woman could not be assigned in ancient Semitic society); we have Ruth's initial chance encounter with Boaz in chapter 2, Naomi's subsequent direction behind the scenes of Ruth's secret nocturnal proposal to Boaz in chapter 3, and then, finally, as the consequence of their prior agreement, Boaz' public negotiation for the right to marry Ruth in the context of the law governing the remarriage of a childless widow in chapter 4. Though the placing of widow and daughter-in-law in the center of the story thus complicates the narrative (and in fact gives it much of its interest and effectiveness), it still clearly follows the same stages and addresses the same theme—the need for progeny—as *Krt*. It is indeed even closer to *Krt* than Gen 24, in that it has a prologue in which Naomi's loss of her husband and two sons is succinctly stated (1:2, 4).

Clearly the same theme and structure are evident in all three stories. Certain differences are determined by the setting. The peculiar nature of the negotiations and their conclusion in Ruth is determined by the choice of the two widowed women as subjects. The character of the negotiations in Gen 24 is determined by the private, family setting, the piety of the servant, and the polite conventions of guest and host. In *Krt*, the status of the king requires a show of military strength, and lengthy, formal diplomatic communications (a presumptuous request by a weak king for a strong king's daughter is ridiculed in 2 Kgs 14:9; for lengthy diplomatic negotiations v. e.g., 1 Kgs 20:1-11; 2 Kgs. 18:17-37). Despite such differences of setting and emphasis, all three stories follow the same sequence of events; all three face the same fundamental need of anyone in these societies, the need of a family; and all three treat at great length that delicate and momentous task of negotiating a marriage agreement with the right spouse.

The same theme and structure seem to have had a role in shaping the final form of the present complex version of the Jacob story. Isaac instructs (the unmarried and therefore childless) Jacob to go to Paddan-Aram to get a wife (Gen 28:1-2), invoking El Shadday's blessing on him (anticipatory marriage blessing? See Chap. 3 D) (3). Jacob undertakes the journey (28:5, 10; 29:1). He negotiates for his chosen bride (29:15-30). (There is reference to the marriage feast in conjunction with the first, undesired marriage—v. 22). The narrative of the births of Jacob's progeny follows.

The peculiar significance of the negotiation of a marriage may be demonstrated by further comparative evidence. It is the subject of the narrative section of another ugaritic text: 1.24. Yarikh sends a request to "king" *Ḫrḫb* for the hand of his daughter, promising a generous bridewealth. *Ḫrḫb* replies with the suggestion that Yarikh marry one of Baal's daughters. Yarikh insists on *Ḫrḫb*'s daughter. The isolated episode concludes with her family managing the scales on which the bridewealth will be weighed (1.24.16-37).

Actual negotiations between kings for one to take the daughter of the other in marriage are recalled in Tushratta's letter (roughly contemporary with our copy of *Krt*) to Amenophis IV, in which he claims that numerous messages were sent by

Tuthmosis IV to Artatama, and later by Amenophis II to Shuttarna, before the Mitannian kings were finally ("the seventh time") prevailed upon to give their daughters in marriage to the Egyptian kings. Tushratta claims that he himself agreed promptly to give Amenophis IV his daughter in exchange for an enormous *tirḫatu* (EA 29:16-27). EA 3-5 constitute the actual correspondence between Amenophis III and Kadashman-Enlil concerning the marriage of each to a daughter of the other.

The reluctance of the bride's father or family to give her up, seen in *Pbl*, Laban, *Ḫrḫb*, Artatama and Shuttarna, is probably a frequent motif in each type of tale—and probably also common in actual experience. The beauty of the bride, noted (in order of increasing detail) of Rachel (Gen 29:17b), Rebeccah (Gen 24:16a) and *Ḥry* (1.14.6.25-30 and 3.40-45) is probably also a common motif. On the other hand, coincidence surely accounts for the fact that all three of the longer narratives that we have compared also include instructions to the party that is to negotiate the new relationship—Naomi instructs Ruth, Abraham instructs his servant and El the king. All three sets of instructions arise from different causes peculiar to the setting of each narrative. Naomi must guide the younger Moabite woman, *after* their journey, in what are for Ruth the strange community and institutions of Bethlehem. The narrator is interested in the relationship between the two women and the way they manage to move from the edges of society to a central place in it. The aging Abraham cannot undertake the journey to his kinsfolk, and so must direct his servant to act on his behalf, commissioning him at the beginning of the narrative to undertake the whole enterprise. The narrator is interested in the role of the emissary as such (see Roth 1972, 180-84), Abraham playing no further role in the chapter after his initial charge. Similarly El commissions Keret at the beginning to undertake his expedition. But this is determined by the choice of the dream theophany with instructions as a vehicle for extending and structuring the narrative.

One common stylistic feature shared by *Krt* and Gen 24 is the lengthy, step-by-step repetition of the main action, including speeches, and with only minor deviations—in El's instructions and predictions and Keret's execution of them in *Krt*, and in the servant's experiences and then his account of them to Laban in Gen 24. In both cases there are internal repetitions—e.g. in the correspondence of prayer (Gen 24:13-15) and fulfillment (15-20) in the narrative and then in the servant's report (43-44 and 45-46); in the correspondence of Pbl's offer and

Keret's rejection in El's instructions and predictions, and then in their execution and fulfillment as repeated to the messenger and then to the addressee. This is a stylistic feature, obviously revealing what is considered particularly important or pleasurable in each narrative, but not otherwise significant in the relationship between them.

On the basis of the common structure of *Krt*, Gen 24 and Ruth, it is reasonable to propose an earlier, simpler form of *Krt* A, consisting solely of Keret's expedition for a wife, but distinguished by its peculiar interest in his preparations for the campaign (1.3.52-4.12), the character of his army (1.4.13-31), the situation of the siege (1.14.4.49-5.12 [+ ?]), the diplomatic negotiations (1.14.5.31-1.15.1. ?), and the scope of his promised family (1.15.2.23-3.15)—a tale of a king of legendary greatness. The balance between the acquisition of such an abundant family, and the total loss of a full family as described in the prolog, may also be original (cf. Ruth, Job). By the same token, a case may be made that the account of the dream, and the material that introduces and motivates it (1.14.1.26-35), are a secondary embellishment, modelled on the standard form (and experience) of the dream theophany with instructions. It may have been suggested by Keret's claim that El had given him Hurraya in a dream (1.14.6.1-2). Whether or not this is so, its effect, apart from the aesthetic aspects mentioned previously, is to emphasize the role of El, who responds immediately to Keret's plight (not only on Baal's intercession, as in *Aqht*), and dictates virtually everything that Keret is to do to get his wife. The story already has each king claiming that El has given him his city or wife respectively, neither questioning the other's claim. It also has El presiding at Keret's wedding, and pronouncing a blessing which spells out the details of the abundant family Keret will now enjoy—a blessing which is immediately and summarily fulfilled in the conclusion of the narrative. With the addition of El's response to and direction of Keret, Keret now owes everything to El, who appears as a beneficient, omniscient and omnipotent tutelary deity of the otherwise helpless king. Keret, who, in the hypothetical older, simpler narrative, would have been the successful leader of a great expedition, is now the totally dependent, obedient servant of the god.

It is noteworthy that the theme of divine guidance is clearly present also in Gen 24 and Ruth, though it is conveyed through different means in each. In Gen 24 Abraham is too old to undertake the mission, and Isaac must not leave the promised land (vv. 6-7a) and indeed is no more than a name until the last few verses, when the mission is accomplished. Abraham assures the servant, lacking confidence of success (v. 5) that Yahweh will send his envoy before him (v. 7). The servant later prays for guidance (13-15), his prayer is granted, and he acknowledges Yahweh's guidance (26-27). In his subsequent account to Laban, the servant repeats each of these references to Yahweh's leading (40, 43-44, 48), and Laban immediately acknowledges, "This is Yahweh's doing" (50). The suitor's claim that the deity had designated the bride for him is common to Gen 24 and *Krt*, and may well reflect actual custom. (I have known of suitors who have made such a claim today!)

The more extraordinary circumstances of Ruth require a different kind of treatment of the theme, but divine guidance is still explicitly there. Thus Boaz prays that Yahweh will grant Ruth a full reward for giving up her own family and seeking refuge among Yahweh's people (2:11-12). On learning of Ruth's meeting with Boaz, Naomi recognizes that Yahweh has kept faith with her depleted family (2:20a). When the marriage of Ruth and Boaz is concluded, Yahweh grants Ruth conception (4:13), and the women register that Yahweh has provided Naomi with a new family (4:14). While these may all be regarded as conventional expressions of piety (all but 4:13 occur in speeches), they nevertheless balance Naomi's pronouncements at the end of the first chapter, where she charges that Yahweh has treated her badly. They thus express the author's intention to show that Yahweh has in fact reversed Naomi's fate (as first in chapter 1).

It is likely that the search for a spouse and conclusion of a marriage agreement were among the most momentous and sensitive undertakings of a person's life. People would have been peculiarly aware at such times of their dependence on the beneficence, wisdom and guidance of a higher power. All three of these stories in their present form reflect such awareness, and it may have figured frequently in the traditional tales on which all three are surely modelled.

There are two loose ends at this point in the poem. The first is the outcome of Keret's vow to Athirat. Keret must have brought Hurraya to his palace at the beginning of 1.15.2, thus fulfilling the condition laid down in the vow for his promised gift to Athirat. Its fulfillment, as was noted above, is impressed on us by the reiteration of the language of the condition in the opening cola of El's blessing. Seven years later Keret has evidently done nothing about fulfilling that promise, as becomes immediately apparent in the next bicolon: *wtḫss aṯrt ndrh*//*ilt* ["Then

Athirat recalled his vow//the goddess [" (25-26). But, again as was noted above, the vow is intrusive in the account of Keret's expedition. The poets did not include it in El's instructions to him, but forced it into Keret's execution of them by displacing the instructions' seven-day sequence with a three-day sequence, leading into the vow, and then an unparalleled four-day sequence, to bring Keret to Udm at the right distance and time (see Chap. 2 D 5). The vow actually has no function in the tale of El's response to Keret's need of a family.

The second loose end is the outcome of El's announcement at the end of the marriage blessing that he would assign first-born status to the youngest daughter, which stands in tension with the special attention to the privileges of the first-born at the beginning of the blessing, and has no relationship to any other material in the larger narrative.

While 1.14.1.1-1.15.3.25 is a complete story without the vow or the reference to the change of status of the youngest daughter, the former provides the basis for the complication begun in 1.15.3.25-26 (Merrill 1968, 9-10, 14)—that is, for the next story—and the latter seems to anticipate developments in the third major block of narrative beginning in 1.16.6.

B. Keret's Recovery from Sickness

Immediately following the completion of Keret's family in 1.15.3.20-25, Asherah recalls Keret's vow (25-26), and the narrative introduces a speech by her (27) in which she apparently notes Keret's failure to fulfil his vow (*uṯn ndr*["or change [his] vow . . ."), and threatens to cancel (*apr*) something (28-30). The root *prr* is used of breaking vows in Num 30:9, 13-14, 16 and may have been used in 1.15.3.28 (following *ap k[rt* and paralleling *ṯn* "change" in 29) of Keret's breaking of his vow, as several commentators have suggested. In any case, the force of the verses seems to be that as Keret has denied her something, she will deny him something. The increasingly damaged text now fails altogether. Approximately seven lines are missing from the bottom of 1.15.3 and another five from the top of 1.15.4.

The non-fulfillment of a vow was a serious matter in the ancient Near East. It explains the terrible compulsion felt by both Jephthhah ("I have spoken to Yahweh—I cannot go back [on my word]" Judg 11:35b) and his daughter ("You have spoken to Yahweh—do to me as you said you would" Judg 11:36a) in the story of Jephthah's vow. In each speech there is an implied "therefore" between the two clauses.

Warnings on the subject appear in Israel's legal and wisdom

literature. Deut 23:22-23 warns against delay in fulfilling a vow, "for Yahweh will be sure to require it of you, and you will be found to be at fault." Num 30:3 says simply: "If someone makes a vow to Yahweh . . . let him not profane (*hip'il* of *ḥll*) his word (i.e. cancel his promise)." Qohelet reiterates at length that one should not procrastinate when one has made a vow to God—God is not pleased with such behavior—but fulfil it promptly. It is better not to make vows at all than to make one and then not fulfil it. Such rash speech will bring down God's wrath, and God will bring one's accomplishments to nothing (Qoh 5:3-5; cf. Prov 20:25).

Several references in second millennium Akkadian texts spell out consequences of the non-fulfillment of a vow that bring us even closer to *Krt*. An old Assyrian letter urges upon the recipient: *ikribam ša ana Tašmetim takrubuni apputum la tamašši iltum irtibi* "Be sure not to forget the votive gift you promised to (the goddess) Tashmetum—the goddess has become angry" (TCL 19, 35:15). In another Old Assyrian text: *aššumi kaspim ša ikribi annakam* PN *tamraṣ* "PN has become ill here because of the silver she had vowed" (KTS 24:4; the clear implication is that she had not given what she had promised to a deity). The final outcome of such failure to fulfil a vow may be (according to an old Babylonian omen text): *šarru imâtma; ikribišu šanûm anaddin* "The king will die; another will fulfil his vow" (YOS 10, 17:72). (The preceding are all cited from *CAD* s.v. *ikribu*, section 2.) The goddess' wrath is implied in the verses of *Krt* we have just reviewed; the illness of the person who has failed to fulfil a vow is clear in what follows; and the prospect of the king's death is certainly in view in 1.16.1-2.

As Loewenstamm (1979, 511) has observed, it is likely that tales of such unfulfilled vows circulated in the ancient Near East. They would have followed the course of the institution itself, recounting the making of the vow, the deity's fulfillment of his or her part, notice of the supplicant's failure to do the same, and the consequences suffered by the supplicant, with whatever final resolution was deemed appropriate. Such tales would have served to warn the audience of the dire consequences of not fulfilling vows, and reinforced the institution by encouraging the listeners to pay their vows promptly.

A late, secularized, example of such a tale is found in Ovid. Laomedon, king of Troy, promised gold to Apollo and Neptune, if they would rebuild his city's defences. They did so, but then Laomedon refused the gold (and tried to protect himself from harm by falsely swearing that he had made no such commitment). Neptune punished him by first bringing a devastating flood over his land then demanding his daughter as a sacrifice (*Metamorphoses* XI 199-212; though Ovid's text does not spell out that the contract was a vow, the identity of Apollo and Neptune as gods assures the religious character of the transaction originally envisaged).

Against this background it is reasonable to see in *Krt* B—the second major narrative unit of the larger poem—such a tale of an unfulfilled vow, and to build on these few lines at the end of 1.15.3 a connection between Keret's failure to fulfil his vow and his sickness in the sequel. Keret had vowed a gift to Asherah conditional upon his winning of Hurraya as his bride. Seven years after his marriage to Hurraya, the king still has not fulfilled his vow. Asherah now takes note of the fact, swearing that she will treat him in a way analogous to the way he has treated her. The sickness with which we see Keret afflicted in the following columns is Asherah's punishment of him for his non-fulfillment of his vow.

In the next three columns there are almost no undamaged lines, only a couple of dozen completely restorable lines, and fewer than seventy of which any part is preserved. The remains are sufficient for us to conclude with confidence that we have to do with a banquet or series of banquets; but further claims than that must be judiciously supported and moderated.

The first lines of 1.15.4 largely restored, but formulaic, have Keret addressing his wife. The speech is introduced in 1.15.4.2. Keret instructs Hurraya (3; cf. 14) to prepare meat and wine (4-5) and summon his seventy//eighty nobles (6-7), identified as "the bulls of greater *Ḫbr*//the gazelles of Lesser *Ḫbr*" (8-9; on this use of animal names see Miller 1970). No sense can be made of the traces of the next four lines. Since the execution of instructions, here beginning in line 14 (*tšmʿ mṯt [ḥ]ry*), usually follows directly on the instructions, Keret's speech may continue through line 13. However, it is quite possible that some other action intervenes, as elsewhere. In any case, following Hurraya's execution of his instructions in 15-20 the text clearly does not correspond with the remains of 10-13. Thus if the latter were a continuation of Keret's instructions (e.g. telling Hurraya what to announce to the guests, as proposed by De Olmo Lete 1981, 262), Hurraya's execution of them must have been postponed until what is now the gap at the end of the column (cf. *Dnty*'s postponement of the second part of Danel's instructions until after the arrival of the visitors in 1.17.5).

Hurraya brings Keret's bulls//gazelles into her (or his?) presence (17-18; corresponding loosely to Keret's instructions to her to summon them: 6-7). 19-20 are identical with 8-9. 21-23 shifts to the guests as subject, and speaks of their entry into Keret's house, after which they reach for dish and knife (24-25). Line 26 introduces a speech by Hurraya, which begins: "I have summoned you to eat and drink" (27). Line 28 has been reconstructed on the basis of 1.15.6.5, which follows the same two lines as line 28 does here. Hence: "Keret, your lord, is holding a feast." However, the word for lord is there *adn*, here *b'l*; the corresponding line in 1.15.5 is entirely different; and, as Herdner points out, there is space for another couple of letters here (Caquot and Sznycer 1974, 544, n. c).

The surviving material in this column thus tells the following: the king instructs the queen to prepare a feast and invite the guests; she prepares the feast and brings the guests in; they reach for the food and she addresses them. Perhaps she goes on to state the purpose of the feast. Unfortunately we cannot say what that was.

The general setting and sequence of events and speeches here is well-known, and perhaps most fully developed in the third tablet of *Enūma eliš* (cf. Irvin 1978). Here Anshar sends his assistant, Gaga, to the other gods to invite them to a banquet (1-8; the entire speech proceeds to line 66). Gaga carries out his master's instructions (67-124). After a brief reference to the gods' reactions to the message (125-28), the poem tells of their journey and entry into Anshar's presence (129-332), and their enjoyment of the food and drink (333-37). They then proceed to the business for which they were invited (338 and IV 1-34). The banquet is only the setting and occasion for the real business: to make Marduk their champion against Tiamat and Kingu—it is this subject that composes most of the speeches of Anshar and his messenger. Indeed the invitation to the banquet, made clear to Gaga by Anshar, is taken for granted in Gaga's message to the gods.

The invitation to a banquet, with its components: instructions to summon the guests, summoning of the guests, coming of the guests, enjoyment of the banquet, speech(es) concerning the business at hand, clearly lies behind 1.15.IV-VI as behind *Enūma eliš* III-IV. It is obviously a literary reflex of a common practice at the palaces of the ancient Near East. (For other examples of parts of the invitation to a banquet see e.g. 1.4.6.44-59; 1.20-22; 1.114.1-4; Prov 9:2-5 and Lichtenstein 1968-69a.)

Unfortunately, as *Enūma eliš* shows, the banquet setting, so well revealed in 1.15.4, is merely the background of the essential business, unfortunately missing in 1.15.4. What is distinctive in what remains of 1.15.4 is that Keret himself does not invite nor address his guests. He seems to have Hurraya act on his behalf. Although we do not learn of his sickness until later, it is likely, as agreed by most commentators, that he became sick in the gap between 1.15.3 and 4, that is, immediately following Asherah's resolve to do something about his failure to honor his vow. That would both provide a motivation for the present actions, which otherwise lack narrative justification; and would put Keret in a plight at the beginning of this narrative segment comparable to that of the loss of his family at the beginning of the first segment. It is therefore likely that Hurraya's address to the bulls/gazelles has to do with Keret's sickness, as seems to be the case in 1.15.5.

There are about fifteen lines now lost to us at the bottom of 1.15.4 and another one or two at the top of 1.15.5. When the text resumes, the bicolon in which Hurraya prepares the feast can be restored (1.15.5.1-2). The restoration of the following four lines is less sure, but they seem to treat of people associated with *Ḫbr* (line 4; *bḫr* [erroneous transposition?] line 5) coming into Keret's dwelling (*lmṯb* line 6). Whether these are the "bulls" again (so Herdner and Del Olmo Lete), or a different group, cannot be ascertained (but see the suggestion below). In any case the seven lines of 1.15.4.17-23 are here reduced to just over four (lines 3-7). In lines 7-8 the guests again prepare to cut the meat (cf. 1.15.4.24-25). Line 9, like 1.15.4.26, introduces a speech in which Hurraya first tells the guests that she has summoned them to eat and drink (line 10; cf. 1.15.4.27). Only four letters of line 11 are preserved—enough to indicate that it does not duplicate 1.15.4.28 or 1.15.6.5 (both following the same first line of Hurraya's speech).

In line 12 Hurraya appears to call on the guests to weep over Keret ( ]*krt tbkn*). Though the reading is very difficult the following lines seem to refer to the bellowing of bulls ( ]*rgm ṯrm* 13), and again to weeping (14). The remains of lines 15-17 yield no sure, continuous sense, though some individual words are unambiguous: *blb* "in [someone's] heart," *uṣb[t* "fingers"). Lines 18-20 comprise a clearer bicolon: Keret will arrive (or: let Keret arrive) at sunset. Lines 20-21 then announce the sequel: *wymlk [y]ṣb ʿln* "and Yassub will rule over us." Is the reference to Keret's arrival a euphemism for his reaching the underworld? Or an explanation of why Hurraya is now presiding, and an assurance that he will appear later? Though the present context sheds no light on these questions, the subsequent text supports the former more than the latter. Is the reference to Yassub's rule a reassurance that there will be a regent to fill the vacuum left by Keret's withdrawal to his bed, or a cause for concern? Del Olmo Lete (1981, 264) surmises that we may have a palace intrigue to assure a certain succession, comparable to that recounted in 1 Kgs 1. The characterization of Yassub in the marriage blessing already indicates that Yassub is the assured heir. If Hurraya is plotting, it must be to see that Yassub does not take his father's place. The broken state of the text unfortunately does not permit more than speculation at this point.

The verb of the next colon is unfortunately partially missing. Whether this colon formed a bicolon with the preceding (*wy[ ]y [kr]t t̠ʿ ỉln*), or introduced a speech by Keret (restoring *wy[ʿn]y*, and taking *ỉln* as the first word of the speech) is unclear. In any case the second person singular of *at̠tk* "your wife/wives" in line 23 poses a problem. What individual would Hurraya or Keret address? But again, the context is hopelessly damaged, and the most we can say of the remaining lines is that they refer to Great *Ḫbr* (25) and to El (26).

In this column we appear to have a repetition of elements of the invitation to a banquet: Hurraya's preparation of a feast, the arrival of guests, and Hurraya's address to them (1.15.5.1-10 corresponding roughly to 1.15.4.15-27). The more fully preserved state of Hurraya's speech allows us to see that Hurraya is calling on the guests to weep for Keret, and referring to his arrival at sunset and the anticipated rule of Yassub. Lines 11-21 (and further?) must have corresponded in some way with 1.15.4.28ff. Thus the gap between the two columns may have been occupied almost entirely by Hurraya's first speech, after which she might have dismissed her first guests, and immediately made preparations for the second guests. If her first speech was much shorter, then Keret may have first given her instructions for the second feast, as he did for the first (1.15.4.2-9/13).

We have most of only eight lines of col. 6. Some one is addressing someone (*šmʿl*["Hear . . ." line 1), and referring to their eating and drinking (line 2—a formulaic line). Line 3 introduces a speech by Hurraya, in which she begins as before by telling her guests that she has summoned them to eat and drink (4 = 1.15.4.27 = 1.15.5.10). Here she continues with the announcement that Keret, their lord, has a feast (5), and an appeal to the guests to weep for Keret (6, reading *tbkn* with Herdner [Caquot and Sznycer 1974, 548, n. p]), with a reference to the roaring of bulls (7), and to something *bd̠rt* "in a dream" (8).

Here then is Hurraya's third speech. It substitutes for the

second line of her second speech (1.15.5.11) the announcement that Keret is holding a feast, echoes the next two cola of the speech, then diverges. The gap between cols. 5 and 6 allows for Keret to give Hurraya a new set of instructions, and for her to act on them up to the point where she begins her speech. However 1.15.6.1-2 show again that the text is not following a consistent pattern.

The constant in all three columns is the introduction to and opening colon of Hurraya's speech. It seems reasonable to draw two conclusions: first, that the repetition of the opening of the speech implies three different audiences, that is, three different sets of guests (so Ginsberg 1946, 9); second, that the divergences in the rest of the speech imply three different appeals or directions, each related to the particular character or abilities of the particular set of guests. It may be that the second set were the dead ancestors of the king. The surviving letters allow the following restoration in col. 5:

(3) *[tšʿrb] rp[i arṣ*	She ushered in the dead rulers of the Earth
(4) *[rpi ḫ]br[rbt]*	The dead rulers of Great *Ḫbr*,
(5) *ḫb(!)r[ṯrr]t*	Of Little *Ḫbr*.

The restoration of the last two lines is supported by both the remains and the comparable 1.15.4.8-9, 19-20; that of the first is suggested by the surviving *rp* and by the comparable bicola 1.15.4.6-7 and 17-18. In 1.161 we have a ritual invocation of the *rpi arṣ* alongside the late king and on behalf of the ruling monarch of Ugarit; and we know from 1.15.3.2-4, 13-15 that the *rpi arṣ* are treated as the ancestors of Keret. Whether it is significant that their title means "healers" is obviously uncertain. Presumably they may also have been regarded as counsellors in a situation like this.

However confident we may be of the use of the invitation to a banquet and the repetition of that motif three times with different guests each time, the substance of the hostess' announcement and its effect on each set of guests remain unknown. That it had something to do with the prospective loss of Keret and succession of Yassub is suggested by 1.15.5.12 and 20-21. Whether it concerned the healing of Keret or the succession cannot be determined on the basis of these poorly preserved columns.

Approximately forty lines are missing from the remainder of the last column of 1.15. We have the beginning of the next tablet, the first line of which bears the colophon *lkrt*. All the lines of the first column are preserved, though the last dozen lack their first few letters. The text begins at line 2 with a speech which, with some omissions and additions, is repeated in 1.16.1.14-23 and 1.16.2.36-49. The first bicolon of the first version is preceded in the other two versions by another bicolon, which should probably therefore be restored at the bottom of 1.15.6.

Since the introduction to the speech is among the lines lost from 1.15.6, we have to infer the identity of the speaker from 1.16.1.46. At that point, after he has addressed Keret and received Keret's reply, he is mentioned by name as he goes to do Keret's bidding. It is *Ilḥu*. The speech that *Ilḥu* is reciting at the beginning of the tablet he immediately repeats before his father (1.16.1.11ff.) Evidently the speech he then delivers to Keret in 1.16.1.14-23 he first rehearses in a speech in which he tells himself to deliver it—a literary device used in the presentation of Yassub's address to his father in 1.16.6 (see Chapter 2 C 1 a; first suggested in Ginsberg 1946, 25). Preceding the first bicolon of the speech at the bottom of 1.15.6 the text therefore would have introduced a speech by *Ilḥu* (cf. 1.16.6.25-26), followed by *Ilḥu*'s directions to himself to go to his father and address him (cf. 1.16.6.27-29). In view of the similarities of this passage to 1.16.6.25ff., it seems more likely that *Ilḥu*'s visit to his father was spontaneous (like Yassub's), than that it was in response to a summons conveyed by Hurraya, comparable to that in 1.15.4 (as suggested by Del Olmo Lete 1981, 265; cf. also the summons conveyed by *Ilḥu* to Thitmanit, to be discussed shortly).

Ilḥu's speech would have begun with a bicolon expressing joy in Keret's life (cf. 1.16.1.14-15; 2.36-37), but continues with two bicola expressing grief at the prospect of his dying (2-5). Two parallel bicola refer to the very mountain of Baal as weeping for him (6-9). The final bicolon of the speech asserts that Keret is the offspring of El (9-11). The speech appears to be modelled on the lament for the dead, which would have expressed the mourner's delight in the deceased's *past* life, and *called on* the mountain to mourn for him (using the jussive instead of the imperfect *tbkyk*; cf. the Akkadian *libkika* [pl. *libkūka*] in Gilgamesh's lament over Enkidu [*Gilgamesh* VIII 1 5-23; Gurney 1954, 90-95], and the imperative *bkynh* in 2 Sam 1:24; on the lament for the dead see Müller 1978). The poets here use components of the lament for the dead, but in an address to one who, though evidently mortally ill, is still alive.

Having rehearsed this speech to himself, *Ilḥu* now goes in weeping to his father and addresses him (11-14—the first colon is identical with that used of Yassub in 1.16.6.39-40; the following bicolon corresponds with that used to introduce another version of the same speech as *Ilḥu*'s by Thitmanit in 1.16.2.35-36).

Ilḥu's actual speech to his father, however, departs from the proposed model (see chapter 2 D 1) by dropping the references to the weeping of Saphon, and moving directly to the bicolon concerning Keret's divine paternity. But this is now quoted in a question (*ikm yrgm* "how can it be said?") and beside that question is set the alternative (*uilm tmtn/špḥ lṭpn lyḥ* "or do gods die//the offspring of the Gracious One not live on?"). The aesthetic effect of this is to produce a nice balance between the opening and the concluding bicola of the speech, between Keret's life//"not-death" (*ḥyk//blmtk*) and the gods' dying//not living (*tmtn//lyḥ*). The rhetorical questions may reflect the model of the lament—cf. Del Olmo Lete 1981, 265-6—but they also express a scepticism that we shall have occasion to comment on later.

Keret's reply is introduced immediately (24). In a speech extending from line 25 to line 45, he first bids his son not to dry up his head with weeping (25-28), but to call upon Thitmanit to weep for him (28-30). The following lines, though containing many familiar words, are too damaged to be translated confidently. *Ilḥu* is (not) to say something to his sister (*al trgm laḫtk* line 31). Someone (Keret?) knows that someone (Thitmanit?) is compassionate (*yd't k rḥmt* line 33), Thitmanit is (not?) to shed her tears (*mmh//ṣat npšh*) in the open fields (34-35), something is to happen at dusk (36-38).

Keret next tells *Ilḥu* to convey a message to Thitmanit (using the formulaic colon used to instruct a messenger: *rgm l* + personal reference). Within Keret's speech to *Ilḥu*, then, we now have the speech that *Ilḥu* is to deliver to Thitmanit. Commentators are divided over whether that message is limited to the bicolon 39-41 (so Watson 1976; Gibson 1978; Del Olmo Lete 1981) or whether it extends to the end of Keret's speech (Caquot and Sznycer 1974; De Moor and Spronk 1982, 183). All agree that *Ilḥu* is to tell Thitmanit that Keret is having a banquet (39-41). But are the following instructions also intended for her, or is Keret again speaking directly to *Ilḥu*?

A decision on the reading and interpretation of the following lines must precede an answer to that question. Although some follow Virolleaud and read *apk* in line 41 (Watson 1976; De Moor and Spronk 1982) the reading preferred by Herdner and KTU is *tpk* (so already Ginsberg 1946; followed by Caquot and

Sznycer 1974; Del Olmo Lete reads *tpk* but translates "your nose"). This renders unnecessary the relation of *mrḥ* (47) to √*rwḥ*. Further, the traces at the beginning of 42 do not allow, according to *KTU*, the restoration of *grgr*, although the latter remains the most likely reading in 48. But since every other word makes good sense in this context in its most usual meaning, it is *grgr* that requires special explanation. In line 43 Virolleaud and CTA read *škn*, for which KTU now reads *šr*. While it was tempting to see in the *šknt*[of 1.15.2.53 an execution of the instruction *škn* in line 43, it is perhaps more compelling that *šr ʿl ṣrrt* follows on the instruction *qḥ tpk byd* "take your timbrel in your hand" (1.16.1.41), and may be related to *bd aṯt . . . ṣrry* (1.16.1.5 and repetitions; so De Moor and Spronk 1982, 183) or to *al tšt bšdm mmh//bsmkt ṣat npšh* "let her (not?) put her waters (i.e. tears) in the fields//the outpouring of her soul in the *smkt*" (1.16.1.34-35).

Pending further clarification of the possibilities and constraints imposed on our readings by the physical remains of the tablets, I prefer the second of the alternative readings in both cases and the interpretation of the rest of Keret's speech as the message *Ilḥu* is to convey to Thitmanit. According to this construction of the text, the message consists of three bicola with a monocolon between the second and third. *Ilḥu* is first to tell Thitmanit that Keret is having a banquet (39-41), then to direct her to take her timbrel (41-42) and sing on the heights (43), and finally to direct her to bring gifts of [silver]//gold (44-45). (Del Olmo Lete asks whether the silver and gold are to fulfil his vow to Asherah, in hopes of then having his health restored—Del Olmo Lete 1981, 267, n. 98.)

Thitmanit's singing on the heights in this context may be compared with the activities of Jephthah's daughter and her associates in the face of her impending fate (Judg 11:37-38; the passage is mentioned in this context by De Moor and Spronk 1982, 183). This unnamed young woman went into the hills with her companions and bewept her girlhood (*btwlyh*, i.e. her unfinished life). A similar situation is probably envisaged in the more poetic language of Jer 7:29. Because Yahweh has rejected and abandoned his people, the addressee (feminine singular!) is called upon to raise a lament on the heights. In each case the rite is performed by a woman (women in Jdg 12:37-38), and anticipates, rather than follows, the approaching loss.

With the end of line 45 Keret's speech to *Ilḥu*, and within it the speech that *Ilḥu* is to deliver to Thitmanit, are concluded. *Ilḥu* is introduced afresh at the beginning of his ensuing actions (*apnk ǵzr ilḥu* 46). He takes up his spear (47-48), and comes to his destination at dusk (49-50). His sister has gone out (51) so he sets his spear aside (51-52). At the gate (52-53) his sister sees him, and her reaction is described in language drawn from the sterotypical "reaction to bad news" (53-55; see chapter 2 B). The preserved part of line 55 has her weeping, and this introduces a speech consisting of one bicolon, in which she mentions sickness and the king (56-57)—presumably enquiring whether the king is sick. *Ilḥu*'s reply is introduced in line 58. He too mentions sickness and the king (59-60)—either denying (according to most commentators) or confirming that Keret is sick—and then begins the message that Keret had directed him to convey to her, announcing that Keret was having a banquet (61-62; cf. 39-41). It will be consistent with the preceding interpretation to understand *Ilḥu* as here confirming Thitmanit's suspicions. She in any case knows he is sick twenty lines later, since she enquires of *Ilḥu* how long he has been afflicted (1.16.2.19-20). Having been sent to Thitmanit by Keret, presumably to engage her assistance in ministering to his condition, and having begun to repeat the message that Keret had given him, it seems unlikely that *Ilḥu* would then attempt to conceal his condition from her.

What is significantly new in this column (and the end of the preceding column) is *Ilḥu*'s proposal to go to Keret, and his speech to his father, in which he speaks of weeping for him, and raises the question of his mortality. Nevertheless, there appears to be clear continuity between this column and the last three columns of 1.15. Here, as there, the king gives instructions that include reference to a royal banquet and the person instructed speaks of weeping for the king. But whereas the queen played a crucial role in 1.15.4-6, conveying the invitation and addressing the guests, and whereas the invitation to the banquet appeared to be addressed to larger groups in the kingdom; here it is the hitherto unknown son *Ilḥu* who plays the messenger role, and the message about the banquet is addressed to another of Keret's offspring, namely one of his daughters. In other words, there is a shift from the larger public realm to the smaller sphere of the family.

Whether the rest of the message that *Ilḥu* was directed to convey to Thitmanit (41-45) is repeated in 1.16.2.1-4 cannot be finally determined from the odd letters preserved only at the beginnings of those lines—the amount of space is a little less than one would expect. The beginning of line 5 reads *pǵ[t* which suggests a third person reference to Thitmanit following the delivery of Keret's message to her. While individual words become increasingly distinguishable in the following lines, it is only with line 18 that syntax and versification become clear enough to allow continuous translation.

Thitmanit is evidently speaking, as questions are being posed to which her brother replies in 22ff. (in a speech introduced in 21). She asks, in the bicolon 19-20, for how many months Keret has been ill. (Obviously she has by now definitely had her suspicions of 1.16.1.56-57 confirmed—presumably in 1.16.1.59ff.) *Ilḥu* answers that Keret has been ill for three//four months (22-23). There follows a passage of considerable difficulty and decreasing completeness. Keret's "arrival" (*mǵ[y* 24), i.e. at the end of his days (?), is again mentioned (cf. 1.15.5.18-19). Lines 25-6 apparently mention a grave (*qbr*), though whether in the context of second person instructions to Thitmanit, later (34) fulfilled in the third person (as proposed by Caquot and Sznycer 1974, 557-58, n. f.), or in the first of two sets of instructions to her (Del Olmo Lete 1981, 267) is uncertain. The two passages both contain the words *tṣr trm*, but otherwise differ in form, and the second is preceded by a reference to *ǵzr ilḥu* (33). 27-28 contain the parallel constructions *km nkyt//km škllt*, but both nouns are *hapax legomena*. Where *Ilḥu*'s speech ends, and what, if anything, follows it prior to line 35 must remain moot. (A new speech by Thitmanit is introduced in line 30, where the text reads]*ʿny* [, and another by *Ilḥu* in line 33, where the prince is mentioned again, according to Del Olmo Lete 1981, 269; 314.)

In lines 35-36 the bicolon used in 1.16.1.13-15 to introduce *Ilḥu*'s speech to Keret is converted into feminine forms and applied to Thitmanit. There follows (1.16.2.36-49) the third version of the speech previously seen in the mind and then the mouth of *Ilḥu* (1.15.6. -1.16.1.11 and 1.16.1.14-23). This is close to a conflation of the other two, including all the material from the first version, and the last two lines of the second version (see chapter 2 D 1). In the present state of the surrounding text it is impossible to build on these differences claims about the particular relevance of this version to its present context.

The general assumption is that the following two lines: *bkm tʿrb*[ ]//*tʿrb ʿ[* *]* (50-51) refer to Thitmanit's entry into her father's presence (so already Ginsberg 1946; followed recently by Caquot and Sznycer 1974; Gibson 1978; Del Olmo Lete 1981), thus implying that the preceding utterance was a kind of rehearsal of her actual speech, comparable to that in which *Ilḥu* was engaged at the beginning of the tablet. But the introduction to the speech is identical with the introduction to *Ilḥu*'s delivery to Keret of the speech he had previously composed to himself, and lacks any hint of that peculiar introduction that is attested immediately before Yassub's soliloquy (1.16.6.26-29). Moreover, there is no evidence in the remains of the following lines that Thitmanit repeats her speech to her father, as do *Ilḥu* and Yassub immediately after their respective mental rehearsals. It seems likely, then, that the narrative was here compressed in comparison with those other two passages, and that this speech was delivered directly to Keret. Thitmanit would then have immediately "gone in" (50-51) somewhere else. Only the initial word of the next six lines is preserved. Apart from an individual letter there are then four lines missing from the bottom of the column and about another thirty from the beginning of the next.

Up to this pint it seems that Keret has been suffering from a mortal sickness since his failure to keep his vow to Asherah. At his direction, his wife has three times invited special groups to a banquet. On each occasion she made a speech, which, on at least the second occasion, had apparently referred to Keret's "arrival" at sunset, and probably to Yassub's rule in his stead. Next, one of his sons, *Ilḥu*, comes on his own initiative to the king, bewailing the mortality of this figure supposed to be the offspring of El. Keret bids him dry his tears and let his sister do the weeping. He is to go and inform Thitmanit of Keret's banquet, and tell her to go and sing on the heights with her timbrel. After a break she enquires how long Keret has been sick, and he tells her. After further difficulties in the text, we see Thitmanit deliver her own speech, similar to *Ilḥu*'s, to Keret.

One recurrent motif that seems to bind these various episodes together is that of weeping, mourning or grieving for the sick king. While nowhere else do we have such a lengthy exploration of social reactions to a royal sickness, perhaps the closest analogue is the visit of Job's friends to comfort and console the sick Job. They engaged in acts of mourning: weeping, tearing their clothes and throwing dust over their heads (Job 2:11-12). The purpose of this mourning before death is made clear in the story of David's mourning for his sick son in 2 Sam 12:15-23. After the child's death, David's servants asked why he fasted and wept while the child was alive, and then rose and ate a meal when the child died (v. 21). David replied that he fasted and wept while the child was alive because he thought that God might let the child live, but now that the child was dead no amount of fasting could bring him back. Mourning over the sick was doubtless designed to prevail upon the gods to spare the sufferer. So in *Krt* the weeping and lamentation probably serve the same purpose.

The proper response to Keret's plight lay first of all with his "bulls"//"gazelles" and the other guests of the initial banquet(s). In these first two columns of 1.16 that responsibility seems to shift to his daughter, Thitmanit. We are reminded of the responsibility assumed by Pughat on Danel's behalf in 1.19.4.

There are approximately forty lines between the last line of Thitmanit's speech and the first preserved words of column 3. On this column only seventeen lines are preserved, the first and last two of those only partially. These are without obvious connection with what has preceded (Caquot and Sznycer 1974, 490). Initially, oil is being poured (*yṣq šmn* 1.16.3.1). This one phrase leads many commentators to conceive of the whole passage as narrating the performance of a human rite of some sort (but a ceremony held in Baal's abode on Mt. Saphon, according to Gibson 1978, 22). Yet there are only two other uses of the phrase, neither of which supports this assumption. In the first Anat has just sated her lust for slaughter. In the following description of her washing the blood off herself comes the colon: *yṣq šmn šlm bṣ*ʿ "oil of peace was poured into/from a bowl" (1.3.2.31-32). The same colon recurs in the last lines of 1.101 (lines 14-18) as the first of several from 1.3.2-3. Here the preceding context is too damaged to make continuous sense. But it is clear from both texts that the subject is Anat's toilet, not a ritual offering (so, on 1.3.2.31-32, Caquot and Sznycer 1974). Again, since there are no prefixing verb forms in what follows (as in the rites enacted in 1.19, for example), the question must be raised whether in the rest of the column we have to do with narrative at all, and not rather with part of a speech. Then the question will be: what kind of speech? Since the last part of this passage is the least ambiguous, it will be discussed first.

Lines 12-16 consist of a bicolon and a tricolon. The former speaks of the plowmen lifting their heads heavenward, and the latter of the containers of bread//water//oil being exhausted. This is a description of the state of affairs when the agricultural produce has all been used up before new crops are ready to be harvested. Preceding this description is another bicolon and tricolon that speak of how good Baal's rain is for the earth//field (7-8)—good for the grain in the furrows (9-11). Since, following this statement, the plowmen are looking up, while their food supplies are exhausted, this must be not an appreciation of something now happening (as believed by Gibson 1978, 22), but a reminder of what is needed. The preceding bicolon (4-6) is identical to 7-8, except that *nʿm* "good" is replace by *ʿn* at the beginning. The meaning of this word is uncertain, but that it belongs with this bicolon is clear both from the parallel bicolon that follows and from the fact that the preceding words conclude a verse, as confirmed by their occurrence at the end of a verse in 1.5.6.5.

The initial boundary of the preceding verse (3-5) is also confirmed by its counterpart in 1.5.6.3. 1.5.6.3-5 is less well preserved than 1.16.3.3-4. Only the verb (*sbn[y*)—the first word—and the second prepositional phrase (*ʿd ksm mhyt*)—the last words—are complete, and the remains between suggest that the first, parallel, prepositional phrase may not have been identical with that in 1.16.3.3. However, the immediate context of 1.5.6.3-5 is much clearer than that in 1.16.3, so that it may give some slight assistance in the interpretation of the latter. 1.5.6 opens with formulaic language narrating the arrival of two messengers at El's residence and introducing their speech (1-3). They say that they have been around to the limits of the waters and arrived at a place where they came upon the dead Baal (3-10). In our text the first person dual of the suffixing tense is replaced by the form *sb*. The whole bicolon, here complete, is prefixed by another, parallel colon, referring to a tour (*tr*, parallel to *sb*) of heaven and earth, with which it forms a tricolon. If indeed this whole passage is a speech, then these two verbs may be imperatives—someone would be directed to go around heaven and earth (*arṣ wšmm*), even to the ends of the earth (*qṣm arṣ//ksm mhyt*). The speech would continue with the statement of the value of Baal's rain for the earth (4-11) and of the anxious searching of the sky by the agricultural laborers (12-13), whose supplies are exhausted (13-16). These statements would justify and motivate the command to mount the search. The purpose of the search would be to find, not the dead Baal, as announced by the divine messengers in 1.5.6, but at least the missing or absent Baal.

Such a search is mounted in the Hattic Telepinus myth (also told of the storm god). Telepinus' departure has the consequence that grain and spelt thrive no longer. The sun god sends a messenger to look for the missing fertility god: "Go! Search every high mountain!" "Search the deep valleys! Search the watery depth!" When this envoy is unsuccessful, another is sent to search "the streaming rivers . . . the murmuring springs." (The translations are taken from that of A. Goetze in Pritchard 1969a, 127.) The situation is similar to that portrayed in

1.16.3.14-16. The speeches are strikingly reminiscent of 1.16.3.2-4, and tend to confirm the interpretation of the verbs there as imperatives.

There is a similar speech in the Baal myth, following the dream by which El is assured that the buried Baal is in fact alive. El sends Anat with a message for Shapash, noting that the furrows of the fields (*ʿnt šdm*) were dried and cracked, and asking the question: "Where is Baal?" (1.6.4.1-4=12-16). In effect, his message is substantially the same as that of 1.16.3, namely: Go and find Baal since his rains are essential for the soil. Conversely, in 1.16.3 the speaker is saying substantially the same as 1.6.4, drawing attention to the barren condition of the fields and furrows and asking: where is Baal? The rhetoric employed in each case is different, but the situation and message are essentially the same.

Given the fact that both in the Baal cycle and in the Telepinus myth the speeches comparable to that in 1.16.3 are delivered among the gods (as well as the specific similarity of 1.16.3.3-4 and 1.5.6.3-5), and that the reference to the pouring of oil in 1.3.2.31 and 1.101.14 has a divine setting, it is likely that 1.16.3 also had a divine setting, rather than a human one. This links it more significantly with the divine scenes of cols. 4 and 5. What is its relationship to the preceding columns? Presumably, the imminent death of the king has deleterious effects on the natural world, and it is at this point that the gods take note, or at least action. The connection of the exhaustion of the products of nature and of Keret's state may have been spelled out in the sequel, of which we have only two words, the last two preserved on the column: *bt krt* "the palace of Keret." The following *t*[may be the first letter of a second person imperfect verb (Virolleaud: *t[bun*]), which would further confirm the interpretation of the preceding as a speech.

To conclude, 1.16.3 is best explained on the assumption that the king's sickness has repercussions in the natural sphere, as is generally granted. Rain ceases, the food supplies are exhausted and there is no promise of a new harvest. Court, royal family and now land are bearing the consequences of the mortal sickness of their monarch. Now, finally, the gods take note of the situation. One (El?) addresses the problem by giving directions to another or others to search to the ends of the earth. Whether the search was explicitly for Baal and his rain—in recognition of their connection with Keret's sickness—or for a specific means of healing Keret, cannot be determined. The urgency of the search is motivated by references to the goodness of Baal's rain alongside others to the exhaustion of past produce. The gods have now begun to search for a remedy for the plight of Keret and his kingdom.

Approximately thirty-four lines are missing between the las;t words of col. 3 and the first of col. 4. The first two words of 1.16.4.1 (*il šmʿ*) cannot be construed with certainty for lack of context, but it is most likely that the first word is a vocative and the second an imperative ("hear, god,"—so Del Olmo Lete 1981). That a deity is told to listen fits well with what follows: first, a bicolon in which the deity's wisdom is extolled (*amrk* [ ] *kil//ḥkmt kṯr lṭpn* "Your perception [like El's//(your) wisdom like that of the Kindly Bull" (1-2); second, a command to summon the god *Ilš* and his wife or wives (3-4). The next line, damaged and incomplete, probably also belongs to the speech. The preserved and understood part of this speech thus consists of a call to attention, compliment, and then commission. Since shortly it is El who addresses *Ilš* after his arrival (9), it is likely that it is also El who initially sends some deity to summon him. There is no clue as to whom he addresses and sends (so Caquot and Sznycer 1974, 490-91). (Some conclude from the phrase "wise as El" that it must be Baal, e.g. Gibson 1978, 22).

That unknown deity proceeds to summon *Ilš* and his wife or wives in the tricolon 6-8. *Ilš*'s fuller title here associates him with the palace of Baal. Line 9 introduces El's addresses to him with the usual formula. El's speech begins with the formulaic call to attention *šmʿl* PN "listen, so-and-so," which is here built into a tricolon by the repetition of the names and titles of *Ilš* and his wife or wives already used in 6-8.

The substance of El's address to *Ilš* follows. He is told to go to the top of some structure (the form of the bicolon 13-14 is clear, but the precise reference of the individual nouns is not). The next line (15) has not been satisfactorily explained and the next two lines (16-17) are only partially preserved. The clearest sense may be derived from the two words at the end of line 16: *gm ṣḥ* "cry aloud," which must begin a colon, since in every clear context *gm* occurs as the first word of a colon. Immediately preceding these is the phrase *lǵr* "to/from the mountain."

The problem with this passage is the opposite of that we have encountered in the preceding columns. There the text was often damaged or obscure and there was little use of general stereotypes or specific patterns, so that while we could discern the sense of particular phrases or bicola in isolation, we had great difficulty making continuous sense of many passages.

Here there is a rather well preserved passage using familiar structures (A tells B to summon C, B summons C, A addresses C) and a particular set of formulae attached to the name *Ilš*, so that we have a good grasp of the general situation and development; but there are no specific references to the larger purpose of this development or the particular content of the message toward which it is leading.

It may be significant that there have been several passing references to Ball through cols. 1-4 of 1.16: the *ǵr bʿl* "mountain of Baal" wept for Keret according to *Ilḥu*'s speech to him in col. 1 and Thitmanit's in col. 2; the goodness (and need) of Baal's rain for the earth was mentioned in the divine speech in col. 3; and the deity who is now in col. 4 summoned and commissioned to do something has a function in the palace of Baal. It is perhaps significant that this has to do with a mountain (*ǵr* 16). It may be that the weeping of Baal's mountain for Keret implies Baal's preoccupation with mourning and neglect of the rains, thus causing the situation which col. 3 regrets and seeks to address by finding Baal and bringing him back. The fact that a member of Baal's household is now called upon and that the message to him refers to Baal's mountain suggests that that previous attempt to recall Baal was unsuccessful, and that now a new attempt is being made by drawing on those closer to Baal himself. There is certainly no explicit reference in col. 4 to Keret or his plight. Yet, as here interpreted, there is continuity and progression between cols. 3 and 4. (Anticipating the scene of the next column, some think rather that the commission in 4 would have been a simple convocation of the gods, leading to their assembly in 5; but I would see a divine assembly already presupposed in the addresses of cols. 3 and 4.)

The missing remainder of col. 4 amounts to some twenty-seven lines. The damage to the upper right of col. 5 leaves only two letters preserved at the beginning of the first line, but the preserved portion of the following lines gradually increases until with line 21 we have a complete line. Only two to five letters appear at the beginnings of the first nine lines, which, since they suggest no precisely corresponding passage elsewhere, is minimal ground for restorations. However, some suggestions of De Moor and Spronk are worth notice. Their restoration, *ʿr[b* DN] "In came DN," in lines 1-3 fits the remains and the sequel (De Moor and Spronk 1982, 188), and suggests that the same verb might have originally accompanied the divine names in 1.15.1.2ff. Further, their assumption that *bdk* in line 7 indicates direct speech ("in your hand"), that the *y* at the beginning of the preceding line should then be understood as a vocative particle, and that the name of the goddess Asherah should be completed there (*yaṯr[t]* "Oh, Asherah) leads to an interesting and plausible proposal; namely that the two numerals in lies 8, 9 (*ṯnnth*[and *ṯlṯth*[ ) refer to the amount of silver//gold now being placed in Asherah's hand, to placate her wrath at her deprivation of what was her due (v. 1.14.4.42-43; 1.15.3.25-30). This would be necessary in order to clear the way for an uninterrupted healing of Keret (De Moor and Spronk 1982, 189). (If this surmise were correct, the commission in the preceding column may have had to do precisely with this settling of Asherah's account.)

Whatever the merits of the preceding, the pattern clearly discernible in the remains of lines 10-22 (see Chap. 2 D 5) allows a virtually certain complete restoration of those lines. El is addressing the assembled gods, asking: *my bilm ydy mrṣ//gršm zbln* "Who among the gods will dispel the sickness//drive away the illness?" (10-11, 14-15, 17-18, 20-21). At each repetition of the question, *in bilm ʿnyh* "none among the gods answers him" (12-13, 14, 19, 22). A unique numerical sequence of verbs in pairs, beginning with even numbers ("to repeat a second time, to repeat a third time," etc.), extends this one-sided exchange through seven unanswered repetitions of the same question. Finally, in line 23, a different speech by El is introduced. He bids the gods be seated (24-25), and announces that he himself will work magic (*iḥtrš*) and *aškn ydt mrṣ//gršt zbln* "produce a creature (female) who will dispel the sickness// drive away the illness" (27-28). The repetition of the verb and direct object from the preceding refrain heightens the contrast between the gods' inadequacy and El's ability to create a deity who can do what they cannot.

This is a variation of a widespread traditional episode in ancient Near Eastern literature—the meeting of the divine council, in which the high god appeals for a volunteer to undertake a mission (Müller 1963). Typically the high god says: "Who will do X?" Some member of the council volunteers: "I will do X." The high god then commissions him: "Do X." A familiar example is found in 1 Kgs 22: 19b-22. Yahweh is seen sitting on his throne, and all the forces of heaven are standing around him. Yahweh calls for a volunteer: *my ypth ʾt-ʾḥʾb* "Who will deceive Ahab?" One member of the assembly comes forward and says: *ʾny ʾptnw* "I will deceive him." Yahweh concludes: *tpth* "You will deceive (him)" (cf. Isa 6:8-9). A common motif in this traditional scene is the confusion or helplessness of the assembly prior to the appearance of the volunteer. Thus in 1 Kgs 22 the immediate sequel to Yahweh's challenge is that "one said one thing and one said another" (v. 20b)—only after this does the successful volunteer come forward. Usually this motif is used to heighten the prestige of the volunteer by setting his act against the general inadequacy of all the others in the assembly. Thus the seven silences following the seven repetitions of the question in *Krt* clearly serve to expose the total inadequacy of the assembled gods (rather than their fear of the mother of the gods, Athirat, as the one responsible for Keret's sickness, as proposed by Del Olmo Lete 1981, 270.) But this is contrasted not with the role of a volunteer from the assembly, but with that assumed by El: El himself proposes to make a creature to perform the task—and does so.

The Assyrian version of the Zu myth has a comparable conclusion. Here the high god, Anu, has asked: "Who will slay Zu?" Different gods are called and commissioned by Anu, but each in turn declines. Finally, Anu announces: "I will find a god" who will be "the vanquisher of Zu" (Tablet I, 106-107; for the translation of the whole see Pritchard 1969a, 112-13 and 514-15).

Ginsberg has argued from the participles in El's announcement of 1.16.5.27-28 that the verb-forms in El's previous questions must also be participles. He would then translate the questions: "Who among the gods is an ejector of sickness, and expeller of disease?" (Ginsberg 1973, 133). Against this must be placed the consistency with which the prefixing conjugation is used in the initial question of the other examples of this traditional episode; and the evidence of the Zu myth in particular, which also uses the prefixing verb-form in the question, but then, after showing the inadequacy of each of the volunteers, concludes, like *Krt*, with the first person form of the prefixing tense of a different verb—with which the high god announces that he will produce for himself someone to perform the desired task.

The state of the text now rapidly deteriorates, but it is clear that El immediately pinches (*yqrṣ*) clay (*rṯ*) (29)—suggesting a model used also in a common description of the making of humankind (see, e.g., Job 33:6; *Babylonian Theodicy* 277; and, for an Egyptian portrayal of a divine potter making a king: Pritchard 1969b, no. 569). Closer analogies to the present act of El, however, are those stories which portray the creation of a special being for some particular purpose, as Aruru's forming of Enkidu, at Anu's command, as a match for Gilgamesh (*Epic of Gilgamesh* I ii 29-35); and especially Enki's creation from the soil in his fingernail of the *kurgarra* and *kalaturra* (*Inanna's De-*

scent 219ff.), whom Enki commissions to revive the dead Inanna (244-45), and who then successfully carry out the commission (270ff.). Enki's address to his new creatures is introduced, but only the end is adequately preserved. (Abusch *apud* Ginsberg 1973, 133, n. 15 refers only to the later Akkadian version of this Mesopotamian myth, *Ishtar's Descent*, which lacks any reference to the manner of creation of the creature who is to revive Ishtar.)

Following line 30 there are two lines in which only the final letters are preserved, four lines in which not even a single letter can be clearly reconstructed, and then sixteen lines in which the first one to four letters are preserved. Following this, approximately eight lines are missing altogether before the beginning of the next column, which is almost completely preserved.

5.41 begins *at š*[, which has been restored appropriately *at š[ˁtqt* "You, Sh[aˁtiqat . . ." This would represent the beginning of a commission or proclamation of the destiny of the newly created creation, comparable with that with which Enki addresses the *kurgarra* and *kalaturra* in *Inanna's Descent* (see above). We may also compare 1.2.4.11-12 (and 19), in which Kothar proclaims the name and destiny of the two clubs he has created.

wypˁr šmthm	Then he proclaimed their names:
šmk at ygrš	"Your name is Let-him-expel!
ygrš grš ym	Let-him-expel, expel Yamm!"

If De Moor is correct in interpreting the first word of the next line as the causative stem of √*ˁdy* (De Moor 1979, 646, n. 43), we should perhaps restore in 1.16.5.40-43:

šmk] at š[ˁtqt	"Your name is Moved!
šˁtqt] šˁd[mrṣ	Moved, remove the sickness!"

This would however produce less satisfactory word-play than that which justifies the names in 1.2.4.

The beginnings of the two preceding lines read: *ks* . . . //*kr[pn]*, which have now generally been restored on the basis of 1.15.2.16-18 (cf. 1.17.1.34): *ks[yiḫd il byd[//kr[pn bm ymn*] "El took a cup in his hand//a goblet in his right hand." This gesture, used as El prepares to bless Keret (and Danel), would here replace the introduction to the proclamation of the name that is used in 1.2.4. The letters required for both the above restorations fit perfectly in the number of spaces estimated by Herdner.

It is in any case virtually certain that by line 40 El has completed his creation of the healing agent, and that in line 42 he has begun a speech addressed to the new creation. There is nothing in the remaining lines to suggest that his speech ends before the beginning of the next column. On the contrary there are two clear indications that El continues to address Shaʿtiqat. *di* at the beginning of line 49 is most likely a feminine singular imperative, corresponding to the third person feminine singular of the prefixing conjugation in 1.16.6.6, 7 [*tdu*]. *li* in the second line of col. 6 is also a feminine singular imperative, corresponding to the third person feminine singular of the suffixing conjugation in 1.16.6.14 (supposing a dittography of the two wedges of *a* in *lan* [a nominal form], and correcting this to read *lat*). In fact, 6.1-2 correspond as instructions to 6.13-14 as the execution of the instructions (see Chap. 2 C 1 a). Immediately following *li* in 1.16.6.2 the text shifts to third person feminine singular forms of the prefixing conjugation. Up to this point El has been addressing Shaʿtiqat. Now she is acting on El's commission. We might expect this to correspond to the last part of the last column in the relation of execution to instructions. in fact, if we assume that 6.2-14 was the execution of instructions concluding in 6.1-2, we can restore everything preceding that last bicolon in the three lines following *zb[ln* in 5.51 and the eight missing lines at the end of 5.

But this leaves some eight lines following the address to Shaʿtiqat in 5.42 without any counterpart in the execution of the instructions—even though there is at least one imperative (*di*) in those eight lines. Indeed, there are further correspondences between those eight lines and the execution of the instructions. There is a possible reference to the plant (?) *ṭr* of 5.44 in 6.8 (according to Herdner, not acknowledged by *KTU*); a reference to the towns and the verb *d'* of 5.46-48 in 6. 6-7; to the sickness (*zb[ln*) of 5.50 (but not to the *mr[ṣ* of 49) in 6.9. Clearly, these correspondences do not occur in the same order in the two passages. Moreover, some of the remains in 5.43-50 have no corresponding groups of letters in 6.2-12 (e.g. those in 5.45, 46, 49).

What are we to conclude from this? First, El's speech was far longer than the account of Shaʿtiqat's enactment of her destiny. Perhaps the early part of the speech concerned her general character and role, and only in its latter half did El give her specific directions for dealing with Keret. This would account for some of the same vocabulary being used in both sections of the speech. Alternatively, we would have to assume that the poets drastically abbreviated and rearranged the instructions in recounting Shaʿtiqat's execution of them.

The last bicolon of El's speech (6.1-2) bids Mot, Death, be crushed, Shaʿtiqat be victorious. The following bicolon (2-3) has

Sha'tiqat leaving for Keret's house, which she enters as a mourner (4-5). Of the next bicolon (6-7), clearly referring to towns//villages, it is otherwise difficult to make good sense. (By reading *mt*! for *mh* Del Olmo Lete is able to translate: "Drive Mot from the city//The Enemy from the town".) The following line is even more uncertain, but a verb is presupposed by the next colon (9): *zbln 'l rišh* "the sickness from (upon) his head." Sha'tiqat proceeds to wash Keret's sweat from him (10), and to restore his appetite (11-12). With this Mot is indeed crushed, (the same verb is used of the fate of a defeated god in Jer 50:2) and Sha'tiqat victorious (13-14). Her destiny is fulfilled, and that is the last we hear of her.

Keret immediately orders his wife to prepare food for him. His speech is introduced in the unique colon 14-15 and the formulaic 15-16. It occupies 16-18, and consists of the standard call to attention (*šm'* + personal reference) and a unique bicolon calling for the slaughter of animals that he might eat. Lines 19-21 note precisely her execution of the instructions and his realization of his desire: she obeys and slaughters, he eats. This third reference to eating (by use of the traditional pair √*lḥm*//*ṯrm*) in eleven lines of text places considerable weight on this sign of restoration to health.

A numerical sequence is now introduced (21-22), with a tricolon (22-24) in which Keret sits once again on his throne—the characterization of his royal seat in the second two cola is well-known from a formulaic bicolon in *B'l*. The numerical sequence is not pursued, so that Keret's resumption of his throne is marked by this single statement.

We know that this segment of the poem opened with Asherah's recollection of Keret's unfulfilled vow to her (1.15.3.25-26). It must have continued immediately with notice of her punishment of him with a mortal sickness and his consequent abandonment of his royal throne and duties (in the twelve lines missing between what is preserved of 1.15.3 and 4), since it was already Hurraya, not Keret, who was presiding at the banquet of 1.15.4. Those missing verses would then be balanced by these final reports of his return both to personal health and also to his royal position. His restoration to the condition and status that he enjoyed before Asherah's punishment marks the end of the second major segment of narrative (*Krt* B) in the larger poem. (Del Olmo Lete takes 1.16.6.21-24 to be the opening of the next segment of narrative, claiming that the numerical clause is typical of transitions in the narrative—1981, 272.) The brief notices of Keret's recovery of his appetite and resumption of his throne following Sha'tiqat's visit and ministrations at the end of this narrative echo the brief references to the conception and birth of Keret's sons and daughters following El's visit and blessing at the end of the first narrative (1.15.3.20-24).

Krt B thus begins with Keret's being struck with mortal sickness, proceeds to explore the various effects of this and the various attempts in different spheres to cure it, and concludes with El's creation and commission of a creature who does effect a cure, restoring his appetite to Keret, and Keret to his throne. This is a literary exploration of a situation to which we have a historical counterpart in the sickness of the Hittite king, Hattusili III, as seen through the prayers and vows of his wife, Queen Puduhepa (cf. Chap. 3 C).

As a literary work, the preserved material in this second major narrative segment appears to fall into three parts with an introduction and conclusion:

Introduction: Asherah strikes Keret with sickness (1.15.3. 25-);

1) the response to Keret's sickness in the court (1.15.IV-VI; actors: Keret, Hurraya, the nobles [and other groups? e.g. *rpum* "dead rulers"?]);

2) the response in the family (1.16.I-II; actors: Keret, *Ilḥu*, Thitmanit);

3) the response in the pantheon (1.16.III-VI.14; actors: El and ? Baal? Asherah? Sha'tiqat);

Conclusion: Keret's restoration by El (1.16.VI.14-24).

There is one text which on a miniature scale discloses a similar overall structure to that of *Krt* B, and that is the table of Job's sickness (Job 2; 42:7-10):

Introduction: a member of the heavenly council strikes Job with sickness (2:7);

1) The response of Job's wife to his sickness (9-10);

2) The response of his peers (11-13);

3) The response of God (42:7-10);

Conclusion: Job's restoration (42:10)

The traditional character of the basic material underlying both texts is suggested by this common structure. The differences between the two literary products discloses their different present character and purposes. In Job the bare outline of the story is presented, with Job's wife serving as a foil to Job's quietistic piety in chapter two, and the friends as a foil to Job's existential honesty in chapter forty-two, both parts of the story now separated by and serving the interests of the great poem of 3-42:6. By contrast, *Krt* B, in part through the use of conventional scenes and episodes such as the banquet scene and the divine council, and in part through the use of epic repetition, expands extensively on the relationships and actions in each part of the story. Unfortunately the damaged state of the text leaves the particular purposes of much of the elaboration rather obscure.

It is clear from 1.16.5-6 that the restoration of Keret is the final goal of the narrative, but it is not clear that everything before that tends directly toward the same end. Some recent commentators have suggested other interests. One question that arises here is whether there was also a move to make some adjustment in the succession, as may be suggested by the reference to Yassub in 1.15.5.21 (so Del Olmo Lete 1981, 264). The preserved text gives no further support to that suggestion.

A second question concerns the necessity for appeasing Asherah, the author of the sickness. As noted above, Del Olmo Lete has suggested that the gold mentioned at the end of Keret's speech to *Ilḥu* (1.16.1.45) might be intended for Asherah; and De Moor and Spronk have proposed to restore the name of Asherah as the addressee in 1.16.5.6, to whom (*bdk* line 6) gold and silver would then be given in the proportions promised by Keret in 1.14.4.42-43 (*ṯnnth*//*ṯlṯth* 1.16.5.8-9). Even if neither of these suggestions could be sustained, the question remains whether the narrative would have required some conciliatory move toward Asherah by or on behalf of Keret.

The answer to this question must be that no such move was necessary. When Enlil ordered various plagues in *Atra-hasis*, Enki, Atra-hasis and the god of the particular plague were able to stop the plague without any reference to Enlil. Further, if Asherah were directly appeased, one might expect that she would herself withdraw the punishment—there would be no need to continue the search for a cure for Keret. In view of these general considerations, as well as the testimony of that part of the text that has been well preserved, it seems best to conclude that the appeasement of Asherah was not a necessary part of *Krt* B.

A third question is posed by the remains of 1.16.3. Granting that this passage presupposes that Keret's mortal sickness implicates Baal and his rains, the vegetation and the food supplies; why does the search for a solution now shift from Keret's sickness to the problem of the infertility of the fields and to Baal as the one able to remedy that situation? It seems likely that the gods in *Krt* notice first the crisis in the food supply, and so direct their attention to Baal as the one who can address that problem, as, similarly, on the human plane, Danel and his daughter first addressed the immediately visible problem of the infertility of the fields, and only later learned about and addressed directly the problem of Aqhat's murder.

It is striking that, as in the book of Job the story of Job's sickness and recovery is combined with the story of the loss and recovery of Job's family, so in *Krt* the narrative focusing on Keret's sickness and restoration is combined with that treating of his loss and recovery of family. But whereas in Job the former story is inserted into the latter (and both then split by the great poem that forms the bulk of the present book), in *Krt* the sickness story is appended to the family story, and rooted in the latter by the insertion into 1.14.4.32-45 of the episode in which Keret makes a vow to Asherah—the non-fulfillment of which at the end of the family story justifies Asherah's striking him with sickness.

C. Keret's Repression of Rebellion

Immediately after Keret's resumption of his throne, the narrative shifts to a new subject. Yassub is abruptly introduced (*ap yṣb . . .*), sitting in the palace taking counsel with himself (1.16.6.25-6). Yassub's speech to himself (lines 27-38) begins with a tricolon (27-29), in which he tells himself to go to his father and say—and within Yassub's speech to himself there now comes the speech with which he proposes to address his father (29-38). An opening appeal for his father's ear (29) leads into an indictment of his father's behavior, including references to his misrule (30-32) and his failure to give justice to the widow and the despairing (33-34). (Or possibly the reference to his misrule is balanced by an appeal to give justice to the widow and the despairing—cf. below.) There follows a reference to Keret's being tied to his sickbed (35-36), and finally an appeal to him to step down from his rule in Yassub's favor (37-38).

Yassub now executes his instructions to himself. The poets do not repeat the language of the directions in lines 27-29, but fall back on a cluster of more general formulae to report Yassub's approach to his father and to introduce his speech to him (39-41). The actual speech with which he addresses his father (41-54) also exhibits some variations from that which he had rehearsed to himself. The opening appeal for his father's ear is preceded by a version of the more familiar call to attention (41-42—*šmʿ mʿ lkrt ṯʿ* "Hear, now, Keret the Noble"). The charge that Keret has failed to (or the appeal to Keret to) give justice to the widow and the despairing is extended by three cola which speak of his driving away those who exploit the poor and feeding the orphan//widow around him. This extension produces a chiastic structure of five parallel cola, of which the first two and the last two each form a more fully parallel bicolon, and in which the first and the last both concern the treatment of the *almnt* "widow" (cf. Greenfield 1969, 65, n. 51).

We have here a second (the first complete) example of that peculiar kind of instruction and execution in which an individual instructs and obeys himself. The main part of this device is the speech which appears first in the individual's proposal to himself, and then is repeated in its actual delivery to the intended audience. As in the first example in 1.15.6. -1.16.1.23, so here there is some variation in the two forms of the speech. In this case the first version is shorter, moving us more rapidly to the actual confrontation, in which Yassub's appeal for a hearing is slightly fuller and more formal, and his indictment more extended and thus more insistent.

As observed above, this introduces into the action a character who has not appeared before. It also moves the plot in a new direction. Keret is now under attack, being charged with incompetence and neglect, and threatened with displacement. As *Krt* A introduced Keret's loss of family and *Krt* B his loss of health, this new section also introduces a new threat: loss of throne. The one curious think about Yassub's speech is that, whereas *Krt* B had concluded with the cure of Keret's sickness and his return to full health and to business as usual, Yassub now still refers to his being tied to his sickbed. While this well explains Keret's neglect of his duties, it seems to be out of place in the progression of the plot. It may, of course, be explained by hypothetical factors that are not made explicit by the composers: Yassub may have been ignorant of recent developments by reason of his isolation or preoccupation with something else; or he may have assumed earlier that Keret would probably die, making his intervention unnecessary, so that now, faced with Keret's cure, he has to act fast and build as good a case as he can. But such hypotheses are outside the scope and interest of the narrators, who are silent on the question.

The reference to Keret's sickness also interrupts the progression and detracts from the integrity of Yassub's speech. It is the preceding indictment that justifies and leads into the final bicolon: the call for Keret to step down and let Yassub take over. As we shall see, the direct connection of indictment and displacement is found elsewhere. But further, Yassub's call for Keret's abdication seems to assume that he is in fact exercising his office on his throne—he is to leave his royal office (*mlk*), to "come down" (*rd*) so that Yassub may "sit" there (*aṯb an*). This assumption is not compatible with a claim that he is sick in bed.

The best explanation for Yassub's present action and his reference to Keret's sickness is that this is the beginning of a new story, which the narrators have linked to the preceding one by the reference to the sickness which was the subject of that preceding story. Apart from the names of Keret and Yassub, this one bicolon provides the sole link between this new story (so far as we have it) and the preceding one. The poets thus smooth over the join between lines 25 and 26 by soon referring back to the antecedent narrative—but without developing such a connection. The audience is invited, not to dwell on the reasons for the timing of Yassub's move, but rather to follow this new development with the general feeling that it grows out of what had been told previously.

Gibson has suggested, on the basis of this section of *Krt*, that 1 Kgs 15:5 might reflect Jotham's deposition of his sick father, Azariah (Gibson 1977, 23, n.2). Del Olmo Lete echoes this suggestion, and also thinks that, once David's impotence becomes known, the pretenders to the throne in 1 Kgs 1 makes essentially the same claims as Yassub (Del Olmo Lete 1981, 273). But Jotham's assumption of responsibilities for the royal household and for the more general government of the people seems to be an appropriate accommodation to his father's incapacity. In the more complicated story of the succession to David, Adonijah is certainly portrayed as a rebel, pursuing a strategy not unlike that of Absalom, but building on a base that David had accepted for years (1 Kgs 1:5-6). The aging and presumably incapacitated David responded by having Solomon proclaimed king (1 Kgs 1:30, 34-35). Whether or not this is to be interpreted as a coregency (see Jones 1984: 32-33), David's cooperation in the move—not to say his sponsorship of it—is patent. I should therefore prefer to say, on the basis of these two passages in Kings, that the reference to Keret's sickness in Yassub's speech alludes to circumstances in which there may be a normal, agreeable and understandable displacement of father by son—and that, since at this point those circumstances no longer obtain, the proposed displacement is not normal, and the allusion can only reveal the poets' development of the story, and possibly, in consequence, Yassub's bad timing.

The new story begins by narrating a bid by the heir to the throne to supplant his father. This has invited comparison with the account of Absalom's rebellion in 2 Sam 15. Specifically, Absalom appeals to those with a suit (*ryb*), coming to the king (*mlk*) for justice (*mšpṭ*). He tells them their case is a good and sound one, but that the king will take no notice of them. On the other hand, if they made Absalom √*šôpēṭ* "ruler-judge" in the land, he would deliver justice to them (2 Sam 15:2-4). In both *Krt* and 2 Samuel the son's charge of incompetent rule by the father—defined specifically in terms of neglect in the administration of justice—leads to the proposal that the son assume that responsibility in his father's place. Certainly, the poetic and narrative strategies in each work are quite different. In the one case the son speaks to those who may be most easily convinced, telling them that the king does not attend to his judicial duties, and suggesting to them that they would be better off if he held his father's office. In the other case the son addresses his father directly, charging him with neglecting his judicial duties, and calling on him to step down in the son's favor. In the first case the son's plan is revealed to the readers only as he prepares the ground for his public acclamation. In the case of *Krt* the audience is fully informed of the son's plan, even as he conceives it in his speech to himself; and the larger political environment is completely ignored as the son confronts the king directly with his accusation and proposal. Absalom not only avoids confrontation with the king, but deliberately conceals his plans from him, even hoodwinking the king into facilitating one stage of his strategy (2 Sam 15:7-9). In the one case we see the son calling directly on his father to abdicate in his favor; in the other case we see the son building a political base from which to supplant the king.

For all these differences, the two narratives share an essential link: between the son's charge that the king has not fulfilled his role as administrator of justice, and his proposal that he should replace his father. In both texts, the proposal is justified by the charge.

The same connection has shaped the mythic drama of Psalm 82. Here the forum is the divine assembly (v. 1). God (the God of Israel) addresses the ruling gods:

ʿd-mty tšpṭw-ʿwl	*wpny ršʿym tśʾw(-slh)*
špṭw-dl wytwm	*ʿny wrš hṣdyqw*
plṭw-dl wʾbywn	*myd ršʿym hṣylw*

"How long will you judge unjustly,
and favor wrongdoers?
Give justice to the weak and the orphan,
vindicate the oppressed and the poor,
Rescue the weak and the needy,
save (them) from the power of wrongdoers!"
Ps 82:2-4

Since the gods do not respond, but continue in their ways, thus threatening the stability of the universe (v. 5), God speaks again: "Though you are gods . . . yet . . . you will fall like any ordinary ruler" (vv. 6-7). To which the worshipping community responds: "Arise, God, give justice to the earth//for you claim an inheritance among all the nations" (v. 8).

God is here portrayed as accusing the gods of unjust administration of the world—by rhetorical questions and calls to administer justly. The confirmation of their continued abuse of their office leads God then to announce their downfall (like any human ruler). The audience responds by calling upon God to assume the judicial office in the place of those who had abused it.

Different as it is in literary genre, the psalm brings us in many ways closer to *Krt* than the account of Absalom's conspiracy. God, like Yassub, confronts the present ruler(s) directly. The first part of Yassub's speech may, like God's, consist of rhetorical questions (so Del Olmo Lete 1981), followed by appeals. The announcement that the gods will "fall" and the call upon God to "rise" corresponds to Yassub's appeal to Keret to "come down" so that he may go up and sit on Keret's throne.

While the literary character of the psalm and its mythological setting make for a very different form of presentation, the connection we have observed in *Krt* and 2 Sam 15 is present here also. The charge that the present rulers have not fulfilled their judicial responsibilities leads directly into the consequence: the expectation that they will be replaced by the one who brought the charge. This constant element in the three otherwise very different texts suggests that we may have to do with a literary motif, based on the ideal of the just king. Any bid to depose or replace the king must be based on the claim that he has neglected and/or abused his judicial powers. It may be noted at this point that there is nothing in Ps 82 or 2 Sam 15 analogous to the references to Keret's sickness in Yassub's two speeches, which tends to confirm the claim that those references are inserted into the speeches purely to provide a connection with the preceding story.

We know the outcome of the events described in 2 Sam 15 and Ps 82. David fled in fear before Absalom's rebellion, and Yahweh became ruler of the entire world. From the remaining lines of *Krt* we learn only what Keret's immediate reaction was. That reaction is expressed in a speech, introduced in 1.16.6.54 and extending from line 54 to the end of the tablet (58). We know nothing of the consequences of his reaction, or of any further complications or attempted resolutions of this latest threat to Keret's wellbeing. We do not even know whether this initial speech of Keret ended at line 58 or continued on the next tablet.

The speech consists of a tricolon (54-57) and a bicolon (57-58). The tricolon is a curse calling upon Horan//Athtart-Name-of-Baal to smash Yassub's head. (Smashing skulls is what is done to bad people generally, perhaps by the sun-god, according to the proemium of the Hurrian tale of *Appu* [Vs. I 4-6; v. Siegolová 1971, 28].) The bicolon is more difficult and its construction and meaning disputed. It seems fairly certain that it is a wish for Yassub's fall, *tqln* of 1.16.6.57 corresponding to *tpln* in 1.2.1.9. Indeed the same curse, with an additional colon between the tricolon and bicolon of *Krt*, seems to be addressed to Yamm in 1.2.1.7-9. Unfortunately the fragmentary state of 1.2.1 and the disputed order of the preceding damaged columns forbids a more precise comparison of the larger narrative.

The ninth-century inscription of Kilamuwa, from Zinjirli, some 100 miles north-northwest of Ugarit, may be fruitfully compared with this last section of *Krt*. In the second half of this inscription Kilamuwa boasts of having been a father, mother or brother to different groups of his subjects (11. 10-11). He claims to have vastly increased the fortunes of the poorest in his land, making those who had never seen a sheep owners of flocks, and those who had never seen an ox owners of cattle and silver and gold, so that his people were as devoted to him as a fatherless child to its mother (11. 11-13). He then anticipates the possibility that one of his sons ruling after him (*'š yšb tḥtn*), might damage his inscription (and hence his record before the gods) (13-14). He utters a curse (of civil unrest) on such a son, and adds another curse on anyone who might smash the inscription: "May DN smash his head!" The curse is repeated twice, each time with a different divine name associated with a different predecessor, with a third divine name added, identified as *b'l bt* "Lord of the (present) dynasty" (15-16).

This text is obviously spoken by the king in the first person. He claims to have helped the poor and disadvantaged, anticipates a possible post-mortem challenge to this record from one of his sons (or descendants), and pronounces a curse ("May DN smash his head!") on any such challenger. Although *Krt* narrates in the third person such a challenge during the king's lifetime, the challenge takes the form precisely of a charge that Keret has not helped the poor and disadvantaged. In response, Keret pronounces a curse on the upstart ("May DN smash your head!"). In both texts the king's record of justice toward the care for the powerless is at issue, a challenge to the king's record by one of his offspring is envisaged, and a virtually identical curse on a challenger is pronounced. If to us Kilamuwa's predicament seems to be of a totally different order from Keret's, the commonalities between the two texts illustrate the reality for these people of the continuity of life and status beyond death, and the importance for one's position in the afterlife of maintaining a permanent record before the gods and those who have the responsibility for the care/cult of the dead. The circumstances anticipated and portrayed respectively in these two very different literary genres doubtless reflect a recurrent preoccupation in the courts of the city-states of the East Mediterranean littoral—a preoccupation that would have found expression in more royal inscriptions and court tales than have been preserved.

To conclude: this third major section of the larger *Krt*—*Krt* C—introduces a third threat to the wellbeing of the king. Following his loss of family and lack of an heir, he has faced mortal sickness, and now faces usurpation by his son. While the inscription of Kilamuwa ends with the curse—as is customary in such inscriptions—I shall argue that Keret's curse of Yassub is only his first, immediate reaction to the young man's challenge, and that the narrators would have gone on to develop a third story, whose course we unfortunately cannot follow.

D. The Interpretation of *Krt*

No other material belonging to the story of Keret has been found among the other Ugaritic texts published to date, or elsewhere; and, to my knowledge, no other text has been reasonably claimed as belonging to *Krt*. (The one claim made for 1.101 has been aptly dismissed; see Del Olmo Lete 1981, 242.) However, as mentioned above, there is some disagreement as to whether the poem ended with Keret's curse on Yassub, or whether it continued beyond 1.16.6 on another tablet.

Most commentators favor the latter alternative (see Del Olmo Lete 1981, 243, n.14). Gray allows for either possibility (Gray 1964, 9-10; 1965, 17-18), but Merrill sees the work as completed in the present three tablets. With Keret's curse of Yassub "the stability of the house of Keret is established as the final point" (Merrill 1968, 17). Merrill designates this a pessimistic conclusion that is more realistic than a happy ending (Merrill 1968, 11). Allowing for the lacunae in the three tablets that we have, Gibson follows Merrill in judging that the story "forms a satisfactory thematic whole" (Gibson 1977, 20). Most recently Del Olmo Lete has argued for the integrity of the present three tablets. Admitting that to our taste the ending of 1.16.6 is extraordinarily abrupt and leaves much unsaid, Del Olmo Lete argues that such is characteristic of primitive epic style. Keret's curse of his son is, as a magic formula, understood to be immediately operative. The present crisis is thus resolved, and the authors see no need to go beyond the immediate situation to describe how the king "lived happily ever after" (Del Olmo Lete, 1981, 273; cf. 62). But, by the same token, one could argue that Asherah's resolve to punish Keret for his failure to honor his vow in 1.15.3.25- would have been equally efficacious, and that the poets might equally well have concluded the poem with her speech, without spelling out how Keret's punishment affected his family, kingdom and land, or how it was brought to an end. In fact, not infrequently in Ancient Near Eastern literature a divine word of condemnation—certainly regarded as no less efficacious than a curse—served as the starting point of a story, witness especially the Egyptian tale of *The Doomed Prince* (Lichtheim 1976, 200-203; Simpson 1973, 85-91), but also the story of Saul's displacement by David, starting with his rejection by Samuel (1 Sam 15:23, 26, 28), and, on a smaller scale, many of the prophetic legends in the Hebrew Bible. A more immediate objection to Del Olmo Lete's argument is that the curse in 1.2.1.7-9—virtually identical with that at the end of 1.16.6—by no means concludes the story of the relations between Yamm and Baal. That story continues at a characteristic pace, and concludes not with the literal fulfillment of the curse, but rather with Baal's defeat of Yamm with the aid of Kothar (1.2.4).

It is characteristic of *Krt* that each of the first two crises—the loss of Keret's family, and the onset of his sickness—is addressed in a long, slow-moving development extending over more than eight columns in each case. One expects that the third crisis which has just been introduced—the threat of usurpation—would not be disposed of in a mere thirty-four lines. Of course, if this episode were in fact a part of the treatment of Keret's sickness (Yassub basing his claim on Keret's *inability* to rule), it would be reasonable to think of it as an ill-timed bid to take advantage of Keret's debility—a bid easily quashed by the newly restored monarch. In that case, it would be a kind of appendix to the story. It would also raise the question why the composers on the one hand added this exhibition of the folly and destruction of the divinely suckled heir to the throne (cf. 1.15.2.25-), and on the other hand left undeveloped the last line of the marriage blessing in which there appears to be a promise of the irregular assumption of the rights of the first-born by the youngest of Keret's daughters (1.15.3.16).

It seems altogether more satisfactory to recognize the completion at 1.16.6.24 of the second major story about Keret, and to see in the remaining lines of the tablet the beginning of a third story, bound to the preceding material by the reference in Yassub's speech to Keret's sickness. While Keret may be thought to be securely fixed on his throne as he pronounces his curse on Yassub, the question of his heir—and thus of the future of the dynasty—has been thrown wide open. The last line of the marriage blessing, the tantalizing hints of the partially preserved lines 1.15.5.20ff., and this latest challenge to Keret and his maledictory response all cry out for development and resolution. It is reasonable to suppose that the last line of the marriage blessing (which, in the mouth of a god, is really a promise) and Keret's curse on Yassub were both fulfilled—that is, that in the unfolding of this third story on a fourth tablet we would see the demise of Yassub and the ultimate succession of Keret's youngest daughter to the throne. A rough analog to such a narrative might be the biblical story of the fulfillment of the divine pronouncement to Isaac (Gen 25:23) and of Isaac's blessings on his two sons (Gen 26:27-29 and 39-40); or that of the fulfillment of Samuel's oracle, that God was removing the monarchy from Saul (1 Sam 15)—actually from Saul's descendants—and giving it to the youngest son of Jesse (1 Sam 16).

Interpretations of *Krt* have generally fallen into one of two broad categories: mythico-cultic or historico-political (for summaries of earlier interpretations see Herdner in Caquot and Sznycer 1974, 492-98; Caquot 1979). The priority of the question of its literary character was emphasized and pursued by Bernhardt (1955/56), later resumed in different ways by Merrill (1968), Liverani (1970) and Parker (1977). On the basis of the preceding literary analysis and comparisons, I now offer my interpretation of the poem in terms of its (diachronic) formation and its (present, synchronic) structure.

I would see the origin of the poem in a story about a king who undertook a campaign against another king to claim that king's daughter as his bride. Negotiations between the kings resulted in the ceding of the woman in question, and hence in the marriage of the two and the birth of children (for the fundamental structure of this story, cf. Gen 24, Ruth).

It is this much that forms the most solid basis for those who claim that the poem reflects historical events. Thus Gibson: ". . . that Keret and Pabil . . . were actual historical figures, the story of whose clash in war and subsequent alliance became in time the basis of a myth about the nature and value of kingship, is difficult to deny" (Gibson 1977, 23). While a historical basis for such a story is certainly a possibility, it is equally possible that the story was even initially a fictional exploration, in the royal sphere, of a man's dependence on the deity in the delicate and momentous business of getting a wife who will produce good offspring.

The historicity of the larger poem as we now have it was appropriately discounted by Bernhardt, who pointed out the prevalence of the typical, the formulaic and the stereotyped, and the lack of any specific, concrete events or internal chronology (Bernhardt 1955/56, 116-7, 120; similarly Merrill 1968, 6-7). Wyatt, while only toying with the possibility of the historicity of the story, does commit himself to claiming that "it is presented as a history—that is, as a series of events in the lives of people, historical or fictitious, who are believed to stand in a significant relationship with the present." He concludes that "we have here an important historiographical document" (Wyatt 1979, 828). A recent rehearsal of the arguments against the historiographic character of the poem is to be found in Van Seters 1983, 200-202.

In the core story, which I have isolated on literary grounds, the king's demand for Hurraya is based on the claim that the god El has promised her to him in a dream. This perhaps suggested to the tellers of the story an elaboration of it: they supplied and prefixed to the original story an account of a dream theophany in which El appeared to the king, asked him what he wanted, and then gave him detailed instructions—corresponding to his subsequent actual experiences—on how to proceed. The original story now functioned as the execution and fulfillment of the instructions and predictions of the deity. (For the structure of the story at this stage, cf. the several accounts of dream theophanies with instructions discussed in Chap. 5A). Whether the initial loss of the king's family was a part of the original story (cf. Ruth) or was introduced as a separate motif (cf. *The Tale of the Shipwrecked Sailor*) at this stage in its development, to provide an overarching frame (cf. Job) is obscure. In either case the story is now vastly extended and given a chiastic shape:

Loss of family
    Divine approach—king's request for progeny
        Instructions for campaign and negotiations
        Execution of campaign and negotiations
    Divine approach—blessing/promise of progeny
Birth of children

As noted above, the last four lines of the dream theophany (1.14.3.46-49) serve as a kind of fulcrum at the center of this structure, pointing back over El's response to Keret's plight and forward to the ultimate consequences:

dbḥlmy il ytn	Whom El has given me in my dream,
bḏrty ab adm	the Father of Humankind in my vision;
wld špḥ lkrt	to bear offspring for Keret,
wǵlm lʿbd il	and a boy to the Servant of El.

It may be noted that the story as we now have it contains elements of historical realism, such as the offer made by the besieged king to buy off the invader; and of psychological realism, such as the transition from the king's loss of family to the dream theophany; as well as elements of hyperbole and fantasy, such as the composition and scope of the army, and its siege tactics. Doubtless the history of the composition of the story was more complicated than sketched here. The present proposal is simply what I believe is authorized by the preceding analysis and comparisons.

To this story of a king's campaign for a bride (and hence family) has been added a story of the search for a cure for the king's sickness (*Krt* B). Sickness is generally understood to be the result of the malevolence of a god or demon. In this case, the goddess Asherah is posited as the cause of the sickness, and, in order to link this new story to the preceding one, Asherah's punishment of Keret in this way is attributed to his failure to fulfil a vow he had made to her—commonly perceived in the ancient world as a reason for sickness. The vow draws on the language of El's blessing of Keret toward the end of the previous story, and is inserted, appropriately, into the middle of his conventional seven-day journey to his destination, which is consequently broken into a three-day and an abnormal four-day journey. (For these reasons I cannot follow Loewenstamm in his hypothesis of an original Asherah epic, in which, without El's instructions and predictions, Keret would have sought the aid of

Asherah on his campaign [Loewenstamm 1979]. The vow is too obviously modelled on the marriage blessing and intrusive in the numerical sequence of Keret's journey. Had the vow been a part of the original story it would surely have appeared—like everything else!—also among the instructions and predictions in the mouth of El. Those who now added the second story, however, wish to intrude minimally into the previous material—and probably wish to avoid making El in any way responsible for what ultimately brings Keret down.) Thus the new story begins with Asherah's noting Keret's failure to fulfil his vow, and resolving to punish him. It continues by portraying the various attempts to deal with his ensuing sickness, by the queen and nobles, his children, and the gods.

First, his wife invites the nobles of the realm to a feast for Keret, where she bids them weep for him. Two other feasts follow, whether for the same guests or others is not clear, as it is not clear whether the same or different speeches or acts are undertaken. Then, one of Keret's sons approaches him in mourning, but is sent to his daughter, to invite her to a banquet for him. She comes to Keret and repeats the same mourning speech as the son. Next, the attention of the gods is drawn to Keret's plight as the consequences of his sickness become apparent in the larger world: there is no rain, the fields produce no vegetation to replace exhausted food supplies. Various gods are sought or sent for. Finally, El appeals to all the gods for one who can heal Keret. None responds, so he undertakes himself to make a creature whom he then commissions to go to Keret and conquer threatening Death. She does so, and Keret takes food and mounts his throne again.

Some have suggested on the basis of hints in and restorations to the text that Keret's daughter produced silver and gold for Keret to fulfil his vow, and that Asherah was subsequently given satisfaction in the divine assembly before El undertook to cure Keret. Such an interpretation of the remains is possible, but does not seem to be necessary.

The only structural similarity between *Krt* A and *Krt* B is that both begin with a calamity and end with restoration. Beyond this, *Krt* B is organized, not chiastically nor by epic repetition like *Krt* A, but by the structure of Keret's universe. The narrative reports the response to Keret's sickness first, in his public, political world; then in his private, family world; and finally, in his cosmic, divine world. Thus *Krt* A and B differ in subject and structure.

Krt B has a closer relationship—in terms of subject and structure—to the second Job story. It shares its initial impulse and final resolution: Asherah smites Keret with illness at the beginning and El accomplishes his cure at the end, just as the Satan smites Job with a disease at the beginning and Yahweh restores him to health at the end. Both narratives also share a similar progression. As in *Krt* B, the Job narrative shows us the response to Job's plight in his private world (wife), then in his public world ("friends" or associates), and finally in the cosmic, divine world (Yahweh).

Further, *both* the Keret stories and *both* the Job stories begin with a calamity and end with restoration. Both works combine a story about the loss and recovery of family with one about the loss and recovery of health. As the book of Job exhibits a single theme in its combination of two such stories, it will be appropriate to ask whether *Krt* also exhibits a single overarching theme in its combination of just these two stories.

As we have observed, the remainder of the poem does appear to begin a new, third subject: a challenge to Keret's fitness to rule. As we have also observed, such a challenge begins a new narrative segment in the books of Samuel (at 1 Sam. 15), and is the starting point of a psalm that treats of Yahweh's displacement of the previously ruling gods (Ps. 82). There is no reason to conclude that Keret's curse of his presumptuous son would take effect immediately; it is more likely that, like many divine promises or prophetic threats, it would set up an audience expectation, but also a narrative tension that might be sustained over a series of events comparable in scope to those pursued in *Krt* A or B. Further, we noted the artificiality of the connection of this new narrative with the preceding material. After the complete healing of Keret and his restoration to office, Yassub, in his indictment of his father and proposal to take his place, refers in an intrusive bicolon to his being tied to his sickbed. This is the only connection between what is preserved of the new story and what has gone before.

The same evidence which suggests the essentially independent character of the subject and plot of each of the three stories also attests to the unity achieved for the new whole. That is, the effect of the way in which each new story is added onto the previous one is to produce a larger narrative in which no sooner has one crisis in the life of the king been resolved than another one arises, ostensibly, but tangentially, growing out of the previous one. Thus *Krt* A, B and C form a chain of stories, superficially linked by plot devices, and sharing the same protagonist (and perhaps other individuals, human and divine).

It is only with the introduction of the third story that the succession to the throne becomes prominent. In his challenge to Keret's fitness to rule Yassub proposes that he, the heir (so designated in El's marriage blessing toward the end of *Krt* A), replace Keret. If Keret's prompt curse of Yassub is not of immediate effect, it raises the question whether Yassub will succeed to the throne—and, consequently, the further question: if not Yassub, then who? It is precisely now that certain details from earlier in the poem begin to acquire significance. In El's marriage blessing we noted beside the characterization of Yassub as the divinely prepared heir to the throne the apparently contradictory promise that El would give the youngest daughter first-born status. We also observed in the midst of the anxiety about Keret's sickness and the concern to effect a cure, which seem to predominate in *Krt* B, a possible passing reference to the eventuality of Yassub's reigning (*ymlk* [*y*]*ṣb* *'ln*—1.15.5.20-21), which, if not contradictory in that context, is at least an isolated reference of marginal concern. If the third story added to the first two introduces an interest in the question of succession, then the placing of these anticipatory references in those two earlier contexts would now appropriately effect a slight shift of emphasis, preparing the ground for the third and concluding interest of the whole poem.

But with so little of that third section, we are severely hindered from saying anything significant, not only about the course or outcome of that story, but also about its effect on the interpretation of the poem as a whole. It is, of course, quite possible that, if the third component story of the whole work pursued the succession question, it may have provided an explicit link with the dynasty of Niqmad. Many commentators have claimed a connection between Keret and the ruling dynasty of Ugarit (Pedersen 1941; Gray 1965, 17; Gottlieb 1974). Recently Kitchen has attempted to relate Keret, chronologically and geographically, to the Ugaritic king list (Kitchen 1977, 141-42). But the conspicuous absence of the names of Keret or any of his family, not only from the king list, but also from the dynastic seal; the fact that Keret is portrayed as living in *Ḫbr*; and the lack of anything in the surviving text to link Keret or his family with the monarchy of Ugarit leaves such connections without any foundation (cf. Caquot 1979). The only connection between the text and the Ugaritic monarchy is the fact that it was copied in Ugarit under the sponsorship of the Ugaritic king of the time—which is equally true of *Aqht*, *B'l*, etc.!

We have so little of this third story that it is impossible to even surmise the subsequent course of the plot. Even if it were possible to sketch it in broad outline, that would not necessarily tell us anything about the theme, for plots are only vehicles for themes, and similar plots may treat of quite different themes. Thus if, regardless of the question of a connection with Ugarit, the plot of the third story did focus on the royal succession, we still could not assume that one of the lessons of the poem was that heredity monarchy is the gods' will for man (as proposed by Caquot 1979, building on Bernhardt 1955-6 and Merrill 1968).

Given our ignorance of the theme and plot of the third story, it is futile to argue about the theme or purpose of the whole work. However, we have the first and second narrative components of the whole, each marked by a significant closure, and each relatively untouched by tangential material related to later developments and interests—material that can be recognized and isolated. In view of this situation the best available option for further interpretation is to settle for the text as we have it; to recognize that at some stage *Krt* A and *Krt* B formed an entire poem; to bracket out, therefore, the truncated third story and the isolated earlier cola that seem to be related to the interests it introduces and unrelated to the interests of the first two; and to ask what is the theme, purpose and setting of the poem as it existed before the addition of *Krt* C. (It is of course quite possible that, whatever the course of the plot of the third story, it sustained the theme established in the present form of the first two. But it is equally possible that it significantly altered the interpretation of the first two.)

What emerges as the predominating interest in the treatment of the various episodes and traditional materials in the poem is the unique benevolence, wisdom and power of El. As Keret pines on his bed at the beginning of the poem, it is El who responds directly (not Baal, mediating between the protagonist and El, as in *Aqht*—1.17.1). El spells out at extraordinary length and in great detail instructions to Keret and predictions of what he will find—instructions and predictions which are realized to the letter. On the basis of these Keret is able to claim to *Pbl* that El has given him *Pbl*'s daughter in his dream. But *Pbl* similarly claims that he holds his city as a gift from El. Each is evidently persuaded by the claim of the other—Keret spares *Udm* and *Pbl* hands over his daughter. El's disposition of a king's realm or children is unquestioned. El then appears in person at Keret's wedding, and—prompted in a thoroughly conventional way by Baal (1.15.2.12-16; cf. 1.17.1.23-24, where, however, the simple call to pronounce a blessing is developed into a speech of epic scope and specific relevance to the immediate context)—pronounces a lengthy blessing on Keret, promising him numerous children. The blessing of the other gods is referred to in a word (1.15.3.17), and El's promise of children is immediately fulfilled (1.15.3.20-25).

Throughout this narrative Keret is thoroughly passive. From the moment that he sinks in despair at the beginning of the action, all is determined by El: the campaign and acquisition of a wife, and the number and future role of the children. The only thing Keret does without El is make his vow to Asherah, and that one sign of initiative lands him in his second tribulation.

While the first narrative exposes Keret's total dependence on El, the second explores the inadequacy of others in Keret's world to accomplish anything without El—his peers, his family, or the gods in general. There is not a hint that Keret is in any way benefitted by any of the gatherings, eatings, weepings, or speeches of the various groups and individuals whom we see responding to the news of his sickness. Even the gods are utterly helpless. In the divine council episode of 1.16.5 the response to the conventional call for a champion is not merely delayed, as in other examples of this stereotyped form, but remains, after the appeal has been made seven times, totally lacking. (As noted in the discussion of the preceding columns above, it is likely that, before this, assistance had been sought from certain specific deities.) El finally has to tell the gods to sit down, and he then undertakes to do what no other god has the slightest notion of accomplishing. He creates a being whom he directs to heal Keret and who promptly acts upon this directive, so that Keret is immediately able to take food and resume his throne.

The common theme of both stories, as we now have them, is the total dependence of the king and his entire world on El. El in turn is shown to be uniquely willing and able to help the helpless king. I know of no other Ancient Near Eastern narrative that so pointedly presents a ruling monarch as utterly helpless and dependent on a god. (The proposal that Keret and El were related by covenant like David and Yahweh [Gottlieb 1974] has been aptly dismissed by Loewenstamm 1979.) This portrayal of Keret stands in stark contrast with the claims of many—recently Del Olmo Lete 1981, 276-7—that the poem exalts the function and destiny of the ancestral king in accordance with the traditional royal ideology. The elements of traditional royal ideology in the poem—or of what Liverani has called "heroic ideology" (Liverani 1970, 867-68)—are precisely that: conventional motifs that contrast with the actual standing and fate of Keret in our poem.

The treatment in 1.16.1-2 of the traditional ideology of the king (see Chap. 2 D 1), according to which the king is "son of El//offspring of the Benevolent" and in some sense immortal, is revealing. While Thitmanit's and the first version of *Ilḥu*'s mourning speech appear to reassert that ideology, the second version of *Ilḥu*'s speech questions it: "How can it be said: 'Keret is son of El//offspring of the Benevolent and her Holiness'?" and raises the alternative possibility that the gods are mortal: "Or do gods die//the offspring of the Benevolent not live on?" The third version repeats the question, but then seems to reassert the traditional doctrine. Thus, on the one hand, the authors seem here to be repeating traditional piety, and, on the other, to be interpreting the traditional terminology quite literally and finding it problematic. Superhuman status is not a feature of Keret's identity as king. His participation in the divine realm is not an essential aspect of his royal status. He is, in fact, all too mortal. Indeed, as the narrative shows, Keret and El, rather than being closely related, as implied by Keret's traditional titulary, are antithetical and complementary. El's strength is made perfect in Keret's weakness. Keret's weakness displays the sufficiency of El's grace.

Sapin has argued from such evidence that *Krt* reflects the opposition of two royal ideologies. The one extols the (functional) divinity of the king, and serves the interests of the city. The other maintains a distance between gods and men—including kings, who are as dependent on the gods as anyone else, and whose power is actually also dependent on the acceptance of their legitimacy by their people—and serves the interests of the tribal groupings outside the city. According to Sapin, the latter strain would reflect an ongoing concern among the ruling elite to justify their role to the tribes in which they had their historical roots (Sapin, 1983). But Sapin's two distinct ideologies seem to be more reflective of contrasts within Israel than of conditions obtaining in the city-state of Ugarit (see Liverani 1979), and it seems highly doubtful that the villagers outside the city would have been envisaged as an audience by the writers or sponsors of *Krt*.

For the coexistence within the same literary context of such tensions as appear in the three speeches in 1.16.1-2, I would turn to the outcome of similar shifts and tensions in contemporary Egypt. Alongside the traditional songs that praised death and the afterlife, there had emerged others that dismissed the afterlife and extolled the virtues of the present life. In a single tomb from the end of the fourteenth century are found three songs, one of which describes the afterlife in traditional ritualistic terms, another mentions and rejects the hedonistic and skeptical theme, and a third attempts to combine hedonistic-skeptical motifs with the traditional piety (Lichtheim 1945, 195-99). In her discussion of these texts Lichtheim observes that the owner of the tomb, Neferhotep, must have lived through the spiritual revolution of the Amarna period and the subsequent restoration. She also notes the lack of solution to the problem posed, or of any embarrassment at the juxtaposition of such contradictory attitudes. She sees the reason for this partly in a human wavering between fear and hope, but more fundamentally in the quality of the Egyptian mind (Lichtheim 1945, 200). I would observe that the coexistence of these different attitudes that the Egyptian scribes have here expressed in one mortuary context is not unlike the coexistence of the different attitudes—traditional faith in the king, skepticism, and an attempt to combine the two—found in the one literary context in 1.16.1-2. I would further suggest that such coexistence has to do not with a peculiar "Egyptian mind", but with the mollifying quality of the repetition of tradition alongside a perhaps apprehensive defiance of tradition.

Returning to the question of the status of the monarch and his relations with the divine, we find such questions to be very live issues in contemporary Egypt. Until Suppiliuma's invasion of Syria c. 1350, Ugarit was more influenced by Egyptian than Hittite politics and culture. As we know especially from the El Amarna letters, the scribes of Akhetaten were in abundant communication with the scribes of Palestine and Syria. Thus what was going on in Egypt in the first half of the fourteenth century may be expected to have had some repercussions in Ugarit.

During this period Egypt witnessed attempts increasingly to bolster the status of the monarch. Amenhotep II had boasted of his unparalleled physical prowess. Amenhotep III gloried in his unprecedented building construction. And now Amenhotep IV (Akhenaten) sought to elevate his position by an exclusive definition of the divine world and his claim to be the sole mediator between the sole deity and the rest of humanity. This ideological revolution in Egypt did not last long. Already under Akhenaten's successor, Tutankhamen, the old order was being reinstated and the old titles of gods and of king revived. Now the King Niqmad under whom our tablets were written was a contemporary both of Akhenaten and Tutankhamen. While there is no evidence of any comparable elevation of the monarchy in Ugarit to that attempted by Akhenaten, it is possible that the exclusiveness of El in *Krt* might have received some stimulus from hearsay reports of developments in Egypt. (De Moor is confident that the news of the Aten revolution would have spread quickly through Canaan [de Moor 1986, 2-3]. His larger discussion of "the crisis of polytheism in Late Bronze Ugarit" treats the problem as a purely intellectual one and cites texts as direct expressions of an intellectual or theological ferment without regard to their literary or social contexts.)

It is of course specifically in the quarters of the high priest of Ugarit that the *Krt* tablets were found, which strongly suggests that the priesthood had some responsibility for the present form and character of the poem. The poetic relegation of the legendary king Keret to a position of complete dependence on the favor of El might then have a real, political counterpart in claims by the priesthood that the current monarch was completely dependent on the favor of the god whom they represented and served. Since El steps in to provide precisely what Keret needs in each crisis, there can be no question of a challenge to the institution of monarchy as such. But there is clearly a challenge to the independent powers and resources of an individual king—a challenge based on a display of the king's weakness and dependence on the powers and resources of the old supreme god, El. El's supremacy would serve the influence and prestige of his representatives in the priesthood, as, in a politically more effective way, the exclusive god, Aten, served the power and prestige of its sole representative, the king, in Amarna Egypt. Such a presentation of the role of the king might have been inspired in particular by the increasing encroachment of the secularising, legal-rational, bureaucratic administration of the kingdom on spheres of life and activity that the priesthood had traditionally disposed of.

Both the location and theme of the tablets would then support a consistent social situation and purpose for *Krt* A + B. The present form of the composition would be the work of the priesthood of Ugarit and intended for a court audience. It would dwell on the vulnerability and helplessness of the monarch and his total dependence on the deity, in order to promote the prestige and power of the Ugaritic priesthood as the real controller—on behalf of the deity—of the destiny of the land.

(Wyatt has recently proposed the childlessness of king Arhalbu and the divorce of Ammistamru [and hence the questionable status of his ex-wife's son] as being the conditions which stimulated the exploration of Keret's sickness and of his rejection of Yassub in *Krt* B and C—Wyatt 1983. The two historical situations mentioned do not seem to me particularly close, since Keret, though sick, now has a large family, and his curse of Yassub contrasts with Utrisharruma's freedom to choose to follow his mother or stay in Ugarit [and so become king]. More seriously, this Arhalbu and Ammistamru both ruled after the Niqmad under whom Ilimilku, the scribe, wrote down our only copy of *Krt*!)

Chapter 5
CONCLUSIONS AND IMPLICATIONS

A. The Value of Ugaritic Narrative Poetry for the Study of Ugaritic Society and Religion

The preceding interpretations of *Krt* and *Aqht* have in each case concluded with an exploration of their possible relation to Ugaritic society and culture. In both cases the conclusions were highly hypothetical, and arose to some extent from the contrast between the social and cultural world in the poems and the social and cultural world of Ugarit.

In her general study of oral poetry, Ruth Finnegan writes: "It is tempting to take clear statements in literatures about, say, the importance of heroism or of love, or the general ethos pervading some genre of poetry, as a true reflection of the moral code held or even followed by members of a society. This view is all the more appealing when we lack other detailed sources about people's behaviour and views, or as part of a theory about literature's role in social control" (Finnegan 1977, 264). Too many writers about the Ugaritic poems, lacking just such detailed sources about the behavior and views of the inhabitants of Ugarit, have fallen prey to just such a temptation. They have assumed that the two poems we have been investigating directly reflect the values of their society, and so have forced both poems (and others) to yield essentially similar values (e.g. those of sacral kingship, or of the religious renewal of fertility), and concluded that the common values thus represented are those of the contemporary society. The preceding study has suggested that the two poems present us with quite different interests and values, and that the interests and values of each stand in a relation of contrast with what we know of Ugaritic culture. The contrast between these two worlds is important. It illustrates the observation of Finnegan that literature like *Krt* and *Aqht* is not directly revealing of the culture in which it is recited or written down. Thus we should expect that further study of the narrative poems will not shed much direct light on the social or religious institutions of Ugarit (and therefore, how much less on the society or religion of ancient Israel). To assume that narratives are descriptive, if not of history, then at least of institutions, habits, values is to make a category mistake. Literature represents, most directly, literary values. If literature is also a social phenomenon, with a place and a role in social life, that place and role can not be read with confidence directly off the subject of the literature itself.

Finnegan admits that there are cases in which there is a fairly direct reflection of the society's values in its literature, or where a literary code is used to inculcate the literature's values in members of a society. "But equally literature can also express the views of minority or divergent groups within the society at large, or convey ideas pleasing in a literary context but not necessarily acceptable in everyday life . . . All in all, though the social norms of any established 'community' may be reflected in a complex way in their literature, it is likely to be in an indirect and subtle fashion. Literature as such does not provide any crude basis for neatly deducing a society's group norms and ideals" (Finnegan 1977, 265).

Although *Krt* and *Aqht* are not descriptive of, nor correlated with, precise institutional contexts in Ugaritic social life, the kind of literary study we have undertaken here does expose something of the cultural activity of literary creation in late bronze North Syria. To quote Finnegan again: "the picture that I derive from this study of oral poetry is of man as an active, imaginative and thinking being—and not as the product of 'social structure,' the arena of unconscious urges, or the result of deep cognitive and symbolic mental structures which are in a sense beyond his power to affect. Literature is, and expresses, people doing things, and making choices" (Finnegan 1977, 273). She goes on: " 'People doing things' does not just refer to the outward and observable acts by which people organize poetic activity or use poetry to achieve political power, economic reward and cooperation, religious satisfaction, aesthetic pleasure—or the other roles already mentioned. There is also a sense in which they use it to 'create' the world around them . . . The imagery and symbolism in poetry and the whole view of the world conveyed there mediates people's experience of that world—creates it according to its own image. For the people involved, the nature of the world *is* what they create and picture it to be in their poetry" (Finnegan 1977, 273-74).

Thus we have seen the way the poets of Ugarit and their antecedents adopted and adapted traditional poetic formulae and tales or episodes of tales, and creatively constructed larger more complex narrative poems out of this material. By their choices in the selection and use of their sources they have mediated their experience and created out of their mental worlds the literary worlds to which we have direct access. While these appear to differ radically from the "real" social world which we can partially reconstruct for the population of Ugarit, they remain valuable precisely because revelatory of that mental world of which, without the poems, we would know nothing from the other sources available to us. Since people's mental world is supremely important for their understanding of their social life, it remains, *as mental, literary construct*, an essential ingredient in any account of the social life of those who enjoyed the poems.

While the poems as wholes are not sources of information about the social institutions of Ugarit, there are parts of them that I have correlated with particular social experiences and events. I have argued from the similarity of form and setting of certain speeches and utterances appearing not only in our poems but also in biblical and other ancient Near Eastern sources, that those similarities are to be attributed not to literary continuity or influence, but to common social origins—thus the birth announcement, the vow and the marriage blessing. Of course, as soon as we start talking about the ingredients of the poem, we have lost our immediate connection with Ugarit. All that we can claim of the social context of such a saying or speech is that it is essentially the same in the different societies and periods. It is precisely the commonality of these social situations—a birth, a marriage, a situation of desperation—that engenders a similar existential and verbal response that persists through the variety of adaptations to different literary contexts (—and which, in the case of the vow, is more directly reflected in the recording of royal prayers and vows in Hittite sanctuaries).

Similarly certain traditional tales, also identified on the basis of their recurrence in different dress in quite unrelated literary works, suggest mental and emotional preoccupations or concerns that, while not directly related to specific events or institutions, are in themselves social facts, part of the mental world of the people who told and retold such tales. We may reasonably suppose that such preoccupations and concerns—childlessness, sickness, the need to make the right marriage, etc.—were shared by inhabitants of Ugarit, and indeed this supposition is supported by limited epigraphic evidence from other sources (correspondence, ritual texts, etc.).

In sum then, Ugaritic narrative poetry is of little value for the study of Ugaritic society or religion except precisely as a narrative poetry—as that peculiarly literary expression of a people's experience and mediation of their mental world. If that poetry makes no contribution to our construction of the social or religious institutions of Ugarit, it may nevertheless be the most significant disclosure of the mental world and life of its people—thus, of their experience and perception of their social and religious worlds.

B. The Value of Ugaritic Narrative Poetry for the Study of Ancient Near Eastern Literature

As one of the more sparsely attested literatures of the Ancient Near East, Ugaritic literature has often been illumined by comparison with the better known literatures, especially of Israel and Mesopotamia, but also of Egypt and Asia Minor. Indeed, it is this kind of comparison that has been of particular interest in the last three essays of this book. But such comparison, if it is not a mere equation, but an attempt to give full weight both to common and to distinctive features of the materials being compared, will, in the interpretation of such commonalities and distinctives, accomplish much more than the elucidation of Ugaritic literature.

Certain general benefits of the undertaking should by now be apparent. First, comparisons involving the Ugaritic narratives reveal particular traditional oral sources used by both Ugaritic and other ancient Near Eastern narrators. Second, such comparisons expose something of the techniques of the different narrators in their use of such sources. Finally, they set in relief the peculiar features of the narratives of the different literatures.

Our analysis of the form and structure of *Krt* and *Aqht* led us to seek confirmation of the analysis and of the boundaries of different narrative components by comparison with other narratives from the ancient Near East. From such comparisons we concluded in many cases that the narrative structure common to the portions of tales being compared was in fact the structure of a common traditional tale, episode or motif taken up and adapted in different ways for their own purposes by the different composers of the larger narratives. One necessary corollary of those conclusions is that the diffusion of such tales was not hindered by language barriers, since we have found different uses of the same tale not only by speakers of the different Semitic languages, but also by speakers of such unrelated languages as Hittite, Hurrian and Egyptian.

What gives the Ugaritic poems a particular interest in this

respect is that the copies we have are close to being the first written versions of those poems. (They were written down toward the beginning of the period from which the retrieved Ugaritic tablets come—by Ilimilku under the king Niqmad who reigned in the second quarter of the fourteenth century. That they were not the first written versions is indicated by the presence in them of copying errors—see Segert 1958). While this may be true of some Mesopotamian or Egyptian stories, the presence in both those societies of a long scribal tradition means that we must always allow for the possibility of earlier written versions that have not been preserved, or at least, found.

If *Krt* and *Aqht* are closer to their traditional oral sources, they may enable us to perceive more sharply than in some of the more developed scribal works of Egypt and Mesopotamia the common Near Eastern oral tales, episodes and motifs which lie behind much of the preserved written narrative literature. Whether this is in fact so depends on the scribes' relative freedom, or pressure, to reshape traditional material, on the degree to which and the stage at which the narratives were fixed, if indeed they were not always treated as free texts. These factors all depend on social conditions which we can no longer recover. On the one hand, we may surmise that in comparison with the more large-scale and more enduring scribal institutions at the centers of power in Egypt and Mesopotamia, the social context of the scribes writing the Ugaritic poems was relatively unconstraining. On the other hand, we may infer from the fact that the poems were found in the house of the high priest—that is, associated with the central institutions of the state—that they were likely to be fixed and to serve ongoing official purposes. In either case, they may have been quite freely transmitted prior to their adoption by the Ugaritic priesthood. But the fact remains, we do not know how relatively free or constrained the transmitters were. Further comparative study may give grounds for claiming that the treatment of traditional narrative materials in the Ugaritic poems was relatively more conservative or more free than their treatment in other ancient Near Eastern literatures.

The oral traditional tales which we have read off the comparisons made above include the following.

1. *The miraculous birth in answer to prayer*, consisting of: the childlessness of the protagonist; the appeal to the deity; the deity's favorable response; the conception and birth of a son. Such tales as this would have grown out of the experience and hopes of the childless, and may indeed reflect a particular ritual

for such people. In any case, by their portrayal of successful supplication in such circumstances, they would have fostered the piety of those longing for children.

2. *The dream theophany*: the protagonist's problem; sleep and dream; the appearance of the deity with instructions to the protagonist; the protagonist's awaking and execution of the instructions. This is a narrative reflection of an experience that we found described with some psychological realism in *Krt* and with some institutional realism in *Setne Khamwas and Si-osire*. As a tale it would have reinforced the institution.

3. *The expedition for a spouse*: the protagonist's need of a family; journey to the land of the potential spouse; negotiations for the spouse leading to the conclusion of a marriage agreement; marriage ceremony or blessing; birth of offspring. This reflects the most significant need and delicate task of people of every generation: to find the right spouse and conclude a satisfactory marriage agreement—and so to assure the continuity of the family. The examples of this story all emphasize the divine guidance of the protagonist, presumably reflecting people's awareness of their special dependence on the gods in such a matter. Again, this traditional tale would have modelled the piety required of the suitor, and reinforced it by the guidance and favor shown by the deity.

4. *Sickness and recovery*: a deity strikes the protagonist with sickness; members of the protagonist's family and peers are unable to cope with the problem; the protagonist's deity finally effects his restoration. This arises from the common experience and interpretation of sickness in the ancient Near East (reflected also in laments and wisdom literature). Again it offers encouragement and consolation to the suffering through faith in the deity.

Other than complete stories, we have found other stereotypes: episodes or motifs, as of the loss of one's entire family; loss and recovery of family; hospitality to visiting deities or representatives of deity; challenge to a monarch based on his failure to practice justice; etc.

The comparison of Ugaritic with other ancient Near Eastern narratives also discloses the techniques which the narrators used in the composition of their tales. At the most general level, one may say that the narrators took traditional narrative material and treated it in a variety of ways, adapting it to their own larger purposes. The variety of ways in which they do this includes superimposition and juxtaposition.

In *Krt* A we see the superimposition of traditional narrative materials in the way the expedition for a spouse is extended by and subordinated to the dream theophany, and both are framed by the loss and recovery of family. In *Krt* the tale of Keret's sickness and recovery is added on to the tale of his acquisition of a family by the insertion in the latter of the vow, the non-fulfillment of which brings on the sickness as punishment. The tale beginning with Yassub's challenge to his rule is added on to the tale of Keret's sickness and recovery by the inclusion in Yassub's opening speech of a bicolon claiming that Keret's sickness (still!) prevents him from administering justice. There remain three distinct stories, each with its own discrete subject and plot, united only by a common overarching theme.

In *Aqht* we can see quite clearly shorter narrative sections based on traditional material that seem to be juxtaposed to one another. But there are significant gaps at several points where the traditional tales join, so that the nature of the joins cannot be observed. At the same time we can see a unity of plot sustained throughout the three tablets of the narrative we possess, that gives *Aqht* a compelling forward movement that is absent from *Krt*. Thus the composers of *Aqht* seem to have had a single vision of a trajectory that is not completed until the end of the poem. Every traditional tale or episode that they use is subjected to that larger vision.

Another technique of composition that we have observed is the expansion or telescoping of traditional tales, episodes or motifs. At one extreme, they may appear as scarcely more than a precis of the plot. At the other extreme, they may be extended and elaborated and woven into a lengthy and complex narrative. What is a lengthy opening narrative in *Aqht* A and is worked into the even longer and more complex opening narrative of *Krt* A is a mere summary three lines of prologue in *The Doomed Prince*. The late story of *Setne-Khamwas and Si-Osire* recounts in less than ten lines the story of a dream theophany which in *Krt* A is extended over columns. The prolog of *Krt* describes in twenty lines *Krt*'s loss of his entire family. The same motif is developed into a series of frame stories in *The Tale of the Shipwrecked Sailor*.

The attestation of the most skeletal versions supports the idea that the poets worked with such structures in mind even as they composed larger and more complicated works. In other words, the basic narrative structure or motif is a traditional given. The poets may use it in its simplest form to initiate another action; or they may use it as a framework on which to develop a lengthy and elaborate version, or as one strand in a complex interwoven narrative, or (more rarely) as the recurrent motif of stories within stories. These compositional techniques of telescoping and expansion are common to the composers of all the ancient Near Eastern narrative literatures.

Finally, the comparative study of ugaritic narratives also enhances our appreciation of individual narratives in other ancient Near Eastern literatures. The isolated study of the literature of Egypt and of Mesopotamia, each with its own long, writing tradition, will continue to instruct us about the cultural continuities of each, including the conscious and deliberate use of earlier narratives preserved in writing. But comparative narrative study, including the narratives of Ugarit, will enable us to perceive more sharply the particular cultural, literary, social or situational use of the common ancient Near Eastern stock of narrative stereotypes in the different literatures.

In some of the comparisons undertaken in the preceding studies of the ugaritic narrative poems, we have already noted the contrasting uses of the same traditional sources in other works of Near Eastern literature. Contrasting with the swift succession of five short speeches that dramatically develops the conflict between Aqhat and Anat in *Aqht* C are the two lengthy, rhetorically developed speeches of Ishtar and Gilgamesh in *Gilgamesh* 6. The contrast points up the more static character of the scene in *Gilgamesh*, but also that poem's richer use of description, metaphor and mythology.

The comparison of Anat's use of *Yṭpn* to kill her enemy in *Aqht* C with Inara's use of a mortal to dispose of the serpent in *Illuyanka* clarifies the original independence of the latter story. The role of the storm god at the beginning and end of *Illuyanka* is exposed as a later frame, adapting the story to its present use in the *purulli* festival.

The comparison of Danel's with Appu's getting of a son shows how conventional is the use of the traditional tale in *Appu*. The purpose of this introductory section of *Appu* is to introduce Appu's two children, Good and Bad. But Bad is born first—as the Sun-god's first answer to Appu's prayer. Looked at in isolation, the story might raise theological questions in the mind of a modern western reader. But looked at in the context of ancient Near Eastern tradition, it is clear that the introduction of these two characters is accomplished by the use of a conventional narrative opening which simply introduces major characters by recounting their birth as an answer to the prayers of their childless parents.

The study of any works of ancient Near Eastern literature

stands much to gain from being comparative as well as analytic. By seeking relations between the work or literature of primary interest and the works of other literatures, including ugaritic, we will be able to develop a sounder understanding both of the common pool of experience and literary formulations shared by ancient Near Eastern peoples and literatures, and of the particular cultural presuppositions, social constraints, artistic conventions and visions of the world that are represented in the literature of each individual culture or society.

C. The Value of Ugaritic Narrative Poetry for the Study of Biblical Literature

Since their decipherment, the Ugaritic poetic narratives have been compared most often with the language and literature of the Bible. Biblical comparisons have also predominated in the preceding chapters. This is not a function of the perspective of biblical scholars. Rather, a broad view of ancient Near Eastern languages and literatures suggests that Ugaritic represents better than any other second millennium language or literature the antecedents of the language and literature of ancient Israel. The cultural continuities between the second and first millennium literatures of the Levant, so far as we know them, seem to be stronger than those among the various regional or national literatures of the second millennium or the first millennium.

Most pertinent to the present study is the series of comparisons (of both content and form) made by Westermann between the patriarchal narratives of Gen 12-50 and *Krt*, *Aqht*, 1.23 and 1.24 (Westermann 1980, 165-86; see earlier Eissfeldt 1944). Westermann noted especially the predominance of the family—family life, institutions, and expressions—in the Ugaritic as in the patriarchal stories. Even when the central character is a king, his wife and children are the chief concern of the story (Keret A), or the chief actors (Keret B and probably C). Childlessness, conception and birth are a particularly prominent motif in both bodies of literature, though the Bible is marked by its particular interest in the plight and the point of view of the woman.

Well before the discovery of Ugarit, biblical scholars were analysing biblical narratives and finding in them adaptations of traditional stories. Sometimes such claims were based entirely on internal analysis of the biblical material; other times evidence from the folklore of other societies—including, occasionally, other ancient Near Easter societies—was adduced to support the claims. Ugaritic literature contributes in several ways to this enterprise.

First, Ugaritic not only confirms the oral use of such material, but provides direct evidence of its presence and availability specifically in the period and the cultural area relevant for Israel's ancestors. We have already remarked that Ugaritic literature is demonstrably very close to oral literature—in contrast to the other major ancient Near Eastern literatures, preserved as they are in societies with a long tradition of writing. It confirms, more directly than any other source, that certain traditional episodes or stories were used in the Levant in the period preceding the emergence of Israel. We have seen in the poems several examples of such—including, for example, hospitality to deities, the birth of a son in answer to prayer, the dream theophany.

Second, the preceding analysis of the Ugaritic narrative poems has provided support for conclusions about the sources and the composition of specific biblical narratives. Analysis of the prose framework of the book of Job has suggested that that narrative is composed of two separate stories: an earlier story beginning with the catastrophic loss of the entire family of the protagonist (Job 1:1-15, 13-22) and concluding with the divine provision of a new family for him (Job 42:11-15), and a second story beginning with the divine affliction of the protagonist with a grievous sickness (Job 2) and concluding with his restoration by God (Job 42:7-10). The second story has been inserted into the first (Alt 1937; Horst 1969, IX and 5).

The preceding analysis of *Krt* has shown that the same two traditional stories underlie the first two sections of that work. In *Krt* both stories have been developed into much more complex compositions, and they have been combined by addition rather than insertion. But the fact remains that the Ugaritic *Krt* is based on specifically these two traditional tales. It thus attests to the existence of these two and to their combination in a single literary work in the Levant of the late Bronze Age, and anticipates the work of those who combined the same two traditional stories in what we know as the narrative framework of the book of Job.

The composition of 1 Kgs 19 may serve as a second example. This has been shown to be a very complex composition incorporating several different traditions and interests: the miraculous feeding in the wilderness, the journey to the mountain of God, the reinterpretation of the nature theophany, and the dream theophany (see Würthwein 1970; Jones 1984). Our analysis of *Krt* has shown that there too the composers have used the traditional dream theophany, describing the protagonist's plight, his falling asleep, the instructions and predictions of the deity, and the protagonist's execution of the instructions. But further, the literary treatment of this in *Krt*, as in 1 Kgs 19, is divorced from any specific cultic context. The deity approaches the protagonist out of compassion for his suffering, not in response to a formal prayer or incubation ritual; and the theophany itself consists not just of a divine response to the problem, but of a small conversation in which the deity first enquires after the protagonist's problem, the protagonist tells the deity of his problem, and then the deity proceeds to give him directions. *Krt* thus provides independent evidence of the previous elaboration and adaptation of the basic dream theophany, and suggests the more specific shape of the traditional narrative with which the authors of 1 Kgs 19 may have worked. This in turn directs our attention to other elements in the present narrative which will have been worked into that basic material in order to heighten certain themes and interests.

Fourth, our comparative analysis of the Ugaritic narrative poems allowed us to see something of the compositional technique of the Ugaritic poets. This is valuable extrabiblical evidence of the way in which the narrators of the Levant worked with traditional materials before the composition of the first biblical narratives. We saw how in *Krt* A the expedition for a spouse was expanded and reinterpreted by incorporation into a dream theophany. In Israel too, divine instructions and predictions may be secondary to, and significant reinterpretations of an original simple narrative. The use of the loss and recovery of a family as the outer frame of *Krt* A is replicated in the use of the same skeletal narrative as the outer frame of the whole book of Job. The use of stories of quite different subject in *Krt*—the need for a wife and children, the need for a cure for sickness, the need for a smooth succession—are given some continuity and integrity (so far as we can determine on the basis of an incomplete text) by their treatment of a common theme: the helplessness and vulnerability of the protagonist and his total dependence on a compassionate and powerful deity. In the same way stories about quite different subjects in Genesis 1-11, for example, are given a larger unity by their representation of a common theme.

On the other hand, the succession of different traditional stories in *Aqht*—the birth in answer to prayer, the divine gift, the provocation and vengeance of a goddess, the slaying of the enemy by a woman—achieves a compelling unity of plot. Here too we have an early example of a technique of Biblical narrative in which what is obviously composed of a succession of discrete traditional elements is also consistently single-minded and progressive in plot, e.g. the story of Jacob.

The use of the loss of family as the precipitant of a story in *Krt* recurs in Ruth and, to a lesser extent, Job. The narrative of the birth in response to an appeal to the deity, which is used to begin the story of *Aqht*, is also used to initiate the story of Samuel.

Fifth, the study of Ugaritic literature heightens our appreciation, not just of the sources or compositional techniques, but also of the character and power of biblical narrative. In Ugaritic literature, the plot progresses through largely stereotyped descriptions of actions which may be extended and slowed down by epic repetition or repetition with a numerical framework, or abbreviated and speeded up by a cluster of selected formulaic cola. Speeches too may be quite conventional and may be repeated to fill out a scene (as in 1.17.5). On the other hand, they may be used to portray character and to show changing relationships and so to develop the plot (as in 1.17.6). Fast or slowly, the plot progresses directly forward. There are no asides, no anticipatory confidences to the listener/reader, no summaries or generalizations, no moralizing lessons drawn, no explanations of older customs, no references to the present day.

Biblical narrative, for all its variety, may be characterized generally by contrast with these features. Though stereotyped language and repetition are used, they are occasional rather than pervasive, and generally used for particular artistic effects rather than as a basic means of storytelling. Epic repetition is used very selectively and economically and repetition with a numerical framework never. The more flexible use of language—a function of prose composition, as against traditional verse composition—allows more sensitive portrayal of character and more subtle recounting of and commenting on action. The story line is occasionally punctuated by words directed by the narrator to the audience—introductory interpretation (e.g. Gen 18:1a; 22:1a); parenthetical explanation of older features of the story (e.g. 1 Sam 9:9; Exod 16:36); references to present day connections with some feature of the story (e.g. Gen 26:33; 32:33); summary, retrospective comments (e.g. Judg 16:30b); moral judgments or reflections (e.g. 2 Sam 11:27b; the refrain of the last five chapters of Judges: "in those days there was no king in Israel: everyone did what he wanted"). In every such case, a different point of view is represented (cf. Berlin 1983c). The audience, which loses consciousness of the story-teller and of itself in its immersion in the story, suddenly becomes aware of the storyteller, now commenting on the story, and of itself as audience being addressed more directly.

If biblical narrative is often more direct and explicit in its moral comment or judgment, it is also more allusive and evocative in its presentation of human experience and motivation. Its freer and more subtle use of language enables it to suggest a greater complexity of experience than the more traditional language of the Ugaritic narratives, which generally seem to treat of one subject, one meaning, and one emotion at a time. Auerbach's famous essay contrasting the story of the binding of Isaac with the homeric episode in which Odysseus' nurse recognizes his scar spells out well the suggestive power of the biblical story as compared with the homeric one (Auerbach 1953, 3-23). That power is equally salient when the same story is compared with the Ugaritic narratives. Admittedly, Gen 22:1-19 is one of the high points of biblical narrative. But if we emphasize not the power of the narrative as such, but its suggestion of dimensions of experience that the language does not describe, it will be apparent that such suggestiveness is characteristic in varying degrees of many biblical narratives.

Sixth, of particular interest in biblical narrative is the rendering of the divine, and here too comparison with the Ugaritic poetic narratives will prove fruitful. A provisional classification of the divine role in Ugaritic and biblical narrative follows (earlier comparisons of more restricted view include Cross 1973, 177-87; Clifford 1973; Westermann 1980).

Clearly in neither *Krt* nor *Aqht* do the gods appear as the central actors, as they do in the Baal stories. This is one kind of treatment of the divine that is excluded both from these narratives and from all biblical narrative. In this respect the two poetic narratives and biblical narrative can together be set over against the Baal tablets and all other stories about the gods (contrast the categories in the title of Cross' book: *Canaanite Myth and Hebrew Epic*).

The gods appear in both *Krt* and *Aqht* solely as forces working for or against the people who are the central actors. Even when they appear in a "mythological scene"—that is, talking among themselves—it is the fate of the people that is at issue. Thus the conversation between Baal and El in 1.17.1 concerns the granting of a son to Danel; that between Anat and El in 1.18.1 concerns Anat's revenge on Aqhat; the divine speeches and activities in 1.16.3-6 concern the healing of Keret. The Bible has preserved the occasional example of such "mythological scenes:" in the scenes in heaven in Job 1-2; in the scene and episode recounted by Micaiah in 1 Kgs 22:19b-22. Here too the fate of human actors is at issue. God and the satan in Job 1-2 discuss the interest or disinterestedness of Job's piety, and the discussion issues in God's permitting the satan to put Job's piety to the test. The conversation between God and his spirits in Micaiah's brief narrative is directed toward finding a means of tricking Ahab into attacking and being defeated at Ramoth Gilead.

But these scenes are not a part of normal story-telling in the Bible, as they clearly are at Ugarit. The author of Job has very deliberately constructed his prologue to achieve an archaic effect: the setting, some of the phraseology, and—to our point—the narrative form are archaic. These observations are consistent with the conclusion that the language—and therefore the story as we have it—are late (Hurvitz 1974). The artificial character of the framework is set off against the passionate soul-searching and God-searching of the poem. Similarly, Micaiah's vision, far from being a bit of conventional story-telling, is a deliberate construction for a critical, immediate purpose. Micaiah has told a blatant, mocking lie (v. 15; cf. 16); pronounced his direct prophetic vision (v. 17); and is now seeking to justify this pronouncement by explaining how so many other prophets, who have announced a different fate for the army, could be wrong. As in the first two speeches, the writer is taking a traditional linguistic and literary form and using it with consummate mastery in the context of conflicting prophetic testimony and royal determination to pursue the royal will.

Thus both biblical writers are drawing on a traditional form for special effect. The same form may have figured more commonly and more naturally in serious narratives in early Israel than it does now in the Bible, but the larger history of the form is lost to us. We have only such rare, late, self-consciously artistic uses of what was clearly a common, current narrative technique in ugaritic narrative (as in the Gilgamesh epic, the homeric epics and many others).

The more direct contact between divine and human actors is again portrayed as more natural in the Ugaritic epics than in the Bible. El, Baal and the other gods apparently attend Keret's wedding and pronounce their blessing on him before departing (1.15.2-3). Kothar journeys to Danel and is entertained by him before presenting him with the bow (1.17.5). Aqhat meets Anat and offends her by rejecting both her proposals (1.17.6). Later she journeys to where Aqhat is and talks with him again (end of 1.18.1). She also goes to *Yṭpn* and talks with him (1.18.4).

God does not so naturally visit and converse with people in the Bible. Perhaps the most strikingly similar passage is Gen 18:1-16, where Yahweh (according to the introductory half-verse) or three men (according to verse 2; cf. the changes of number in the references to the embassy in the remainder of the episode) visit Abraham and, after being entertained by him and his wife, promise the barren couple a son. Other passages treat of direct divine-human encounters more darkly and allusively—e.g. Gen 32:25-31; Exod 4:24-26. More commonly in the Bible divine visitors are depicted as envoys of Yahweh. They engage in conversation with the protagonist, but avoid all other contact.

Here, too, we may reasonably suppose that pre-biblical Israelite literature may have more frequently and more readily told of direct divine visitations for various purposes. But we are left with the impression from the surviving literature of a much more stark contrast between the apparent naturalness of such encounters in ugaritic narrative (and elsewhere) and the careful obscuring or stark rejection of such in biblical narrative.

Finally, in ugaritic narrative we see the more realistic portrayal of the activity of the gods or of human dealings with the gods. First, the gods may reveal themselves through the medium of human psychology, as in the case of El's appearance to Keret in a dream after his falling asleep in grief over his lost family. In biblical narratives too God frequently appears to people and speaks to them in dreams or visions (cf. Lichtenstein 1968-69b). Here we may have to do with a rare phenomenon in ugaritic narrative that has become more frequent in a tradition which is not so comfortable as ugaritic narrative with gods who move around among and mix with people. (For some biblical narrators, dreams and visions are an equally inappropriate means of divine communication. They shift away from realism and resort to simple, direct divine speech without appearance or location or medium, as in Gen 12:1.)

The other element of realism, that is particularly prominent in *Aqht*, is the portrayal of human relations with the divine in terms of sacral words and acts. In 1.19, particularly, the gods—who have been so visibly active in Danel's getting of a son, and in his son's getting of a divine bow and suffering the consequences of possessing such an object—are suddenly absent. Danel moves from one ritual act or pronouncement to another in a series of steps designed, first, to deal with the drought, and, second, to deal with the murder of his son. His daughter then takes on her mission of vengeance with Danel's blessing, but without any divine sanction or assistance (so far as our text goes). Here the role of the gods is limited to their assumed observation or hearing of the human rituals and pronouncements designed to sway or direct them.

In biblical narrative, too, religious institutions often represent—as in ordinary social life—the divine role in human experience. But here it is especially divine pronouncements (sometimes in response to enquiries of the deity) uttered by religious functionaries—priests or prophets—that influence, or judge or predict human affairs. And, with rare exceptions having to do with the possible falsity of prophetic claims to divine authority (e.g. 1 Kgs 13), God is in fact the real speaker, not only for the speaker and audience within the narrative, but also for the narrator and the implied audience. Thus religious institutions—especially prophecy—fill the gap left by the withdrawal of the deity from visible participation in the action of the narrative.

Finally, in biblical narrative, the involvement of the deity in the action may be conveyed in a way which is in no way anticipated in Ugaritic narrative—as a power known only by the pious words of the human actors and the relations of events to their words (as in Gen 24, Ruth or the Joseph novella).

If biblical narrative generally has moved away from the full, explicit involvement of the gods in the world of people that we see in ugaritic narrative; it has created, in contrast with ugaritic narrative, the full, explicit involvement of people in a multidimensional world of past, present and future, of events and interpretations, of multiple perspectives, of moral order and of mystery.

LITERATURE CITED

Aistleitner, J.
1964 *Die Mythologischen und Kultischen Texte aus Ras Shamra*. 2d ed. Budapest: Akadémiai Kiadó.

Alexander, T.D.
1985 "Lot's Hospitality: A Clue to His Righteousness." *JBL* 104: 289-91.

Alt, A.
1937 "Zur Vorgeschichte des Buches Hiob." *ZAW* 55: 265-68.

Andersen, F.I.
1971 "Passive and Ergative in Hebrew." In *Near Eastern Studies in Honor of W.F. Albright*, ed. H. Goedicke, 1-15. Baltimore and London: Johns Hopkins.

Astour, M.C.
1973 "A North Mesopotamian Locale of the Keret Epic?" *UF* 5: 29-39.

Auerbach, E.
1953 *Mimesis. The Representation of Reality in Western Literature*. Princeton: Princeton University.

Avishur, Y.
1978 "The Incense and the Sweet Scent: 'The Commandments of the Ideal Son' in Aqhat and Idol Worship in Ezekiel 8." In *Studies in Bible and the Ancient Near East Presented to Samuel E. Loewenstamm*, ed. Y. Avishur and J. Blau, 1-15 (Hebrew volume). (English summary in the English volume, 187-88). Jerusalem: Rubinstein's.

Bauer, J.B.
1958 "Drei Tage." *Bib* 39: 354-58.

Bayliss, M.
1973 "The Cult of the Dead Kin in Assyria and Babylonia." *Iraq* 35: 115-25.

Beckman, G.
1982 "The Anatolian Myth of Illuyanka." *JANES* 14: 11-25.

Berlin, A.

1983a "Ethnopoetry and the Enmerkar Epics." *JAOS* 103: 17-24.

1983b "Parallel Word Pairs: A Linguistic Explanation." *UF* 15: 7-16.

1983c "Point of View in Biblical Narrative." In *A Sense of Text. The Art of Language in the Study of Biblical Literature*, 71-113. JQRSupp, 1982. Winona Lake, IN: Eisenbrauns.

Bernhardt, K.-H.

1955/56 "Anmerkungen zur Interpretation des KRT-Textes von Ras Schamra-Ugarit." *Wissenschaftliche Zeitschrift, Greifswald* 5: 101-21.

1960 "Anmerkungen zum "Sitz im Leben" des *Aqht*-Textes von Ras-Schamra (Ugarit)." In *Proceedings of the XXV International Congress of Orientalists*, Vol. I, 328-29. Moscow.

Boecker, H.J.

1964 *Redeformen des Rechtslebens im Alten Testament*. WMANT 14. Neukirchen-Vluyn: Neukirchener Verlag.

Brichto, H.C.

1973 "Kin, Cult, Land and Afterlife: a Biblical Complex." *HUCA* 44: 1-54.

Briggs, C.A.

1908 *The Book of Psalms, 2*. ICC. New York: Scribner's.

Campbell, E.F.

1975 *Ruth*. Anchor Bible. Garden City, NY: Doubleday.

Caquot, A.

1960 "Les Rephaim ougaritiques." Syria 37: 75-93.

1979 "La littérature ugaritique." In *Supplément au Dictionnaire de la Bible*, vol. 9, ed. H. Cazelles and A. Fueillet, cols. 1361-1417. Paris: Letouzey and Ané.

1985 "Une nouvelle interprétation de KTU 1.19 I 1-19." *SEL* 2: 93-114.

Caquot, A., Légasse, S., and Tardieu, M. eds.

1985 *Mélanges bibliques et orientaux en l'honneur de M. Mathias Delcor*. AOAT 215. Kevelaer: Butzon and Bercker, and Neukirchen: Neukirchener Verlag.

Caquot, A. and Sznycer, M.
1974 *Textes ougaritiques, tome I: Mythes et légendes.* Paris: Editions du Cerf.
1980 *Ugaritic Religion*. Leiden: Brill.
Civil, M.
1983 "Enlil and Ninlil: The Marriage of Sud." *JAOS* 83 (Kramer Volume): 43-64.
Clifford, R.J.
1973 "The Word of God in the Ugaritic Epics and in the Patriarchal Narratives." In *The Word and the World*, ed. R.J. Clifford and G.W. McRae, 7-18. Cambridge: Weston.
Clines, D.J.A.
1976 "Krt 111-114 (I iii 7-10): Gatherers of Wood and Drawers of Water." *UF* 8: 23-26.
Collins, T.
1978 *Line-forms in Hebrew Poetry*. Studia Pohl: Series Major. Rome: Pontifical Biblical Institute.
Considine, P.
1969 "The Theme of Divine Wrath in Ancient East Mediterranean Literature." *Studi Micenei ed Egeo-anatolici* 8: 85-159.
Cross, F.M.
1973 *Canaanite Myth and Hebrew Epic. Essays in the History of the Religion of Israel.* Cambridge: Harvard.
Daube, D.
1973 *Ancient Hebrew Fables*. Oxford: Oxford University.
Day, J.
1980 "The Daniel of Ugarit and Ezekiel and the hero of the book of Daniel." *VT* 30: 174-84.
Del Olmo Lete, G.
1965 "La conquista de Jericó y la leyenda ugarítica de *KRT*." *Sefarad* 25: 1-15.
1981 *Mitos y Leyendas de Canaan Segun la Tradicion de Ugarit*. Fuentes de la Ciencia Biblica 1. Madrid: Cristiandad.
1984 "Antecedentes cananeos (ugaríticos) de formas literarias hebreo-bíblicas." In *Simposio Biblico Español (Salamanca, 1982)*, ed. N. Fernandez Marcos, *et al.*, 83-114. Madrid: Universidad Complutense.

1985 "Frases y formulas ugaritico-hebreas." In Caquot, Légasse and Tardieu 1985, 79-95.

Dietrich, M. and Loretz, O.

1985 "Die 'Hörner' der Neumondsichel—eine Keilschrift-parallele (Ee V 14-18) zu KTU 1.18 IV 9-11." In Caquot, Légasse and Tardieu 1985, 113-16.

Dietrich, M., Loretz, O., and Sanmartín, J.

1976 *Die keilalphabetischen Texte aus Ugarit.* Teil 1: Transkription. AOAT 24. Neukirchen-Vluyn: Neukirchener Verlag and Kevelaer: Butzon and Bercker.

Dijkstra, M.

1979 "Some Reflections on the Legend of Aqhat." *UF* 11: 199-210.

Dijkstra, M. and J.C. de Moor.

1975 "Problematical Passages in the legend of Aqhatu." *UF* 7: 171-215.

Dressler, H.H.P.

1975 "Is the Bow of Aqht a Symbol of Virility?" *UF* 7: 217-20.

1979a "The Identification of the Ugaritic Dnil with the Daniel of Ezekiel." *VT* 29: 152-61.

1979b "The Metamorphosis of a Lacuna." *UF* 11: 211-17.

1983 "Problems in the Collation of the Aqht-Text, Column One." *UF* 15 (1983): 43-46.

1984a "Reading and Interpreting the Aqht Text." *VT* 34: 78-82.

1984b "The evidence of the Ugaritic tablet *CTA* 19 (*KTU* 1.19): a consideration of the Kinnereth hypothesis." *VT* 34: 216-21.

Drews, R.

1974 "Sargon, Cyrus and Mesopotamian Folk History." *JNES* 33: 387-93.

Drower, M.S.

1973 "Syria c. 1550-1400 B.C." In *The Cambridge Ancient History*, vol. 2, part 1. 3d ed, ed. I.E.S. Edwards, C.J. Gadd, N.G.L. Hammond, E. Sollberger, 417-525. Cambridge: Cambridge University.

Eissfeldt, O.
1944 "Mythus and Sage in den Ras-Schamra-Texten." In *Beiträge zur Arabistik, Semitistik und Islamwissenschaft*, 267-83. Leipzig. Reprinted in *Kleine Schriften* II, ed. R. Sellheim and F. Maass, 489-501. Tübingen: Mohr.
1966 "Sohnespflichten im Alten Orient." *Syria* 43: 39-47. Reprinted in *Kleine Schriften* IV, ed. R. Sellheim and F. Maass, 264-70. Tübingen: Mohr.

Finkelstein, J.J.
1966 "The Genealogy of the Hammurapi Dynasty." *JCS* 20: 95-118.

Finnegan, R.
1977 *Oral Poetry. Its nature, significance and social context.* Cambridge, London, New York, Melbourne: Cambridge University.

Fisher, L.R., ed.
1975 *Ras Shamra Parallels.* Vol. 2. AnOr 50. Rome: Pontifical Biblical Institute.

Fontenrose, J.
1980 *Python. A Study of Delphic Myth and its Origins.* Reprint. Berkeley, Los Angeles, London: University of California.
1981 *Orion: The Myth of the Hunter and the Huntress.* Berkeley, Los Angeles, London: University of California.

Freedman, D.
1970-71 "Counting Formulae in the Akkadian Epics." *JANES* 3: 65-81.

Friedman, R.E.
1980 "The *Mrzḥ* Tablet from Ugarit." *Maarav* 2/2: 187-206 and Plates 1-12.

Gaster, T.H.
1961 *Thepis. Ritual, Myth, and Drama in the Ancient Near East.* 2d ed. New York: Harper.
1969 *Myth, Legend and Custom in the Old Testament.* New York: Harper.

Gibson, J.C.L.
1975 "Myth, legend and folk-lore in the Ugaritic Keret and Aqhat texts." In *Congress Volume Edinburgh.* VTSup 28, 60-68. Leiden: Brill.
1977 *Canaanite Myths and Legends.* Edinburgh: Clark.

Ginsberg, H.L.
1945 "The North-Canaanite Myth of Anath and Aqhat." *BASOR* 97: 3-10.
1946 *The Legend of King Keret. A Canaanite Epic of the Bronze Age.* BASOR Supplementary Studies 2-3. New Haven: American Schools of Oriental Research.
1973 "Ugaritico-Phoenicia." *JANES* 5: 131-47.
Good, E.M.
1958 "Two Notes on Aqhat." *JBL* 77: 72-74.
Gordon, C.H.
1953 *Introduction to Old Testament Times.* Ventnor, NJ: Ventnor.
1965 *Ugaritic Textbook.* Analecta Orientalia 38. Rome: Pontifical Biblical Institute.
Gottlieb, H.
1974 "El und Krt—Jahwe and David." *VT* 24: 159-67.
Gray, J.
1964 *The KRT Text in the Literature of Ras Shamra: A Social Myth of Ancient Canaan.* 2d ed. Leiden: Brill.
1965 *The Legacy of Canaan. The Ras Shamra Texts and their Relevance to the Old Testament.* VTSup 5. 2d ed. Leiden: Brill.
Greenfield, J.C.
1969 "Some Glosses on the Keret Epic." *Eretz-Israel* 9: 60-5.
Greenstein, E.L.
1983 "How Does Parallelism Mean?" In *A Sense of Text. The Art of Language in the Study of Biblical Literature*, 41-70. Winona Lake, IN: Eisenbrauns.
Gurney, O.R.
1954 "Two Fragments of the Epic of Gilgamesh from Sultantepe." *JCS* 8: 87-95.
Healey, J.F.
1979 "The *Pietas* of an Ideal Son in Ugarit." *UF* 11: 353-56.
Herdner, A.
1963 *Corpus des Tablettes en Cunéiformes Alphabétiques.* Paris: Geuthner.
Hillers, D.R.
1965 "A Convention in Hebrew Literature: The Reaction to Bad News." *ZAW* 77: 86-90.

1973 "The Bow of Aqhat: the Meaning of a Mythological Theme." In *Orient and Occident*. Essays presented to Cyrus H. Gordon. AOAT 22, 71-80. Ed. H.A. Hoffner. Neukirchen-Vluyn: Neukirchener Verlag.

Hoffner, H.A.

1965 "The Elkuniršа Myth Reconsidered." *RHA* 23: 5-16.

1968 "Birth and Name-giving in Hittite Texts." *JNES* 27: 198-203.

1975 "Hittite Mythological Texts: A Survey." In *Unity and Diversity. Essays in the History, Literature, and Religion of the Ancient Near East*, eds. H. Goedicke and J.J.M. Roberts, 136-45. Baltimore and London: Johns Hopkins University.

Hoggart, R.

1966 "Literature and Society." In *A Guide to the Social Sciences*, ed. N. MacKenzie, 225-48. London: Weidenfeld and Nicolson.

Horst, F.

1969 *Hiob 1*. BKAT 16/1. 2d ed. Neukirchen: Neukirchener Verlag.

Horwitz, W.J.

1972 "Discrepancies in an Important Publication of Ugaritic." *UF* 4: 47-52.

Hurvitz, A.

1974 "The Date of the Prose-Tale of Job Linguistically Considered." *HTR* 67: 17-34.

Irvin, D.

1978 *Mytharion. The Comparison of Tales from the Old Testament and the Ancient Near East*. AOAT 32. Kevelaer: Butzon and Bercker; Neukirchen-Vluyn: Neukirchener Verlag.

Jackson, J.J., and Dressler, H.H.P.

1975 "El and the Cup of Blessing." *JAOS* 95: 99-101.

Jirku, A.

1960 "Doppelte Überlieferung im Mythos und im Epos von Ugarit?" *ZDMG* 110: 20-25.

1962 *Kanaanäische Mythen und Epen aus Ras Schamra-Ugarit*. Gütersloh: Mohn.

Jones, G.H.

1984 *1 and 2 Kings*. 2 vols. New Century Bible Commentary. Grand Rapids: Eerdmans.

Kaddari, M.Z.
1973 "A Semantic Approach to Biblical Parallelism." *JJS* 24: 167-75.

Kapelrud, A.S.
1969 *The Violent Goddess. Anat in the Ras Shamra Texts*. Oslo: Universitetsforlaget.

Kirk, G.S.
1970 *Myth. Its Meaning and Function in Ancient and other Cultures*. Berkeley and Los Angeles: University of California; and Cambridge: Cambridge University Press.

Kitchen, K.A.
1977 "The King List of Ugarit." *UF* 9: 131-42.

Koch, K.
1967 "Die Sohnesverheissung an den ugaritischen Daniel." *ZA* N.F. 24: 211-21.

Kramer, S.N.
1982 "BM 98396: A Sumerian Prototype of the *Mater-Dolorosa*." *Eretz-Israel* 16: 141*-46*.

Kraus, H.-J.
1960 *Psalmen 1*. BKAT, 15,1. Neukirchen: Neukirchener Verlag.

Kugel, J.
1981 *The Idea of Biblical Poetry. Parallelism and its History*. New Haven and London: Yale.

Labuschagne, C.J.
1967 "The Crux in Ruth 4 11." *ZAW* 79: 364-67.

Lebrun, R.
1981 "Studia ad civitates Samuha et Lawazantiya Pertinenta, I. Voeux de la Reine à Istar de Lawazantiya." *Hethitica* 4: 95-107.

Leveque, J.
1970 *Job et son dieu; essai d'exégèse et de théologie biblique*. 2 Vols. Etudes bibliques. Paris: Gabalda.

Lichtenstein, M.
1968-69a "The Banquet Motifs in Keret and in Proverbs 9." *JANES* 1: 19-31.
1968-69b "Dream-Theophany and the E Document." *JANES* 2: 45-54.
1969-70 "A Note on the Text of I Keret." *JANES* 2: 94-100.

Lichtheim, M.
1945 "The Songs of the Harpers." *JNES* 4: 178-212 and plates I-VII).

Lichtheim, M.
1973 *Ancient Egyptian Literature. A Book of Readings.* Vol. 1, *The Old and Middle Kingdoms.* Berkeley, Los Angeles, London: University of California.
1976 *Ibid.* Vol. 2, *The New Kingdom.*
1980 *Ibid.* Vol. 3, *The Late Period.*

Liverani, M.
1970 "L'epica ugaritica nel suo contesto storico e letterario." Accademia nazionale dei Lincei: Atti del Convegno Internazionale sul tema *La poesia epica e la sua formazione.* Quaderno N 139: 859-69.
1979 "Histoire." In *Supplément au Dictionnaire de la Bible,* vol. 9, ed. H. Cazelles and A. Feuillet, cols. 1295-1348. Paris: Letouzey et Ané.

Loewenstamm, S.E.
1969 "The Expanded Colon in Ugaritic and Biblical Verse." *JSS* 14: 176-96.
1979 "Zur Götterlehre des Epos von Keret." *UF* 11: 505-14.
1980 "The Address 'Listen' in the Ugaritic Epic and the Bible." In Rendsburg 1980, 123-31.

Lord, A.B.
1960 *The Singer of Tales.* Cambridge, MA: Harvard.

McCarter, P.K.
1980 *I Samuel. A New Translation with Introduction, Notes and Commentary.* Anchor Bible. Garden City, NY: Doubleday.

Marcus, D.
1986 *Jephthah and His Vow.* Lubbock, TX: Texas Tech.

Margalit, B.
1975 "Studia Ugaritica I: Introduction to Ugaritic Prosody." *UF* 7: 289-313.
1976 "Studia Ugaritica II: Studies in *Krt* and *Aqht.*" *UF* 8: 137-92.
1980 "Interpreting the Story of Aqht: A Reply to H.H.P. Dressler, *VT* 29 (1979), pp. 152-61." *VT* 30: 361-65.
1981 "The Geographical Setting of the AQHT Story and Its Ramifications." In Young 1981, 131-58.
1982 "Ugaritic Lexicography I." *RB* 89: 418-26.
1983a Lexicographical Notes on the *Aqht* Epic (Part I: KTU 1.17-18)." *UF* 15: 65-103.

1983b "The Messengers of Woe to Dan'el: A Reconstruction and Interpretation of KTU 1.19.II.27-48." *UF* 15: 105-17.

Maróth, M.
1973 "Bemerkungen zum ugaritishen Text *Krt*." *Acta Orientalia* (Acad. Scient. Hung.) 27: 301-7.

Mendelsohn, I.
1949 *Slavery in the Ancient Near East*. New York: Columbia.

Merrill, A.L.
1968 "The House of Keret: A Study of the Keret Legend." *SEÅ* 33: 5-17.

Miller, P.D.
1970 "Animal Names as Designations in Ugaritic and Hebrew." *UF* 2: 177-86.
1988 "Prayer and Sacrifice in Ugarit and Israel." In *Text and Context. Old Testament and Semitic Studies for F. C. Fensham*, ed. W. Classen, JSOT Supplement Series 48, 139-55. Sheffield: JSOT.

Montgomery, J.A. and Z.S. Harris
1935 *The Ras Shamra Mythological Texts*. Memoirs of the American Philosophical Society, 4. Philadelphia: American Philosophical Society.

Moor, J.C. de
1973 "Ugaritic Lexicography." In *Studies on Semitic Lexicography*, Quaderni di Semitistica, 2, 61-102. Florence: Istituto di Linguistica e di Lingue Orientali.
1974 "A Note on CTA 19 (I AQHT): I.39-42." *UF* 6: 495-96.
1978 "The Art of Versification in Ugarit and Israel. I, The Rhythmical Structure." In *Studies in Bible and the Ancient Near East Presented to Samuel E. Loewenstamm*, ed. Y. Avishur and J. Blau, 119-39. Jerusalem: Rubinstein's.
1979 "Contributions to the Ugaritic Lexicon." *UF* 11: 639-53.
1986 "The Crisis of Polytheism in Late Bronze Ugarit." *Oudtestamentische Studiën* 24: 1-20.

Moor, J.C. de and P. van der Lugt
1974 "The Spectre of Pan-Ugaritism." *BiOr* 31: 3-26.

Moor, J.C. de and Spronk, K.
1982 "Problematic Passages in the Legend of Kirtu (I) and (II)." *UF* 14: 153-90.

Müller, H.-P.
1963 "Die Himmlische Ratsversammlung." *ZNW* 54: 254-67.
1978 "Gilgameschs Trauergesang um Enkidu and die Gattung der Totenklage." *ZA* 68: 233-50.
Mustafa, A.H.
1975 "Einige Bemerkungen zu Lexikalishen Problemen in den Epischen Texten des Ugarit." *Acta Orientalia* (Hung.) 29: 99-105.
Nielsen, K.
1986 *Incense in Ancient Israel*. VTSup 38. Leiden: Brill.
Nougayrol, J.
1955 *Le Palais Royal d'Ugarit III*. Mission de Ras Shamra 6. Paris: Imprimerie nationale.
Nougayrol, J., Laroche, E., Virolleaud, C., Schaeffer, C.F.A.
1968 *Ugaritica V*. Missiqon de Ras Shamra 16. Paris: Imprimerie Nationale.
O'Connor, M.
1980 *Hebrew Verse Structure*. Winona Lake: Eisenbrauns.
Oppenheim, A.L.
1956 *The Interpretation of Dreams in the Ancient Near East*. Transactions of the American Philosophical Society 46,3. Philadelphia: American Philosophical Society.
Otten, H.
1973 *Eine althethitische Erzählung um die Stadt Zalpa*. SBT 17. Wiesbaden: Harrassowitz.
Pardee, D.
1977 "An emendation in the Ugarit AQHT Text." *JNES* 36: 53-56.
1980 "The New Canaanite Myths and Legends." *BiOr* 37: 269-91.
1981 "Ugaritic and Hebrew Metrics." In Young 1981, 113-130.
1981/82 "Ugaritic." *AfO* 28: 259-72.
Parker, S.B.
1974 "Parallelism and Prosody in Ugaritic Narrative Verse." *UF* 6: 283-94.
1976 "The Marriage Blessing in Israelite and Ugaritic Literature." *JBL* 95: 23-30
1977 "The Historical Composition of *KRT* and the Cult of El." *ZAW* 89: 161-75.

1979-80 "Some Methodological Principles in Ugaritic Philology." *Maarav* 2/1: 7-41.

n.d. "The Birth Announcement." In *Old Testament and Ugaritic Studies in Memory of Peter C. Craigie*, ed. L. Eslinger and J.G. Taylor. JSOTSup. Sheffield: JSOT Press.

Perry, M.

1928 *L'Epithète traditionelle dans Homère. Essai sur un problème de style homérique*. Paris: Société Editrice Les Belles Lettres. (Trans.: "The Traditional Epithet in Homer." In *The Making of Homeric Verse. The Collected Papers of Milman Parry*, ed. A. Parry, 1-190. Oxford: Clarendon, 1971.)

Pedersen, J.

1941 "Die Krt Legende." *Berytus* 6: 63-105.

Pitard, W.T. and Zuckerman, B.

1987 "Figures for Pitard, 'RS 34.126'." *Maarav* 4/1: 111-55.

Pritchard, J.B.

1969a *Ancient Near Eastern Texts Relating to the Old Testament*. 3d ed. Princeton: Princeton University.

1969b *The Ancient Near East in Pictures Relating to the Old Testament*. 2d ed. Princeton: Princeton University.

Reiner, E.

1954 "Deux Fragments du Mythe de Zû." *RA* 48: 145-48.

Rendsburg, G. *et al*

1980 *The Bible World. Essays in Honor of Cyrus H. Gordon*. New York: Ktav.

Ribichini, S.

1982 "*udm e šmk*. Due toponimi 'mitici'." *Materiali Lessicali ed Epigrafici* 1: 51-52.

Richter, W.

1966 "Die Überlieferungen um Jephtah. Ri 10, 17-12, 6." *Bib* 47: 485-556.

1967 "Das Gelübde als theologische Rahmung der Jakobsüberlieferungen." *BZ* 11: 21-52.

Roth, W.M.W.

1972 "The Wooing of Rebekah: a tradition-critical study of Genesis 24." *CBQ* 34: 177-87.

Rummel, S., ed.

1981 *Ras Shamra Parallels*. Vol. 3. AnOr 51. Rome: Pontifical Biblical Institute.

Sapin, J.

1983 "Quelques systèmes socio-politiques en Syrie au 2° millénaire avant J.-C. et leur évolution historique d'après des documents religieux (légendes, rituels, sanctuaires)." *UF* 15: 157-90.

Sasson, J.

1979 *Ruth. A new translation with a philological commentary and a formalist-folklorist interpretation*. Baltimore: Johns Hopkins University.

Segert, S.

1958 "Die Schreibfehler in den ugaritishen literarischen Keilschrifttexten." In *Von Ugarit Nach Qumran*, BZAW 77, ed. J. Hempel and L. Rost, 93-212. Berlin: Töpelmann.

1979 "Ugaritic Poetry and Poetics: Some Preliminary Observations." *UF* 11: 729-38.

1983 "Parallelism in Ugaritic Poetry." *JAOS* 103: 295-306.

Selms, A. van

1954 *Marriage and Family Life in Ugaritic Literature*. Pretoria Oriental Series 1. London: Luzac.

Seow, C.L.

1984 "The Syro-Palestinian Context of Solomon's Dream." *HTR* 77: 141-52.

Siegolová, J.

1971 *Appu-Märchen und Ḫedammu-Mythos*. SBT 14. Wiesbaden: Harrassowitz.

Simpson, W.K.

1973 *The Literature of Ancient Egypt. An Anthology of Stories, Instructions and Poetry*. 2d ed. New Haven and London: Yale University.

Solomon, A.V.

1985 "Fable." In *Saga, Legend, Tale, Novella, Fable. Narrative Forms in Old Testament Literature* (JSOTSup 35), ed. G.W. Coats, 114-25. Sheffield: JSOT.

Stoebe, H.J.

1973 *Das Erste Buch Samuelis*. KAT 8/1. Gütersloh: Mohn.

Stuart, D.K.
1976 *Studies in Early Hebrew Meter*. HSM 13. Missoula: Scholars/Harvard Semitic Museum.

Thompson, S., ed.
1955 *Motif-Index of Folk Literature*. Bloomington: Indiana University.

Tigay, J.
1982 *The Evolution of the Gilgamesh Epic*. Philadelphia: University of Pennsylvania.

Trigger, B.G., Kemp, B.J., O'Connor, D., Lloyd, A.B.
1983 *Ancient Egypt: A Social History*. Cambridge: Cambridge University.

Ullendorff, E.
1977 *Is Biblical Hebrew a Language? Studies in Semitic Languages and Civilizations*. Wiesbaden: Harrassowitz.

Van Seters, J.
1983 *In Search of History*. New Haven: Yale University.

Vansina, J.
1965 *Oral Tradition: a study in historical methodology*. Chicago: Aldine.

Vaux, R. de
1965 *Ancient Israel*. 2 vols. New York: McGraw-Hill.

Wansbrough, J.
1983 "Metra ugaritica: pro et contra." *BSOAS* 46: 221-34.

Watson, W.G.E.
1976a "A Suppliant Surprised (CTA 16 I 41b-53a)." *JANES* 8: 105-11.
1976b "Puzzling Passages in the Tale of Aqhat." *UF* 8: 371-78.
1977 "The Falcon Episode in the Aqht Text." *JNWSL* 5: 69-75.
1983 "Introductions to discourse in Ugaritic narrative verse." *Aula Orientalis* 1: 253-61.

Weiser, A.
1950 *Die Psalmen*. ATD 14/15 Göttingen: Vandenhoeck & Ruprecht.
1960 *Das Buch des Propheten Jeremia Kapitel 1-25,14*. ATD 20. Göttingen: Vandenhoeck & Ruprecht.

Wendel, A.
1931 *Das Israelitisch-jüdische Gelübde*. Berlin: Philo.

Westenholz, J.G.
1983 "Heroes of Akkad." *JAOS* 103: 327-336.

Westermann, C.
1980 *The Promises to the Fathers. Studies on the Patriarchal Narratives*. Philadelphia: Fortress.
1981 *Genesis. 2 Teilband: Genesis 12-36*. BKAT I/2. Neukirchen-Vluyn: Neukirchener Verlag.
1985 *Genesis 12-36. A Commentary*. Minneapolis: Augsburg.

Whitaker, R.E.
1981 "Ugaritic Formulae." In Rummel 1981, 207-19.

Wildberger, H.
1972 *Jesaja*. BKAT 10/1. Neukirchen-Vluyn: Neukirchener Verlag.

Wilson, G.H.
1982 "Ugaritic Word Order and Sentence Structure in Krt." *JSS* 27: 17-32.

Würthwein, E.
1970 "Elijah at Horeb: Reflections on I Kings 19.9-18." In *Proclamation and Presence: Old Testament Essays in Honour of Gwynne Henton Davies*, ed. J.I. Durham and J.R. Porter, 152-66. Richmond, VA: John Knox.

Wyatt, N.
1979 "Some Observations on the Idea of History among the West Semitic Peoples." *UF* 11: 825-32.
1983 "A Suggested Historical Context for the Keret Story." *UF* 15: 316-18.

Xella, P.
1976 "Una 'Rilettura' del poema di Aqhat." In *Problemi del mito nel Vicino Oriente Antico* (Annali dell'Istituto Orientale di Napoli Supp. 7), 61-91. Naples: Istituto Orientale.
1978 "L'épisode de Dnil et Kothar (KTU 1.17 [=*CTA* 17] v 1-31 et Gen. XVIII 1-16." *VT* 28: 483-86.
1984 " 'Tu sei mio fratello ed io sono tua sorella' (KTU 1.18 I 24)." *Aula Orientalis* 2: 151-53.

Young, D.G.
1950 "Ugaritic Poetry." *JNES* 9: 124-33.

Young, D.G., ed.
1981 *Ugarit in Retrospect. Fifty Years of Ugarit and Ugaritic*. Winona Lake, IN: Eisenbrauns.

Zevit, Z.
1976 "The *'egla* Ritual of Deuteronomy 21: 1-9." *JBL* 95: 377-90.
1983 "Nondistinctive Stress, Syllable Constraints, and Wortmetrik, in Ugaritic Poetry." *UF* 15: 291-98.